Praise for *Mission 27*

"For all of us on that team, 2009 was *the* year to remember. Mark and Bryan have done that season justice with this book. It took me right back into that clubhouse with my brothers."
—Alex Rodriguez, ESPN and FOX commentator/former Yankees third baseman

"The 2009 Yankees were an unforgettable group of guys who made my first year in New York the most memorable season ever. *Mission 27* gives you a firsthand look at what went into putting together a championship team and what it took for that team to win it all."
—CC Sabathia, Yankees pitcher

"2009 was the year of CC, A-Rod, Swisher, Tex, and more. Mark Feinsand and Bryan Hoch bring you every moment—on and off the field—of that wonderful championship season. I smiled through this whole book, reliving this magical year. Yankees fans, I promise you won't be able to put *Mission 27* down."
—Suzyn Waldman, Yankees' radio color commentator

"*Mission 27* truly gives you a behind-the-scenes look at the 2009 Yankees straight from the players and coaches who experienced it together. Reading this book takes me back on the field and in the clubhouse to relive that special season."
—Mark Teixeira, ESPN analyst/former Yankees first baseman

"Often the best stories about a team surface only after diligent reporting years later. *Mission 27*, through the hard work of two beat writers who covered the 2009 Yankees, features a level of detail and inside access rarely seen in daily coverage. Readers will be astounded to learn about players with whom they are familiar but actually are getting to know for the first time."
—Ken Rosenthal, MLB on FOX reporter/MLB Network insider

"Feinsand and Hoch take you on an insiders' journey of the Yankees' magical 2009 season. We all watched what happened on the field, but the stories behind the scenes make the organization's 27th title even more compelling. Although it's been 10 years, *Mission 27* makes it seem like it happened yesterday."
—Michael Kay, YES Network play-by-play broadcaster

"The 2009 Yankees had it all: pinstriped legends yearning for one last ring, pricy imports under pressure to deliver, a glitzy new palace for the fans in the Bronx—and the game's biggest star, Alex Rodriguez, embroiled in an outrageous saga of shame and redemption. If you love the Yankees, you remember it well, but you don't really know the story until you read this book. I covered this team with Mark Feinsand and Bryan Hoch, and nobody had better connections—then or now—than they did. With fresh and fascinating insights never revealed before, this isn't just a walk down memory lane. It's a riveting, rollicking ride down the Canyon of Heroes."
—Tyler Kepner, *The New York Times* national baseball writer

"*Mission 27* paints the inside corner for all baseball fans who want a true look at the magic of the summer of 2009. Every page brings back incredible memories and stories that can only be told by two trusted writers who were with us for every pitch. Get your ski goggles ready and chill the champagne."

—Phil Hughes, former Yankees pitcher

"*Mission 27* is packed with stories and anecdotes you either forgot or never knew. For Yankees fans, it's like another go-round on a great amusement park ride: the thrills all come back."

—Tom Verducci, *Sports Illustrated* writer/FOX and MLB Network studio analyst

"A decade after the Yankees' last championship comes the story of how it happened. Mark Feinsand and Bryan Hoch offer fresh details from inside the clubhouse, the front office, and the dugout. Finally, a book worthy of the incredible 2009 Yankees."

—Jeff Passan, ESPN MLB insider

Mission 27

A NEW BOSS, A NEW BALLPARK, AND ONE LAST RING FOR THE YANKEES' CORE FOUR

Mission 27

A NEW BOSS, A NEW BALLPARK,
AND ONE LAST RING FOR
THE YANKEES' CORE FOUR

Mark Feinsand and Bryan Hoch

30 YEARS
TRIUMPH
BOOKS

Library of Congress Cataloging-in-Publication Data

Names: Feinsand, Mark, author. | Hoch, Bryan, author.
Title: Mission 27 : a new boss, a new ballpark, and one last ring for the
    Yankees' core four / Mark Feinsand and Bryan Hoch.
Description: Chicago : Triumph Books LLC, [2019]
Identifiers: LCCN 2018059426 | ISBN 9721629376806
Subjects: LCSH: New York Yankees (Baseball team) | World Series (Baseball)
    (2009)
Classification: LLC GV875.N4 F44 2019 | DDC 796.957/64097471—dc23 LC
    record available at https://lccn.loc.gov/2018059426

This book is available in quantity at special discounts for your group or organization. For further information, contact:

Triumph Books LLC
814 North Franklin Street
Chicago, Illinois 60610
(312) 337-0747
www.triumphbooks.com

Printed in U.S.A.
ISBN: 978-1-62937-680-6
Design by Nord Compo
Photos courtesy of AP Images

To Dena, Ryan, and Zack: my own championship team.

—Mark Feinsand

To Connie, who made 2009 my most magical season.
And to Penny and Maddie, with whom every day
feels like winning Game 6.

—Bryan Hoch

CONTENTS

FOREWORD

When the 2008 season ended, I was in a bad place. It had been such a tough year for me professionally with the Chicago White Sox, and I had no idea what my baseball future would look like. Then I got the call that changed my life.

The New York Yankees had traded for me. *What? Me?*

Given how 2008 had gone, I couldn't imagine someone of Brian Cashman's status would believe in me enough to give me an opportunity to play for the New York Yankees. *Somebody pinch me because this has to be a dream.*

Yet I did end up with the Yankees. And, bro, let me tell you: it was every bit as amazing and badass as I had hoped it would be.

In short, 2009 changed my life forever. I got to play for the greatest organization on the planet. I met and fell in love with JoAnna, the greatest woman I will ever know. I won the World Series. Far too many players never have a chance to experience that. Other than the birth of my two little girls, Emerson and Sailor, 2009 was by far the greatest period of my life.

Getting to spring training and seeing the slogan "Mission 27" slapped on T-shirts and binders was super exciting for me. It was like those were our marching orders. We knew exactly what we were supposed to go out and do.

That was the first time I got a true sense of what being a New York Yankee was all about. Either you win the World Series or you don't. That's it. There are no other objectives. That's the thought process of the Yankees' universe and their fandom.

When you get to be part of that, you immediately buy into it. I'm a pride guy. I'm a passion guy. I'm a tradition guy. The pinstripes have all of that. For me, it was a dream come true, a match made in heaven. I was so stoked just to have the opportunity to be part of it.

So many amazing things happened to me that year, and in my mind, it's all because of New York and the Yankees. I'll always love that city. I'm not a boy from the Bronx, but I feel a connection with that place and its people. There's something special that's almost hard to explain.

When you win a World Series with the New York Yankees, you're remembered forever. You're kind of immortalized. Once a Yankee, always a Yankee. It's a family, and once you're part of that, your life will never be the same.

I'm so amped that Mark and Bryan are telling this story. They were in the trenches with us every step of the way—from the first day of spring training all the way to that unbelievable parade down the Canyon of Heroes.

Every time I hear "Empire State of Mind" by Jay-Z and Alicia Keys, it takes me back to a year I will never forget. I still jam to that song all the time. That was our anthem, New York's anthem, and I am damn proud to have been part of it. It was my year; it was *our* year.

—Nick Swisher
Yankees right fielder
2009 World Series champion
2010 All-Star

CHAPTER 1

THE FINAL ACT:
AN ORAL HISTORY

November 4, 2009, 11:50 PM
Yankee Stadium, Bronx, New York

Mariano Rivera rolled the seams of a baseball over his fingertips as his spikes dug into the reddish brown clay of the Yankee Stadium mound. Electricity reverberated from all five decks of the team's spectacular new home. The most successful franchise in sports history was one strike away from adding title No. 27 to its trophy case, though you would never have been able to tell by examining the hurler's placid expression.

It was all for show. The greatest closer in history had a secret: he was in agony.

Rivera had strained his rib cage while making a 34-pitch appearance in Game 6 of the American League Championship Series, an injury the Yankees somehow managed to keep out of the newspapers at the time. More importantly, as the Bombers battled the Philadelphia Phillies in a taut Fall Classic, the defending champions never had a clue that the all-time saves leader was ailing. "My side, oh my God, that was the worst thing that I ever felt. No one knew about it—only the trainers and my teammates. It was the intercostal, the muscle between the rib. Every time that you throw a pitch, it felt like a knife. That was *pain.* That wasn't soreness. That's pain. My wife [Clara] was like, 'Don't pitch!' I was like, 'Are you crazy?'"

Clara Rivera: "I was begging him. Don't pitch, please. Don't do that. I don't want you to pitch like that."

As the necessary 27 outs ticked off in Game 6, rookie reliever David Robertson had been assigned a covert task. Robertson raced between the clubhouse and the bullpen every other inning, stuffing his pockets with any heating pads or gel packs that could be found in the trainers' office. Rivera would then slide the artificial warmth inside his own jacket, resting in anticipation of a call to warm up.

Roberston: "He had messed up his left oblique pretty bad, and I don't think you guys ever knew about that," Robertson told us. "He was pretty sore. I remember him being sore and in pain. And when you've hurt an oblique, they don't go away. You can't stop it. There's only so much medicine you can take. I remember having to run in and get him hot cream to rub on and I got a hot pad so he could sit there and put it in his jacket on his side before he'd go in and pitch."

Mariano Rivera: "It was so bad that we had a trainer work with me for like five innings, stretching it and using a tool that looked like a knife, sticking it in there. Between innings I needed a heat pack. The guys were good to me. They took care of the old man."

Manager Joe Girardi's call for Rivera came in the eighth inning. Left-hander Damaso Marte completed what would be remembered as a terrific postseason with a swinging strikeout of slugging first baseman Ryan Howard, and Rivera signaled to bullpen coach Mike Harkey that he was ready.

Harkey: "He would've pitched with a broken leg. He's just that type of guy. I knew Joe was going to call in the eighth inning and I knew it was going to be Mo, no matter what the lead was."

The heavy metal strains of Metallica's "Enter Sandman" thumped through each of the 1,784 speakers mounted within the state-of-the-art facility, lending a theatrical quality to Rivera's jog across the outfield grass. The Phillies' scant chances of extending their season fell as Rivera struck out Jayson Werth and then worked around a Raul Ibanez double by getting Pedro Feliz to foul out to catcher Jorge Posada.

Jerry Hairston Jr., left fielder: "We had a four-run lead, and here comes the greatest closer of all time. Game over. You knew that the Phillies were going to be demoralized. They're not going to score four or five runs off Mariano Rivera in an inning and a half. So then to find out later he pitched with that oblique injury makes it even more special. Just the consummate professional, a gamer, greatest closer to ever live."

The Yankees were retired around a Derek Jeter single in their half of the eighth, though none of the 50,315 paying customers seemed to mind. They jumped, clapped, and prayed in anticipation of a party that had been wired to explode since the fifth inning, when designated hitter Hideki Matsui broke the game open with a two-run double. It was part of a six-RBI performance that would secure World Series MVP honors for Matsui, in what would be his final game in pinstripes. "What I did in Game 6—I know it was me, but it didn't feel like it was me," Matsui said. "I felt like it was some kind of mystical powers that was behind that performance. To be able to have that kind of performance in the game that decides the world championship, it felt very surreal. I felt like there was something mystical that was working behind me."

The decibel level spiked as pinch-hitter Matt Stairs smacked a wobbling liner to Jeter at shortstop. Rivera issued a walk to catcher Carlos Ruiz, bringing up shortstop Jimmy Rollins, who had chafed the Yankees during an appearance on NBC's soon-to-be-forgotten *The Jay Leno Show*, guaranteeing that Philadelphia would dispatch the Bombers in five games. Rollins lifted a harmless fly ball to right fielder Nick Swisher, and the title was one out away.

Swisher: "It was so loud in the stadium. You literally couldn't hear yourself think. It was one of the more amazing sounds I ever heard in my life. I also knew that the first year at the old Yankee Stadium the Yankees won the World Series, and the first year of the new Yankee Stadium the Yankees won the World Series. I feel like the ghosts from across the street came on over and really hooked us up."

Philadelphia's last hope was the Flyin' Hawaiian, Shane Victorino, a switch-hitting outfielder from the nation's 50th state. In the prime of what would be a 12-year big league career, including eight with the Phils, his name was about to enter the memory banks of nerds who take pride in an ability to recall the final out of each World Series.

Victorino was intent upon putting up a good battle against Rivera despite a severely bruised right index finger that screamed after each of Rivera's famed cutters. Discovered by accident during a 1997 game of catch with teammate Ramiro Mendoza, the pitch would be responsible for shattering a forest's worth of lumber over 19 celebrated years in the big leagues.

Victorino: "I don't think you can be scared of anyone in baseball. You have to have the resiliency to say, 'This guy is good, but we can beat him'. His numbers show how good he is, but you can't go with that mind-set because then you're beating yourself."

The son of a Panamanian fisherman nestled the ball into his glove and bent deep at the waist. Rivera straightened his wiry frame with several taps of his left foot and then rocked into the smooth, repeatable delivery that would help him save 652 regular-season games over his career—plus 42 more in the postseason; both are records. Rivera got ahead with a called strike, missed inside with one, and then got Victorino to wave at a particularly nasty offering that snapped toward the batter's ankles.

Johnny Damon, outfielder: "I was on the bench ready to celebrate. I loved the fact that we had Mariano out there, a guy who closes out games better than anybody in baseball history. You feel pretty good. But Victorino had just a great at-bat. He was fighting and he still thought they had a chance to win, so we give Philadelphia a lot of credit. They had a really good team. It was just our year and our time."

Andy Pettitte, pitcher: "I came out right to the base of the dugout. You just remember the excitement, the joy, the feeling of accomplishing something that you set out to do eight months before that. Just to be able to get 25 men to come together and to be able to pull that off and to be able to do it for the fifth time, it was even more gratifying, I know, for me and Jeet and Mo and Jorgie. It had been so long since we had won. It seemed like, 'Man, are we ever going to be able to pull this off again?'"

Matsui: "I was in the dugout, closer to the home-plate side, watching the last out. To be honest with you, I was quite calm only because we had a good lead, and Mariano was closing out the game. I felt like, *Okay, now this is it. We're going to win the series. We're going to be world champions.* So I was quite calm watching that last out."

Six more pitches stretched the anticipation. Two missed the strike zone, and four were fouled away. Girardi stood by the dugout railing with his arms crossed, flanked by bench coach Tony Pena to his left and pitching coach Dave Eiland to his right. Hitting coach Kevin Long was about two steps away, hovering close to the bat rack.

Girardi: "Mo's pitch count is what I was worried about. Victorino fouled off a lot of pitches. I'm thinking, *Oh, God. Are we going to get through this? Am I going to make it through this with Mo and his pitch count?* I'm saying, 'Come on, you've got to make it.'"

Eiland: "I recall Kevin Long. When we were on the field and I'm on the railing, Kevin always sat on the bat rack right behind us. I remember when Mo got up, I walked up to the railing and I turn around. Kevin was just sitting over there and he winked at me. Mo gets an out. I turn around, and he winked at me again…Mo was in the game, we had the lead, we were in Yankee Stadium. We just knew it was going to take a few more minutes and we were going to be world champions."

Long: "Each out, I'm going, 'Okay.' A wink meant, 'All right, we're getting real close,' but you don't want to get too excited because it's never over until it's over."

Rivera reared for his 41st pitch of the evening—and his last of the 2009 season—a 91-mph cutter that Victorino chopped to the right side of the infield.

Rivera: "It was amazing. It was like, 'Wow, I'm back here again'. It was a great feeling, being the last guy there standing, throwing the last pitch. It was amazing."

Brett Gardner, center fielder: "I've got a pretty good view for all of it: Mariano's pitching, Jeet's at short, Robbie Cano's at second, Jorge behind the plate. I mean, just crazy, man. Victorino was hitting, and Mariano doesn't like guys dunking balls in front of the outfielders, so I was playing in shallow, praying that someone didn't hit one over my head because I was playing shallow in a World Series game."

Hairston: "I was like, 'Please let the ball be hit to me. I want to make the last out.' I was being a little selfish, but everybody was thinking that."

Second baseman Robinson Cano danced a few steps to flag the ball and then whipped it to first baseman Mark Teixeira. Seeing that his throw was on target, Cano leapt, holding both hands high above his head.

Cano: "I prepared myself from the beginning like, 'Robbie, be ready for the last out, ground ball. Be ready. Don't mess it up.' And it came my way. It happened that way, so I was ready for that. The last thing you want is to make an error right there. I would bite that ball if I had to."

Anchoring his right foot alongside the bag, Teixeira thought, *Don't drop it.* Teixeira gloved the ball in his left hand and raised his right fist. Ballgame over, World Series over.

Teixeira: "I didn't feel the ball hit my glove. If you look at the replay, I actually looked down into my glove to make sure the ball was there. And I just went kind of crazy for 10 or 20 seconds. Once Mo got into the game, I knew the game was over. Running through my head: 'I can't believe I just caught the last out of the World Series.'"

They rushed to the center of the infield, embracing for the most joyous of their 114 celebrations that season—103 in the regular season and 11 more in the postseason.

Jeter: "You forget how good it feels after the final out. But I appreciated the last ones that we won. I knew it was very difficult to do. If it was easy, people would be repeating every year, and no one's done it since we [won three straight titles from 1998 to 2000]."

Posada: "I was looking around at everybody. I'm running behind Teixeira to back up, but once Teixeira catches the ball, I'm looking around. I just wanted to soak it in a little bit more than I did before. I took it all in because I didn't know when it was going to happen again. I'm coming to the end of my career, so I wanted to savor it a little bit more. What a feeling."

Alex Rodriguez, third baseman: "Oh my God, Cano to Teixeira, Yankees are world champs for the 27th time. I just put my hands up, and it was the most happy, liberated, excited freedom I've ever felt on a baseball field. All these years, 36 years or whatever it was, waiting for this moment; it was a dream come true."

CC Sabathia, pitcher: "I remember just trying to get out there fast enough. I was just trying to get into the pile. I remember Robbie catching it, him throwing it to Tex, and then just running full speed to the middle of the field. That's all I remember: just being excited."

Cano: "The last thing you want is to hit someone with your hat, so I had to put it backward. I was jumping, excited. I remember jumping around, all the fans cheering, and the best thing: it was at home in New York. That's something that as a player you will never forget."

Swisher: "Bro, I'll never forget it. Mariano Rivera, Shane Victorino, bro, little jam-sammy to Robbie Cano over to Mark Teixeira, baby. 'The Yankees Win!'—John Sterling with a great call. We will always be remembered as champions, and that is something that I'll take to the grave with me, man."

In the bullpen the relievers clamored for position like thoroughbreds waiting to break from the post at the Kentucky Derby. They were a few hundred feet from the pinnacle of the sports universe.

Phil Hughes, pitcher: "I remember just standing out in the bullpen and knowing it was over, knowing we were going to win, which is pretty cool. It was really kind of a special moment to see Mo get ready. It was pretty much Mo's game. I remember Victorino rolling over on that cutter and knowing that was it and running out there. It was truly something I'll never forget. That's for sure."

Brian Bruney, pitcher: "I remember being on the fence with the guys and just talking about being world champions. I mean, we knew it was over. We were sitting there going, 'I can't believe it.' I just remember waiting in anticipation to open the gate and to run as fast as I ever have. I was with Hughes, and we were standing there and talking, just waiting to open the gate. We wanted to open the gate so bad."

Robertson: "It didn't hit me that we had won the World Series. It just felt like it was going to keep going. I felt like we were going to have another game the next day, but we weren't. That was it. We'd done it."

The mass of pinstriped humanity bounced around the turf as caps and gloves were strewn to the playing field. The air was filled by Freddie Mercury's vocals on Queen's "We Are the Champions."

Joba Chamberlain, pitcher: "I had literally taken my jersey off because I knew they were going to take this, that, and the other thing. I took it off and stuck it in my backpack. I remember talking to Tex, and he was like, 'I don't remember catching that ball.'"

Girardi: "When I think of the '96 World Series, I think of Charlie Hayes running with the ball, kind of high stepping, and he looks like a little kid. That's the image I have in my head. And it's the image of them running together in the infield. I looked for my wife, waved at her, and then went out."

Chad Bohling, director of mental conditioning: "I remember running out on the field and I didn't know what to do. All the players, coaches, and staff ran out there. I remember at one point Joe Girardi jumping on my back, and I was just like, 'Who is this?' I turned around, and he had the biggest smile on his face."

Mick Kelleher, first-base coach: "Just jubilation, love for everybody. The celebration on the field was so special. We were all so fortunate. I often think about players I played with or players that were great players on great teams but never got to a situation like we were in. You'll never know what it feels like until you do it and you never forget the feeling. Just to think about it right now brings me back."

Rob Thomson, third-base coach: "When the ball goes into Teixeira's glove, it was kind of a moment that it almost stops; life kind of stops, so surreal. I turn and I give Mick a hug, and Joe's there, and we all kind of dogpile Joe. It was really the greatest moment in my baseball career."

Dana Cavalea, strength and conditioning coach: "I'm in the dugout, standing next to Andy Pettitte. They gave out these flip cameras before the game that day, so he's like, 'Can you capture the moment?' I got so excited. I ended up dropping the camera. After the celebration he comes up to me: 'Hey man, you got that camera?' I had no idea where it was."

Teixeira secured the ball in the pocket of his uniform pants, planning to present the treasure to managing general partner Hal Steinbrenner.

Teixeira: "I kept it all offseason and then gave it to Hal at the Welcome Home Dinner the next year. I kept it in a safe the whole offseason."

The ball now resides in a museum at the stadium.

A platform was swiftly erected on the dirt behind second base for the presentation of the World Series trophy. Players were handed factory fresh championship caps, T-shirts, and quickie copies of the *New York Post* with '27' printed upon the cover.

A.J. Burnett, pitcher: "Mission 27 is complete. That's all I remember. It happened really fast, and we shot out on the field. Two seconds later, we're all holding newspapers with '27' on stage with the trophy. The lap around the field was probably my favorite part of the night. We got the trophy and we jogged around that whole stadium. That was awesome. I remember [actor] Kurt Russell gave me a hug. He's like, 'I'm so proud of you guys.'"

Brian Cashman, general manager: "I walked down to the field with my daughter, Grace. They were looking for me during the trophy presentation, but I grew up under George Steinbrenner and was taught not to gravitate to those stories. When they were doing those trophy celebrations with ownership, I was down on the field in front of the stage watching. That was by design. They were looking for me, they wanted me to get up there, but I had George in my head saying, "No!""

The words: "Boss, This Is For You" flashed in large gold type on the center-field video screen. Longtime principal owner George M. Steinbrenner did not travel to New York for the final game of the Fall Classic, instead watching on television from his Florida home. For the first time since 2000, the Yankees were champions. Mission 27 was complete.

Rivera: "It was such a great feeling. I was also relieved, like, 'Man, we won it.' It wasn't easy. It wasn't an easy playoff, but we definitely wanted it. It was a great, great feeling."

CHAPTER 2

FAREWELL, YANKEE STADIUM

The first speech took place in a basement classroom of the St. Augustine Cathedral School in Kalamazoo, Michigan. As Derek Jeter stood before two dozen of his fellow fourth-graders with his back to the chalkboard, the nine-year-old announced that he would play shortstop for the New York Yankees. That proclamation had come as part of a sharing exercise in Shirley Garzelloni's class. Jeter never considered that public speaking would join running, hitting, and throwing as part of the job description.

Sixteen years after Jeter's final report card had been perused by his parents, Charles and Dorothy, the future Hall of Famer had another speaking assignment. The evening of September 21, 2008, marked the final game on the grounds of the original Yankee Stadium with a 7–3 victory against the Baltimore Orioles, capping the facility's 85-year history. The team's captain and one of the most popular players in franchise history, Jeter had been entrusted with the stadium's closing words.

Surrounded by his teammates at the lip of the pitcher's mound, Jeter doffed his cap with his left hand, cleared his throat, and raised a microphone with his right hand. He twice said, "Excuse me," quieting the rhythmic chants of his name and "Let's Go Yankees" emanating from the stadium's three decks. "For all of us up here," Jeter said, "it's a huge honor to put this uniform on every day and come out here and play. And every member of this organization, past and present, has been calling this place home for 85 years. There's a lot of tradition, a lot of history, and a lot of memories. Now the great thing about memories is you're able to pass it along from generation to generation. And although things are going to change next year—we're going to move across the street—there are a few things with the New York Yankees that never change. That's pride, it's tradition, and most of all, we have the greatest fans in the world. And we are relying on you to take the memories from this stadium, add them to the new memories that come at the new Yankee Stadium, and continue to pass them on from generation to generation. So on behalf of the entire organization, we just want to take this moment to salute you, the greatest fans in the world."

Showered in love from the 54,610 packing each nook and cranny, Jeter and his teammates again raised their caps, as the cymbal crashes and brass notes of Frank Sinatra's "Theme from New York, New York" were heard for the umpteenth time that day. He led the pack, as everyone wearing a pinstriped uniform walked toward third base and down the left-field line, taking a final lap of the house that Babe Ruth had opened with a home run on the afternoon of April 18, 1923. "Jeter and I spoke for several days about giving that speech, and I don't remember any resistance from him," said Jason Zillo, the team's director of media relations. "Derek wanted to know details as far as when and how it would all go down. It was something he absorbed. It was going to be a big moment in Yankees history. He wanted to be prepared and on point and share the sentiment of the team in an eloquent way."

Even after a $100 million renovation that sent the club across town to play home games at Shea Stadium for the 1974–75 seasons, home plate in the Bronx still sat more or less where Lou Gehrig had given his "Luckiest Man" address in 1939. The outfield grass was the same patch of real estate that had been patrolled by Joe DiMaggio and Mickey Mantle, and Reggie Jackson delighted in pointing to the exact spot beyond the center-field wall where his third home run in Game 6 of the 1977 World Series had struck. Jorge Posada called it "the greatest background in the world," saying that "the ball seems like it glows when it comes in."

Yet there was more than history within the stadium's walls. Due in part to the lax enforcement of building codes in decades gone by, the team was aware of an asbestos issue even before the structure failed inspection in April 1998. Prior to a scheduled game against the Anaheim Angels, a 350-pound expansion steel beam dislodged from the upper deck and smashed into the concrete along the third-base line. Tragedy was averted only because the beam fell four hours before the seats below would have been occupied. The Yankees were relocated to Queens for two games while engineers conducted a structural inspection of the septuagenarian ballpark. Their report indicated that things weren't great. "I know from living in that place: as much history as was there, I saw the infrastructure crumbling," pitcher David Cone said. "I knew that something had to be done and I knew how difficult it would have been to gut and renovate that place. There were some times we were legitimately worried watching the upper deck shake. I was there when part of it fell down. Thankfully, no fans were there, but there were times when we were like, 'Whoa, something could happen here.'"

The beam collapse strengthened the case for a new stadium, a topic that principal owner George M. Steinbrenner had addressed repeatedly. Steinbrenner's complaints concerning underwhelming attendance bounced between the decay of the South Bronx, a shortage of accessible parking, and the lack of a commuter rail train station. A proposal to lure the Yankees to the New Jersey Meadowlands rested upon Steinbrenner's desk as early as the spring of 1986, though many believed the prospect of playing home games in East Rutherford was simply a bargaining chip.

A decade later, Steinbrenner revealed that he conducted discussions with real estate developer Donald Trump to target the West Side of Manhattan, calling the recommendations composed by award-winning architects Hellmuth, Obata + Kassabaum (HOK) "very strong and powerful." The firm's proposal called for a two-sport, retractable dome stadium and won a supporter in New York City mayor Rudy Giuliani, an avid baseball fan who believed both Big Apple teams needed new parks.

The proposed facility was to stand over the rail yards on West 33rd Street, the same location the NFL's New York Jets eyeballed for a home that would have been a centerpiece of the city's bid to host the 2012 Summer Olympics. As preparation Steinbrenner dispatched his youngest son, Hal, to inspect newer ballparks in Baltimore, Cleveland, and Denver, leading a group that composed notes on what made those facilities special and how those concepts could be applied to a new stadium. "You've got to know what options are available to you," Steinbrenner told the *New York Daily News* at the time. "We're going to be doing this and doing it very soon."

Consideration was given to a second remodeling of the stadium site, as both the Boston Red Sox (2006) and the Chicago Cubs (2015) would soon do for their aging parks. Developer Tishman Speyer completed a full feasibility analysis, warning that the financial and environmental cost of retrofitting the structure would be comparable to building a new facility. With that in mind, Giuliani's successor, Michael Bloomberg, and deputy mayor Dan Doctoroff lent their support to a new stadium project.

In June 2005 Steinbrenner attended a press conference to unveil renderings of the team's new 51,000-seat home, which was to be constructed adjacent to and north of the original stadium in Macombs Dam Park. The retractable roof had been lopped off, saving more than $350 million. Now a five-level, open-air ballpark, it would restore characteristics of the pre-1973 stadium while replicating the present field dimensions. Luxury boxes, wider concourses, and improved entertainment options would be added. "We decided we want to stay in the Bronx. We want to do the job here," Steinbrenner said. "We wanted to do something for the people who've always supported this team."

The Yankees offered the ambitious timetable of a 2009 completion with the club financing the majority of the project through taxable and tax-exempt bonds. The announcement was made one week after New York City and the Mets announced plans for Shea Stadium's replacement; Steinbrenner and Mets owner Fred Wilpon had met at the onset of their respective projects, agreeing that they would negotiate together.

Manager Joe Torre inspected the designs, remarking, "Looks like it's going to be a classy joint." Speaking in front of his locker—steps from the stall that had remained vacant since Thurman Munson's demise in a 1979 plane crash—Jeter called it "a great day" and welcomed the entry into baseball's new stadium era. "There's a lot of history here," Jeter said then. "There were a lot of good memories here. Now we'll try to take that over across the street."

The city was tasked with demolishing the existing structure, which was the third oldest ballpark in the big leagues behind Fenway Park (1912) and Wrigley Field (1914). The playing field would be preserved for the use of local amateur leagues. Renamed Heritage Field, the grounds of the old stadium featured three grass athletic fields for baseball, softball, and Little League, plus areas for the discus, shotput, and javelin.

A tree-lined walking trail outlined the perimeter of the old ballpark with plaques and markers to commemorate its place in history. The Bat, a 138-foot boiler stack decorated to look like a Babe Ruth-model Louisville Slugger, would remain. Other elements of the stadium, most notably Monument Park, were to be relocated to the new facility, which would replicate the entry facade, cathedral windows, art deco frieze, and the hand-operated auxiliary scoreboards of the original stadium. "If you look at the 1970s stadium, the old stadium, it didn't really reflect the original Yankee Stadium," team president Randy Levine said. "The idea in building the new stadium was to replicate the original 1923 stadium in a manner that was, of course, state-of-the-art. You never could miss a pitch, the way the concession stands are put in place, a lot of open areas, the Great Hall, a tribute to the great boulevards of New York. The idea was to build a stadium that looked like the original stadium with a grandeur that represents New York City and the Yankees."

The project received regulatory approval in July 2006, following more than two dozen public hearings involving the city council and the state legislature. There had been opposition from parks advocates and residents, who feared increased traffic and pollution, lamenting that the 28-acre Macombs Dam Park and the 18.5-acre John Mullaly Park would be paved over. In response, smaller parks were scattered throughout the area, including some on the rooftops of parking garages.

Groundbreaking was held on the sunny morning of August 16, 2006, coinciding with the 58th anniversary of Ruth's death. Yogi Berra, MLB commissioner Bud Selig, and actor Billy Crystal joined Mayor Bloomberg and New York governor George Pataki, wearing hard hats with Yankees logos while wielding shovels with silver handles in the shape of baseball bats.

Steinbrenner was there as well, though the 76-year-old limped to the podium and appeared pale. His commentary lacked the bluster that had marked his public persona over the previous three decades. As "The House That Ruth Built" gave way to the "House The Boss Wanted," Steinbrenner spoke for only 25 seconds, saying, "It's a pleasure to give this to you people. Enjoy the stadium. I hope it's wonderful."

As was speculated at the time, Steinbrenner's health was failing. Broadcaster John Sterling revealed that Steinbrenner had nearly lost his footing that day. "I'm at the lectern introducing everybody and I introduced George," Sterling said. "He comes up and he started to go and had my arm around his waist. He was a heavy guy, and I held him up. I think he would've gone down."

Three months later, Steinbrenner fainted in a Revolutionary War auditorium at the University of North Carolina while watching his granddaughter, Haley Swindal, perform in *Cabaret*. It was the second time in three years that Steinbrenner had required overnight hospitalization; in December 2003 Steinbrenner had collapsed in Sarasota, Florida, following a memorial service for Hall of Fame quarterback Otto Graham.

Though spokesman Howard Rubenstein repeatedly offered statements touting The Boss' vigor, Steinbrenner had acknowledged his advancing years. "You must let the young elephants into the tent," he said. That process appeared to be underway with Steinbrenner referring to son-in-law Steve Swindal as his hand-picked successor.

Those plans were altered during spring training in 2007, when a St. Petersburg, Florida, police officer spotted Swindal's Mercedes weaving at 61 mph in a 35-mph zone. Six weeks after Swindal was arrested and charged with driving under the influence, Steinbrenner's daughter, Jennifer, announced that the couple was dissolving their 23-year marriage.

With Swindal removed from the hierarchy, the keys were handed to Steinbrenner's sons, Hank and Hal. Their diametrically opposed personalities promised to fill the void left by a swashbuckling Boss, who had publicly clashed with the likes of Reggie Jackson and Billy Martin while also deftly transforming the $10 million purchase of the Yankees from CBS into a fortune of more than $1 billion, including the lucrative formation of the YES Network.

Hank Steinbrenner embraced his father's ability to serve as the organization's mouthpiece, quipping in a gravelly voice, frequently puffing on a cigarette or swigging from a glass bottle of Heineken. He'd occasionally frustrated the baseball operations department for being too forthright with behind-the-scenes details. After the 2007 season, for example, Steinbrenner had provided a daily breakdown of the efforts to acquire pitcher Johan Santana from the Minnesota Twins, emboldening Minnesota to insist upon pitchers Phil Hughes and Ian Kennedy, plus outfielder Melky Cabrera. No trade was made.

By contrast, Hal Steinbrenner proudly referred to himself as a "finance geek," having sharpened his skills by maintaining a modest portfolio of Marriott and Holiday Inn hotels mostly located in Florida. More low-key than his older brother, Hal Steinbrenner was passionate about aviation and frequently used piloting analogies to describe his new duties, telling general manager Brian Cashman on more than one occasion that he liked to observe the team "from 30,000 feet." "The kids wanted to step up for their dad and deliver for their dad, but they were also running a business," Cashman said. "It was a balancing act with Hal. He was quite opposite from his dad. His dad was like an impulse shopper. If he was walking down an aisle in a grocery store and wanted ice cream, he was buying ice cream right there in that moment in time. It was an impulse that he was going to act off of. Hal's not that way. Every decision that he's going to make is going to be one that's well thought out."

With the elder Steinbrenner's trust, the tandem was in charge of ensuring that the new stadium would be a success. Despite numerous overtures from corporate America, the team's new home would be called Yankee Stadium, bypassing the corporate naming rights that represented a windfall for most teams building new parks. That included the Mets, who scored a $400 million commitment from Citigroup—$20 million per year over 20 years—to brand their park as Citi Field. "The dollars we passed were incomparable," chief operating officer Lonn Trost told *The New York Times*. "Having said that, you wouldn't rename the White House, you wouldn't rename Grant's Tomb, and you wouldn't rename the Grand Canyon. This is Yankee Stadium, and this will always be Yankee Stadium."

Trost and the Yankees intended to protect their baby fiercely. In April 2008 he and team president Randy Levine watched with approval while workers used jackhammers to exhume a David Ortiz jersey that rested two feet beneath the surface of the stadium's basement. It had been placed near the entrance to the ritzy Legends Club restaurant by Bronx resident and Red Sox loyalist Gino Castignoli, who worked only one day on the stadium project. Hank Steinbrenner memorably dismissed Castignoli by saying, "I hope his co-workers kick the shit out of him." The tattered Big Papi replica was shipped to Boston and sold at auction to benefit the Jimmy Fund charity, while the hole remains unfilled to this day. "I can't tell you how many times I'm walking somebody through the stadium and people are like, 'Can you show me where the Ortiz jersey was?'" said Doug Behar, the Yankees' senior vice president of stadium operations. "We didn't take it too seriously; listen, if it was buried 100 feet under all the work we did, it'd probably still be there."

Alex Rodriguez's first steps onto what would be the field of the new stadium came in July 2008, as the club announced a deal with the Hard Rock Cafe to open a 7,000-square-foot restaurant past the right-field corner. In all, approximately 172,000 feet of the 634,000-square-foot stadium site would be devoted to premium restaurants, clubs, conference facilities, and high-end retail stores.

As Rodriguez stood over the spot where home plate would rest, he added a looping signature to the sweet spot of a pinstriped guitar, drawing cheers from a group of construction workers milling about in hard hats and jeans. Concrete installation was complete at that time, and as the 4 Train rumbled past what would be the center-field scoreboard, second-deck blue seats were visible running from the right-field corner to the boxes behind home plate. "I had a different prism because I came from the Kingdome in Seattle to Safeco Field and I'm like, 'Oh my God, déjà vu,'" Rodriguez said. "I knew how healthy that move is. We'd miss the history of the old Yankee Stadium, but you gained amenities and comfort and space. I always tell people we have a hundred yards [of clubhouse space], but the media can only see 20. Eighty yards that is all for us."

As their future home rose, the Yankees entered their final season at the old building with a new manager at the helm. Following the team's elimination in the 2007 American League Division Series, Torre refused a one-year, $5 million contract, calling the reduction from his 2007 salary of $7.5 million "an insult." Rising from a seat in a Tampa, Florida, conference room, Torre shook hands and departed for a waiting jet, ending a 12-year run that produced four championships and six pennants.

Torre's bench coach, Don Mattingly, was a fan favorite from his days as a sweet-swinging, Gold Glove first baseman, but Joe Girardi quickly emerged as the leading candidate. A Northwestern University graduate who valued discipline and sported the military buzz cut to match, Girardi caught for three Yankees World Series winners and had been the team's bench coach in 2005 before managing the Florida Marlins in 2006. Girardi guided that young club to 78 wins, earning honors as the National League's Manager of the Year, but was dismissed after one season following clashes with owner Jeffrey Loria.

Participating in an exhaustive interview process with ownership, Cashman, and nine members of the baseball operations staff, Girardi won the team's trust by showcasing his preparation on the topics of game strategy, player evaluation, and advance scouting. Girardi said that he understood the Steinbrenner family's expectations that anything less than a World Series championship would be considered a failure, saying on the date of his hiring, "I expect to be playing in the Fall Classic next October." As a constant reminder of those expectations, Girardi selected uniform No. 27. "I kind of stole the idea from Tony La Russa," Girardi said. "He wore his number on the back of the championships the Cardinals had and he had the next one as well. And I thought, *That's a pretty good idea.* I don't really have a number; 25 is the number I wore, but Giambi's got 25, so I can't ask him for it. I had always been very fond of Carlton Fisk, who I worked out with in the winters, and he wore 72. It was the opposite of that, so I thought, *This fits pretty well.* I thought it was a good statement."

Cashman remembers the discussion differently. "It was my idea," Cashman said. "[Girardi] said, 'What have you got?' and I said, '27. Put the number on your back that our entire mission's about.' He was like, 'I love it.' He could've taken a different number. I suggested 27 and the purpose behind and the reason for it. He liked it and he wore it on his back. That was a story and one that resonated."

The dream of closing the old stadium with a championship waned as a slew of injuries kept the Opening Day lineup off the field through much of 2008. Catcher Jorge Posada played in just 51 games and required surgery to repair a right shoulder injury, and at various times, the Yankees were also without outfielder Hideki Matsui and third baseman Alex Rodriguez. A 19-game winner in back-to-back seasons, ace right-hander Chien-Ming Wang would never fully recover from a right foot injury he sustained while running the bases in a June 2008 game at Houston's Minute Maid Park.

Joba Chamberlain's first full big league season was impacted by injuries, and the club had banked on major contributions from young starters Phil Hughes and Ian Kennedy, who opened the season in the starting rotation but combined to go 0–8 in 18 games (17 starts). Girardi benched promising young second baseman Robinson Cano in September, punishing him for lackadaisical effort on a defensive play, and Melky Cabrera regressed from a starting center fielder into a spare part.

The Yankees' 89 wins ranked third in the American League East behind the Tampa Bay Rays (97) and Red Sox (95), the first full season since 1993 that the club had failed to qualify for the postseason. "For the first time in a long time, there was an 'Oh shit' moment," Rodriguez said. "I came to New York to win a championship, and we came up short…It started in '04 with that disappointment, and then you get to '08 and you're like, 'Fuck. We are not in the postseason.' You could see some of our faces. We were all like sick, so frustrated. You don't know what the hell's going to happen. I personally thought we were letting the entire city down…When you get to the Yankees, it's like you're playing for a public company. The shareholders are the cops, the firefighters, the teachers, all the great people that make up the fabric of the city. And we're like, 'Fuck, we're not going to the playoffs.' I was sick to my stomach."

There were bright spots, such as Jeter surpassing Gehrig for the all-time Yankee Stadium hits record (1,274) and Mike Mussina securing the first 20-win campaign of his career on the season's final day, but the 2008 All-Star Game—a 15-inning affair won by the American League in four hours and 50 minutes, the longest Midsummer Classic ever—would serve as Yankee Stadium's last turn on the national stage.

They were mathematically alive as the home schedule expired, but the last weekend felt like a wake. With the final game scheduled for Sunday evening, many of the players stayed late on Saturday afternoon, enjoying the field as the shadows crept across the diamond. Girardi tossed balls to his six-year-old son, Dante, while Chamberlain, Johnny Damon, and Jason Giambi walked family members around the darkened turf. "As soon as you walked in there, it smelled like baseball," Cano said.

There had been talk of an offseason celebration to mark the official closing, as well as an NHL Winter Classic game between the Rangers and Islanders, but shuttering the gates after a ballgame seemed fitting. Yankee Stadium hosted countless football games, boxing matches, concerts, commencements, and three Papal masses, but baseball was what it had done best.

Fans began filing into the doomed ballpark early on that cloudless, warm Sunday afternoon for the venue's 6,580th game, after which Yankee Stadium would become "Old Yankee Stadium." White message boards attached to the first-base and third-base sides of the park faced the northbound lanes of the Major Deegan Expressway and normally would have black hand-set text reading something like, "BALTIMORE TONIGHT 8:05 PM." Instead, they said, "THANKS FOR THE MEMORIES."

Gates opened seven hours before the scheduled first pitch, and Trost had decided to permit fans to take a lap around the warning track if they wished. The new stadium was visible above where Yogi Berra used to say it would "get late early" in left field, and many rubbed their hands in the dirt, slapping dusty handprints onto the blue padding that covered the outfield wall. A few pretended to tie their shoes, trying to hide a swift pocketing of treasured soil. "We just wanted the fans to be a part of it, to take some part of it with them, even more so than on a normal game or season," Hal Steinbrenner said. "Letting them walk on the field and feel the stadium, we knew that would be special."

A procession of all ages snapped photos against the 408-foot marker in center field and the 314-foot marker in right field. Most used digital and click cameras, as the iPhone had been released by Apple only a year and a half prior. There were laughs, and there were tears. They treated it like hallowed ground because it was. "Everybody was almost misty-eyed," said reliever Phil Coke, who had made his big league debut less than a month earlier. "I was walking in just watching people, and they were saying, 'This is amazing; I'm on the field!' I thought, *You're not kidding. I'm lucky enough to do it every day.*"

As the players arrived outside the press entrance on the stadium's third-base side, they disappeared down a narrow staircase. The visitors followed a painted red line, while the Yankees were guided by a blue line to their club-house. Walls had been stripped bare; photographs of Ruth, Gehrig, Mantle, and others had been removed that week, so, as Andy Pettitte explained, "They wouldn't start walking off." Pettitte admitted that he had his eye on a Whitey Ford lithograph.

Four hours before game time, Girardi sank into an oversized leather office chair, fighting back tears as he compared the pressure of winning that day to a final game of the World Series. He'd just returned from a silent visit to home plate when the realization struck. Miller Huggins had been the first manager to fill out a lineup card at the stadium; Girardi would be the last. "It didn't even dawn on me when I was interviewing for the job," Girardi said. "At no point in my life did I ever think about it. It doesn't really become the last game until you get close. You never think that that point is going to get here."

Batting practice took on the crowded, celebratory buzz of a postseason contest. Red, white, and blue bunting hung from all three decks while celebrities like Richard Gere, Val Kilmer, Bobby Knight, Spike Lee, and Matthew Modine milled about the field. As the turnstiles spun, a slow procession filtered through the concrete concourses. The commemorative programs were $10; pencils, as always, were free.

The DiamondVision screen in right-center field focused on the bronze profile of Gehrig's monument, displaying in large blue letters, "Thank You, Fans." Beyond the wall in left-center field, fans pressed against a chain-link fence, aiming their cameras past a parked ambulance to catch a glimpse of the empty ballpark. A few feet away, others lined five deep to shake hands with Chamberlain's father, Harlan.

The souvenir tables and beer taps were busy at Stan's Sports Bar on River Avenue, and the sound of the stadium's Hammond Colonnade playing a Herman's Hermits tune spilled onto the street. At the will-call window surrounded by the wafting aromas of popcorn, hot dogs, and sausage, dozens crowded to pick up whatever ducats might still be available. They were scarce. A broadcast of the New York Giants' 26–23 win against the Cincinnati Bengals crackled on a nearby radio; few paid much mind.

Fans were urged to be in their seats early, and a stirring 65-minute ceremony did not disappoint, masterfully paying homage to the facility's rich history. The clear, concise, and correct speech patterns of venerable Bob Sheppard spilled out of the public-address system once more; the 98-year-old had recorded his lines from his Baldwin, New York, home due to illness, having last appeared at the stadium in 2007. The "Voice of God" boomed regally as 21 former players, including six Hall of Famers, took the field.

Old-timers like Berra, Don Larsen, and Whitey Ford wore baggy, cream-white uniforms that were intended to evoke the flannel of days gone by. As the generations milled about in the clubhouse, waiting for their call to the field, first-base coach Tony Pena had playfully untucked Berra's jersey. Berra, then 83 years young, grinned, and gave Pena a hard shove. "You hate to see it go," Berra said. "I played here all my life."

During introductions Willie Randolph dirtied his uniform pants in response to a dare from David Wells, sliding into second base. The loudest ovations were heard as Bernie Williams returned to center field, crossing his heart and raising both hands to the sky. It had been two years since the Yankees not-so-gently nudged the switch-hitter into retirement, declining to offer anything more than an invitation to spring training. "It was hard for me because I missed the game," Williams said. "I was always trying to keep track of how the guys were doing. The Yankees were always in my heart."

The 1922 American League pennant had flown on the stadium's first day of service and now it was unveiled on the last day and unfurled across the batter's eye. Outlined in red and proclaiming in blue text upon yellowed white, it read, "NEW YORK YANKEES LEAGUE CHAMPIONS 1922."

The clock rolled back to Opening Day 1923 with fill-ins representing the lineup that had notched a 4–1 victory against the Red Sox. Eddie Fastook, the team's director of security, normally spent his days guarding VIPs and brokering deals with fans who caught milestone home-run balls. On this day, Fastook was asked to stand in right field as Babe Ruth. There was one condition: the burly ex-cop had to shave his mustache.

The children of Roger Maris, Elston Howard, and Thurman Munson took their fathers' positions across the diamond. Mickey Mantle's son, Danny, tipped his cap in center field, bearing a remarkable resemblance to No. 7. Bobby Murcer had lost his battle with brain cancer that July, and there were few dry eyes as his widow, Kay, walked to center field wearing her husband's No. 1.

The cheers grew as Berra emerged from the dugout. The former catcher trotted a few steps before walking the rest of the way. He joked about digging up home plate, saying that it would make a great souvenir. Berra's perfect batterymate from the 1956 World Series, Don Larsen, couldn't wait that long. Assisted by Whitey Ford in full view of the ceremonies, Larsen bent at the waist and grabbed handfuls of mound soil.

A ceremonial first pitch was delivered by Ruth's 92-year-old daughter, Julia Ruth Stevens, who bounced her toss to Posada. "I am very sad that Yankee Stadium is not going to be in existence any longer," she said. "I wish it could have remained as a New York landmark, but I guess, like all things, it has come to its final days and it has to go. But I'll always have the memories of my father hitting those home runs out into the bleachers. And I have a lot of his pictures and I'll just remember those and the glory days of the Old Yankee Stadium. And I hope the New Yankee Stadium brings good luck to the Yankees." A dying Ruth had stood near home plate and told fans in his 1948 farewell address: "I am proud I hit the first home run in Yankee Stadium. God knows who will hit the last one."

After Baltimore got to Pettitte for a couple of quick runs, Damon believed he had etched his name into history with a three-run, third-inning homer off Baltimore starter Chris Waters. Those honors went instead to Jose Molina. The light-hitting, defensive-minded catcher pounced on a fourth-inning offering from Waters, placing a two-run homer atop the netting that covered Monument Park in left-center field. It was Molina's third homer of the season and the most memorable of the 39 he'd hit over a 15-year career. "I wasn't a guy that hit that many homers," Molina said. "To have the last one there, I think a lot about it. It was special for me. I don't know if it was for other people. I think other people thought that other guys that played there for many, many years should've had it, but you know how [unpredictable] homers are. To me, it has a really special place in my heart."

Pettitte went into the books as the stadium's final winning pitcher—part of an effort that included his 2,000th career strikeout. It was the conclusion of Pettitte's second season back in pinstripes after a three-year detour with the Houston Astros, who operated closer to his Deer Park, Texas, home.

Harboring some uncertainty about his baseball future, Pettitte said that the game felt like as much of a must-win as any he had pitched. He normally requested solitude while preparing for a start, but on that night, Pettitte flicked on all of the television screens in the weight room. He did not want to miss a millisecond of the festivities. "The old stadium was just so special," Pettitte said. "There was something about leaving that old, grimy, dirty place—so much magic had been there, magical moments, stuff like that. But then we would make trips over to the [new] ballpark as it was being built. I remember going over there with Lonn Trost a couple times and him showing us around, and it was like, 'Man, this is pretty special, too.' The biggest thing was trying to bring a championship back to New York and being part of that again. As we all were getting older, it seemed like the dynasty was going to be over, and the run was kind of over. We always were trying to get back to that championship-caliber team and bring a championship back to the city and to the organization."

The clock read 11:41 PM as Rivera ended 85 years of history, throwing the stadium's final pitch, a cut fastball that Baltimore second baseman Brian Roberts chopped to the right side of the infield. First baseman Cody Ransom gloved the ball and stepped on first base, securing the Yankees' 4,133rd victory on those grounds. "I probably wasn't as mad as I might be normally against Rivera in the ninth inning with the game on the line," Roberts said. "I didn't want to make the last out. I figured I'd either make the last out or get the last hit or something. I couldn't go wrong. But Mariano is pretty good at getting outs."

A utility infielder from Mesa, Arizona, who batted .213 over 11 seasons with eight organizations, Ransom didn't want to release the ball, but it was the correct choice to pass it to Rivera. The closer promised to relay it to Steinbrenner, who was watching the game on television from his Tampa home. "Closing the stadium was big," Rivera said. "All the championships, all the majestic events, and everything came to end. We still had a team that had a chance to compete and get back into the winning era again."

The stadium's all-time hits leader with 1,274, Jeter was fittingly the final Yankees player to bat. He went hitless but delivered the evening's capper with his rousing speech. Though he had swiftly agreed when Zillo asked him to speak, Jeter wasn't sure what to say. When Jeter was removed from the game with two outs in the ninth inning, he absorbed a standing ovation, a curtain call, and then organized his thoughts. "When I came out in the ninth inning, I said, 'I've got to think of something quick,'" Jeter said. "I knew I wanted to acknowledge the fans. I was scared to death. When I was younger, I used to get really, really nervous when I had to do an oral report in front of 25 people. I guess I've come a long way."

A decade later, those who were on the infield remain impressed by how Jeter held no script yet struck all the right notes in an address that lasted just under two minutes. "I thought it was one of the greatest speeches of all time. I really do," Girardi said. "I sit back and listen to that and think, 'Man, is that really good.'"

"That's Derek. I don't think he's a pen-and-paper person," Chamberlain said. "To touch on every topic that made sense to all of us, that made sense to all of the fans, that made sense to all of the baseball world, that's just Derek and what he does. I don't think there was a better fitting person to close that stadium at the time than Derek."

Rivera had memorably kissed the pitching rubber after Aaron Boone's pennant-winning home run toppled the Red Sox in 2003. Now he pecked at the clay of the mound with his cleats, filling a plastic storage container with whatever came loose. "I remember everybody running like crazy to grab cups and fill those cups with as much dirt as they possibly could, particularly Mariano," said Dana Cavalea, the team's strength and conditioning coach. "I don't know if he had a side deal where he was selling dirt with Steiner [Sports] or what, but I remember him taking more dirt than anybody else."

Radio broadcaster Suzyn Waldman was conducting interviews in front of the home dugout when someone offered her a small plastic bag. She accepted, using it to retrieve dirt from the front of home plate. Cashman pointed her in the direction of a group of authenticators from Major League Baseball, who were overseeing the festivities while they doled out hologram stickers. "[Cashman] says, 'If you want to go over there, they'll put a seal on it for you, so you'll know that it's real,'" Waldman said. "I said, 'I know it's real, I'm doing it myself!' I was there with my little hands putting dirt in a little bag. I still have it. I didn't need it to be certified because I did it myself. I'm not selling it. That's for me."

Rivera wanted one more souvenir, requesting that a photographer capture the remaining cornerstones of the Yankees' most recent dynasty. The group that would come to be known as the "Core Four" gathered shoulder-to-shoulder on the mound with Rivera flanked by Jeter, Pettitte, and Posada. "That's why we wanted to have that picture, so we always remember that moment," Rivera said, "like Mickey and Joe and Whitey and Yogi. That's what we represent in this era. Like Joe DiMaggio said, 'I thank the good Lord for making me a Yankee.' And that's the way it is."

Shortly after the final game, Munson's locker and the carpet underneath it were painstakingly extricated from the home clubhouse and reinstalled as the centerpiece of a museum at the new stadium. Munson's locker had never before been available for public view and for a generation of fans, who vividly recall where they were on the afternoon of August 2, 1979, it would be arguably the most emotional site in the new building. "Our carpenters disassembled the locker in one day and they immediately reinstalled it in the museum," said Brian Richards, the museum's curator. "They wanted to ensure that nothing would get lost or damaged over time. The room was still under construction at that time, but the locker was installed right away. After the carpenters finished installing it, they called me and said, 'This is kind of nicked up. Do you want us to repaint it?' I said, 'No, no, no! Leave it just the way it is.'"

Other items were salvaged for public sale, and the Yankees and Steiner Sports cut an $11.5 million check to the City of New York, acquiring the rights to strip the stadium's guts. Reggie Jackson was among the first in line to purchase items, including his old locker, a section of the black seating area, and the 10-foot-tall electric blue letters that spelled out "YANKEE STADIUM" after the 1974–75 renovation. Curious employees never knew what else they might find. "The top floor of the stadium had rooms that were almost like a haunted house," said assistant general manager Jean Afterman. "They had these incredibly archaic popcorn vending machines with ornate iron work from before World War II. They looked like somebody had pushed them into a room and walked away."

Everything was up for grabs. About 40,000 of the 56,000 seats were sold with a pair listed at $1,499 and single seats at $749. A freeze-dried chunk of grass measuring a few square inches fetched $80. Other items included signage, ticket booths, turnstiles, and even furniture. (A two-drawer file cabinet from the office of team president Randy Levine was still available on Steiner's web site nearly a decade later for $500.) "I have my name plate from my locker," Posada said. "I have the chair somewhere in the house. I wanted to take my locker, but they made it really tough to negotiate that. Steiner took everything."

The future was calling. Tishman Speyer and the project team boasted that they were able to beat the scheduled completion date by a month with a total project cost of $1.5 billion (excluding land and financing). On a rainy November afternoon, former Bombers—Scott Brosius, Jeff Nelson, Paul O'Neill, and Cone—were called upon to help 60 local students transport home plate, the pitching rubber, and dirt from the old stadium to the new one. Standing in the area that would become the home dugout, Cone remarked, "This new Yankee Stadium has got a lot to live up to."

The inhabitants of Monument Park were among the final treasures to travel across 161st Street. Ruth's monument was the most difficult to pry loose. With reporters and photographers looking on, a muddied yellow forklift labored for more than a half hour, trying to unearth the Great Bambino. He'd sat on those grounds since 1949 and was only dislodged by the renovation that relocated the monuments from center field. "It seemed like the Babe didn't want to leave," said Anthony Vespa, part of a five-man crew from the Bronx-based Port Morris Tile and Marble Company, who helped secure Ruth's monument in plywood, foam packaging, and shrink wrap.

Most employees moved to the new stadium on January 23, 2009, packing their possessions into orange plastic crates and carrying them through the loading dock entrance of the old stadium to a waiting truck. The monuments, plaques, and retired numbers were placed into storage and delivered in time for the Yankees to receive the keys from the construction outfits on February 17, 2009. "Seeing people come across the street with that excitement, it was awesome," Behar said. "For some of our special artifacts, our staff put white gloves on and walked the World Series trophies across the street. It was pretty special to watch."

The added glitz was impressive, but the most important hallmark of Yankee Stadium is winning baseball. The franchise still laid claim to the most titles in the sport, but those 26 had been secured across the street. The Philadelphia Phillies were now the defending champs, having defeated Tampa Bay in a five-game, rain-prolonged Fall Classic. It was time to write history in the new place.

CHAPTER 3

A CHANGE
IS GONNA COME

The final turnstile had spun as Brian Cashman walked to his office in the soon-to-be-vacated stadium, and an autumn chill whipped through the thousands of faded blue seats in the grandstand. He'd often said that the Yankees were out of his hands when the postseason arrived; there were no trades or roster moves to make, leaving him to nervously munch popcorn or prank employees while the next nine innings played out.

As Cashman rode the elevator, pulled open a glass door, and passed the two World Series trophies that rested at the entrance of the executive offices, he experienced an even more uncomfortable sensation. The Yankees hadn't been playoff observers for a non-strike season since 1993, and Cashman despised turning on the television to check scores. October baseball belonged in the Bronx, and to make that happen again, he had work to do.

Having risen from a 1986 summer internship to assume the general manager's chair at age 30 prior to the 1998 season—just in time to oversee the winningest club in franchise history—Cashman's shine dulled with the Yankees' two first-round eliminations prior to the playoff miss in '08. A meaty packet of newspaper clippings thudded on each employee's desk shortly after dawn, and when Cashman flipped through, he saw that he was taking fire from the press. One columnist blamed him for a farm system that ranked among the worst in the sport.

That criticism had some validity; Cashman acknowledged that changes needed to be made in the way that the team scouted and drafted players, which was part of the reason why they had no obvious pipeline to supplement an aging roster. Big-money free agents such as Carl Pavano and Kei Igawa had been colossal busts, while a ballyhooed trade for Randy Johnson resulted in an open-palm shove to a CBS cameraman along East 60th Street and a couple of postseason disasters.

Cashman believed that the faulty process that led to those decisions was correctable and that the Yankees were in better condition than when he arrived. For one thing the baseball operations department was less splintered than it had been during George Steinbrenner's heyday, when the New York contingent spent a good portion of each day wondering who was whispering into The Boss' ear down in Tampa, Florida.

Before pressing pen to paper on his most recent extension in 2005, Cashman had insisted upon receiving assurances that the turf war would end, and everyone in the department would report to him. It may not have resulted in playoff success, but at least there was less energy wasted dousing fires with The Boss and his cronies. Now it was time to negotiate again, and Cashman did not appreciate the insinuation that he had been unsuccessful at his job. The *New York Daily News*, in particular, had columnists on staff who seemed to be out for blood, and Cashman grumbled that he wanted to make them pay.

He called upon a favorite saying attributed to Reggie Jackson, who said, "As long as you have a bat in your hands, you can change the story." Cashman hadn't faced a fastball since his days as a scrappy infielder at Catholic University in Washington, D.C., but this job had placed him in confrontations more intense than any batter-pitcher showdown. As he accepted a three-year extension from the Steinbrenner family, Cashman made it clear that he was returning to complete what he viewed as unfinished business. "If I left, I wasn't going to like the story that was going to be written because it wasn't going to be an accurate depiction of my time here," Cashman said. "I've given my heart and my soul to this franchise, and they've given their heart and their soul back to me. I'd be nothing without what the Steinbrenners have done for this person at this table right now. But at the same time, I'm not going to let an inaccurate story stick, and the only way for me to change that is to change the story. So I'm staying to change the story."

To do so, the roster would need to look different. Jason Giambi's seven-year, $120 million contract had expired, and Mike Mussina decided to retire after an 18-year career that would result in his 2019 Hall of Fame induction. Bobby Abreu, a midseason acquisition in 2006, was headed for free agency, as was Andy Pettitte. Pavano and Ivan Rodriguez didn't figure into future plans.

There were pressing issues off the field, too. Joe Torre's exit after 2007 had set the Yankees upon the course Cashman desired; Torre's Godfather-like reputation had given him so much power and popularity that he was considered as influential as anybody in the organization. Yet, Torre's hold on the clubhouse had waned in his final seasons, when some privately groused that unless you were one of "Joe's guys" it was difficult to grab Torre's attention. "The only players he actually had a connection to were the ones he won rings with," a Yankees insider observed. "Anybody else that came in, they were like, 'This is him? This is Joe Torre?' I couldn't tell you how many ones I remember that said, 'I was all excited to play for this guy and then when I got here this fucking guy doesn't talk to me.' Unless you were Bernie or Mo or Jeter or Pettitte, it was as if he looked right past you."

Indeed, Torre was fiercely loyal to those who had helped to place World Series rings on his sizable hands. That attitude leaked into the clubhouse, where Derek Jeter would privately grouse about his new teammates, saying, "Those guys don't know how to win championships." Yet some had: Gary Sheffield won with the Florida Marlins in 1997, Randy Johnson led the Arizona Diamondbacks to a title over the Yankees in 2001, while a bearded, shaggy-haired Johnny Damon had been a part of the Boston Red Sox's 2004 curse-busting gang of "Idiots." If the old guard was unwilling to adjust, Cashman believed that the Yankees needed to change the ethos inside the room. "Culture was an issue in that clubhouse," Cashman said. "We were broken, and it needed to be addressed."

Paced by starting pitchers CC Sabathia and A.J. Burnett, the free-agent class was top-heavy, while the position player front was headlined by sluggers Mark Teixeira and Manny Ramirez. The Yankees had gambled that their rotation—led by the youthful trio of Phil Hughes, Joba Chamberlain, and Ian Kennedy—was ready to enter a new era. That staff was now in tatters because of the troika's inconsistent and underwhelming 2008. For a quick fix, they'd need to spend big. "If all those guys win 20 games, then we wouldn't have done any of it," Cashman said. "We had some areas that were broken that needed to be fixed and we wanted the available market-place to get it done."

Sabathia had showcased his physical and mental fortitude during his three-plus months with the Milwaukee Brewers, going 11–2 with a 1.65 ERA in 17 starts. To the chagrin of his agents, the hulking 6'6", 300-pound left-hander took the ball on short rest in each of his final three starts, helping Milwaukee chase down a postseason berth. It was a stunning sign of sacrifice for a pitcher who was said to be targeting a contract of $150 million or more that winter.

Thrusting aside his own personal stakes for the greater good of the team, Sabathia had proven to be the ultimate teammate. Cashman noticed, recognizing the value of a true ace who could lead the staff on the mound and in the clubhouse. As excellent as Mussina's performance had been in 2008, the veteran was a loner, content to sit at his locker filling out cross-word puzzles or chatting with reporters about cars, movies, or TV. Cashman needed someone like Sabathia. "CC was a massive target," Cashman said. "And not just for what he could do on the field."

Cashman envisioned Sabathia as someone who could add a fresh outlook to the clubhouse, succeeding where Giambi or Alex Rodriguez had failed to wrest control away from staples like Jeter and Jorge Posada. The Yankees had competition, as Sabathia's high-octane fastball and teddy bear personality had the baseball world lining up to wave dollar bills in his direction.

The Brewers hoped to retain their new ace, though they were only able to offer five years and $100 million. He enjoyed his time with Milwaukee but hadn't been there long enough to entertain a hometown discount. The Red Sox were also said to be interested in Sabathia, but the biggest threats to land the southpaw would come from the West Coast. The Los Angeles Dodgers, Los Angeles Angels of Anaheim, and San Francisco Giants were all expected to chase Sabathia, who grew up in the North Bay city of Vallejo, California, 30 miles north of San Francisco and 25 miles from Oakland. To the Yankees' concern, Dodgers owner Frank McCourt reached out to Sabathia personally. Cashman prepared to pitch Sabathia in Las Vegas, joining the millions of annual visitors who dream of leaving Sin City with newfound fortune.

The annual Winter Meetings, which assemble the entire baseball world for four days of rumors, whispers, and signings, took place that year at the Bellagio Hotel and Casino during the second week of December. Exiting a suite that overlooked the Bellagio's iconic fountains, Cashman made the one-and-a-half-mile trek north on Las Vegas Boulevard to the Wynn Hotel, where he scheduled a meeting with Sabathia and agent Brian Peters.

Manager Joe Girardi and Hall of Famer Reggie Jackson—a Bay Area native like Sabathia—tagged along as reinforcements. The Yankees went high-tech in their efforts. Cashman produced a DVD that the team had commissioned, offering Sabathia a virtual tour of the stadium site. It featured video messages from construction workers and team employees, imploring the pitcher to be a part of a new era in the Yankees' rich history. "There were construction workers saying, 'Come, CC,'" Sabathia said of the video, which Cashman still keeps stashed in an office cabinet. "It was a bunch of different people around the stadium, people I still see when I'm walking into the stadium right now. It was dope. That was a huge thing for me: them getting out of the old stadium and me being able to play in the new stadium. I was really excited about that, just the chance to play in a new facility."

As Cashman and Girardi listened, Jackson dominated the meeting. "Mr. October" doled out signed baseballs and regaled Sabathia with stories of his glory years, offering what he believed was his best sales pitch to woo Sabathia. Jackson hit 253 of his 563 homers for the Oakland A's from 1968 to 1975 and then 15 more in 1987, his final season in the majors. Sabathia, who turned seven that year, viewed Jackson as a living legend. At this moment, though, the hurler was more concerned with his own future than Jackson's past. "I was a huge Reggie fan growing up, and my family had been, too, with him playing in the Bay Area for that long," Sabathia said. "It was cool having him be there, but we really couldn't get anything done."

Peters called Cashman the following day and requested a second meeting at the Wynn, which the general manager recalled as "a good, strong talk." Jackson did not attend that meeting, freeing Cashman to lay out a more complete proposal to Sabathia, during which he stressed the need for a strong, team-first personality to mend a clubhouse in need of a makeover. "CC was interested and open to coming here, but there were also concerns because he knew we had a broken clubhouse," Cashman said. "He said that was [the perception] around the whole league. So I talked to him about, 'That's one of the reasons we're talking to you—not just because of who you are as a player but someone who brings people together.'"

During his seven-and-a-half seasons with the Cleveland Indians, Sabathia would routinely invite teammates to Cavaliers games, and cookouts at the hurler's home were commonplace. Those types of group gatherings were not part of the Yankees' culture, and Cashman loved everything he had heard. The fact that Sabathia had averaged more than 14 wins and 207 innings over his first eight years didn't hurt.

The Yankees had made an intriguing pitch, but Sabathia remained uncertain. He and his wife, Amber, had just welcomed their third child, Cyia, in October. Aware that they would not return to Cleveland, the couple had spent the first part of the offseason clearing out their longtime home and shipping boxes to California. "I remember sitting in the offseason and talking to Amber, and we're like, 'Wherever we sign is where we're going to live,'" Sabathia said. "We were tired of moving around. Lil' C [as Carsten, their oldest son, is affectionately known] was starting kindergarten, so we wanted to be set somewhere. We just started looking at possible places we wanted to play. It was the Dodgers, Anaheim, and then New York."

The allure of playing on the West Coast was obvious. Sabathia's extended family still lived in Northern California, so landing in Los Angeles or Anaheim would place their loved ones a short flight away. Any of those teams could make him richer than he had ever imagined. So what would be the deciding factor? Location? Lifestyle? Ballpark? As Sabathia deliberated his future, he kept returning to the same thing. "I felt like I was comfortable on the money," Sabathia said. "But I wanted to win more than anything, so once I kind of figured my No. 1 thing was wanting to win, there was no other place to choose."

He had come close to experiencing victory in 2007. The well-balanced Indians pushed past the Yankees in the American League Division Series, thanks to an assist from a swarm of tiny bugs known as midges, which had caused Chamberlain to blow an eighth-inning lead in Game 2. Rather than leaving Cleveland with a split, the Yankees faced an 0–2 deficit that they could not overcome in the best-of-five series.

The Red Sox outlasted the Indians in a seven-game American League Championship Series, and Sabathia posted a ghastly 10.45 ERA in his two losses to Boston. He won the AL Cy Young Award a month later, but the honor felt empty given his postseason performance. "I should've won the World Series that year in '07," said Sabathia, a tinge of bitterness still present in his voice as he reflected years later. "We had the best team, and I just wasn't ready."

Sabathia had more questions for the Yankees. Peters reached out to Cashman again, requesting a third meeting. This time it wouldn't be at the Wynn; it wouldn't even be in Las Vegas. Sabathia had returned to his home in a gated community near Fairfield, California, where he wanted to sit down one more time with the GM. Peters provided the address, and Cashman booked a one-way ticket to Oakland, leaving reporters and agents to wonder why the public face of the Yankees' front office was no longer representing the team at the biggest event of the winter. "I'm like, 'I'll do whatever you need,'" Cashman said. "I snuck out of there and I remember saying, 'I've got to be John Calipari. I've got to get in that house with a recruit and I've got to get the commitment from the recruit. I'm getting an in-house visit.' All I could think of was John Calipari at the University of Kentucky and I was like, 'I've got to close this recruit out.'"

A car service shuttled Cashman to Sabathia's front door, and the GM produced a selection of Yankees swag for Sabathia's kids—part of a full-court press to win over the family. Cashman told Sabathia that he'd seen the house before on an episode of *MTV Cribs*. Seated in a luxurious double-height living room, Sabathia said that he was giving serious thought to life in New York but expressed apprehension about a future with the Yankees.

According to friends, chief among Sabathia's concerns was the prospect of throwing to Posada, whose defensive reputation around the league was not particularly strong. Cashman assuaged those fears, listing a number of All-Stars and future Hall of Famers who had thrived with Posada calling pitches.

A Connecticut resident at the time, Cashman answered all of Amber's questions about raising a family in the New York area, describing lush, family-friendly suburbs that were close enough for the couple to enjoy Manhattan's nightlife. Selling Sabathia's wife, it turned out, had been as crucial as convincing the pitcher. When Amber mentioned that she loved the Macy's Thanksgiving Day parade, Cashman promised that the Yankees could get her front-row seats. "I wasn't really sold about coming to New York after the very first meeting," Sabathia said. "When Cash came to California, we talked, and he gave me and Amber the chance to ask him questions, selling us on the family side of it and having a place to live. I was just thinking in New York you live in the city, and my kids would be growing up with no grass lawn and stuff. Once we talked about places to live outside the city and I would be comfortable, I felt good."

Once Sabathia acknowledged that he could see himself in pinstripes, Cashman and the hurler swapped dollar figures. Cashman had boosted an initial six-year, $140 million proposal by a year, offering seven years and $161 million, surprising Sabathia by including an opt-out clause after the third year. It was an aspect of the deal that Sabathia said he hadn't even thought about, but Cashman's willingness to add an escape hatch sent a message: we're so confident that you're going to love New York that we'll let you leave if you don't. "I went in there and hit him over the head with a lot of money," Cashman said. "They told me they were worried about making such a commitment and being stuck here. So I remember on the plane, I thought about the opt-out."

While the rest of the baseball world was wheeling and dealing into the wee hours back in Nevada, Cashman prepared to spend the night in a San

Francisco hotel, catching a quick snooze before boarding an early-morning flight back to Vegas. A few hours after exiting Sabathia's home, Cashman received the call he was pinning his hopes upon. Sabathia was in. "With him selling us on a good place to live, the opt-out after three years if I didn't like it, and having a chance to win every year—once they walked out of the house, I was like, 'I'm sold. I'm done,'" Sabathia said. "I was set on being a Yankee. I was excited."

Why wouldn't he be? Sabathia was about to sign the richest pitching contract in history, surpassing the six years and $137.5 million that the New York Mets had bestowed upon Johan Santana the previous winter. According to Cashman, that was just the first part of the plan. "He left the house saying he was going to get some more players," Sabathia said.

Derek Lowe and Ben Sheets were among the other names connected to the Yankees, but the most exciting option was Burnett, who had earned a reputation as a Yankee-killer. A flame-throwing right-hander who sported dozens of tattoos and a wicked curveball, Burnett dominated New York while wearing a Toronto Blue Jays uniform in 2008, posting a 1.64 ERA in five starts. Every time Cashman watched the snarling Burnett slash through his star-studded lineup, the Yankees resembled a Little League team instead of a squad with the highest payroll in the majors. Jeter and Damon were among those who privately lobbied Cashman for Burnett's acquisition. "We needed starters, and he had a big year in Toronto," Cashman said. "All our players down in the locker room were talking to me about, 'We've got to get A.J. Burnett.'"

Burnett had never won more than 12 games in a season before his breakout 2008 campaign, during which he won 18 and led the American League with 231 strikeouts, prompting an opt-out of the final two years of his Blue Jays contract. It was easy to join Damon and Jeter in championing Burnett's acquisition. Given the underwhelming performance of Chamberlain, Hughes, and Kennedy—plus uncertainty surrounding Wang's return—adding two elite arms could return the Yankees to the peak of baseball's mountaintop.

Unlike Sabathia, geography was not a concern for Burnett, who also received significant interest from the Atlanta Braves. It was believed that the Monkton, Maryland, resident preferred pitching in the northeast in part because his wife, Karen, had difficulty flying. That had made his three years in Toronto complicated for their family, but New York City was just an Amtrak ride away. "That was kind of blown out [of proportion]," Burnett said. "That was more early, being so far away from home and in Toronto. She got better; it wasn't like a crazy flying thing. She just didn't care for it."

Burnett said that he'd made his decision after the Yankees' initial pitch. Other teams reached out to Burnett's agent, Darek Braunecker, but none offered the same appeal of the Yankees. Cashman had considered a trip to Burnett's Maryland home, as he had with Sabathia, but that trip was never deemed necessary. "It was kind of an easy decision for me the way New York came at me," Burnett said. "There wasn't any other place or any other contract that I would've went after. I couldn't have gotten a better offer from Cash and the Yankees. It was kind of a quick decision once that 2008 season ended, and I decided I wasn't going back to Toronto. It was just a no-brainer."

Tommy John surgery had cost Burnett a previous chance at postseason play, when his 2003 Marlins defeated the Yankees in six games. His finest moments in a Marlins uniform were a May 2001 no-hitter against the San Diego Padres, in which he walked nine men, and an intentionally errant warm-up pitch that blew out a window of a pickup truck behind home plate, terrifying a guy wearing the Billy the Marlin mascot costume. Burnett decided that a chance at winning needed to be his top factor as he negotiated what was likely the final major contract of his career. "When I was coming up and in the middle part of my career, the Yankees won a lot," Burnett said. "You don't get a chance very often to play in the postseason for any team—much less them. To be able to get a chance to go late in the post-season, maybe to chase a ring, that's everybody's first priority. If not, you're playing for the wrong reasons."

On the morning that news broke of the Yankees' preliminary agreement with Sabathia, Burnett knew he would be joining the big southpaw in New

York. He didn't need to be the No. 1; the opportunity to follow Sabathia's lead was too good to pass up. "Bringing CC in at the same time sealed the deal, being able to go there with him," Burnett said. "I didn't know him that well at the time, but I'd battled against him in Cleveland with the Blue Jays. I knew exactly who he was and what he offered. With what we already had, I figured it gave us a chance to win. He got finalized, and I was like, 'Okay, man, we should probably go there and get a ring.'"

Burnett and Sabathia were introduced together at the old stadium on December 18 and then were led across 161st Street to pose for photographs in the new building. As they inspected the grounds with jerseys draped over their shirts and ties, a Christmas tree rested atop the mound. It was a striking metaphor. With the two big arms leading a rotation that would theoretically include Wang, plus two of the three kids in Chamberlain, Hughes, and Kennedy, '09 had the makings of a happy new year.

The one name missing from that group was Pettitte, whose negotiations had hit an unexpected speed bump. As the Yankees went through their offseason program, it felt *fait accompli* that the wily lefty would be a part of the team that christened the new ballpark. Cashman even made a pit stop in Houston on his way back to New York from the Winter Meetings, hoping to close a deal with the popular left-hander.

With $243.5 million committed to Burnett and Sabathia, the dollars were adding up quickly for Cashman, who was no longer dealing with George Steinbrenner's win-at-all-costs philosophy. Hal Steinbrenner was as committed to winning as his father, recognizing that a winning baseball team was at the heart of the Yankees brand, but he also had a fiscally responsible side.

The Yankees had paid Pettitte $32 million for two steady seasons in 2007 and '08, but with Sabathia and Burnett in place, the team didn't intend to spend as lavishly. Cashman offered Pettitte a one-year, $10 million contract for 2009, to which the pitcher's agent, Randy Hendricks, balked at the $6 million pay cut. Pettitte was an integral part of the clubhouse; would the Yankees really move into their new stadium without him? Pettitte hoped not. "It was like, man, you want to be a part of this," Pettitte said. "I mean, just everything that I had done with the Yankees in the time that I spent there, and you got a new stadium being built. You definitely wanted to see that through also and be a part of the new ballpark. With the guys that were on the team, the guys that were with me all along—Mo and Jorgie and Jeet—everybody was coming back. I didn't want to be the odd man out."

Cashman was holding firm. Other teams had inquired about Pettitte's availability, but the 36-year-old had let it be known that he wanted to return to New York. If that wasn't in the cards, retirement was a legitimate option, and perhaps the only bargaining chip Pettitte had to play. "I think I told my agents, 'If I'm not going back there, I may just go home,'" Pettitte said. "Things were dragging, and there was concern. At that point in my career, it was more just about: I want to be compensated fairly for what I felt like I could bring to the table. There were definitely stressful times there, wondering if I was going to be able to get a deal done."

With the holidays rapidly approaching, it appeared the stalled negotiations would be pushed into the new year. Cashman could not sit back and wait for Pettitte. Circumstances had presented another option—not for the rotation but for the lineup. When Mark Teixeira's expected deal with the Red Sox hit a snag, Cashman jumped at the opportunity, signing the first baseman to an eight-year, $180 million contract.

It had been more money than ownership had allotted for the winter, but Hal Steinbrenner gave his okay, having been convinced that this was an opportunity to add a Gold Glove first baseman with one of the best all-around bats in the game. The Yankees shelled out $423.5 million for the three biggest names on the free-agent market, but to Pettitte's dismay, that left the coffers virtually empty. He was no longer in the team's plans. "Andy called, wanting to know what the hell happened," Cashman said. "I walked him through the experience that we had with the agency in this particular time frame. I think he was caught off guard and was unaware of some of the directions and the twists and turns that the failed negotiation had taken… He was crushed. We didn't have his money anymore."

Cashman had great fondness for the pitcher who had won 149 regular-season games, another 13 in the postseason, and four World Series rings with the Yankees and also Pettitte the person. There was no place for senti-mentality. "You see the team they're putting together and, when you have a championship in your eyes, that's all you are concerned about," Pettitte said. "You start seeing them bringing in CC Sabathia, you bring in A.J. Burnett, you bring in Mark Teixeira. It's like, 'Dude, are you kidding me? I've got to figure out a way to hopefully get me on this team.'"

While the $10 million offer was gone, Cashman had an idea to clear space for Pettitte. He presented a new offer with a base salary of $5.5 million, a shocking pay cut of more than $10 million from the previous season. Yet, as Cashman detailed, Pettitte could earn an additional $6.5 million in incen-tives based on innings pitched and days on the active roster. In other words, if he was able to stay healthy, take the ball every five days, and pitch the way he had in each of the previous four years, he would make $12 million.

Since Pettitte didn't want to open bidding to the other 29 clubs, there was but one move to make. He agreed to the incentive-laden deal on January 27—less than three weeks before pitchers and catchers were set to report for spring training. It had been a long, strange winter for Pettitte and the Yankees, but when the new stadium opened in April, No. 46 would be part of the festivities. "The only way for him to fix that was to be open-minded to taking a different type of deal and unfortunately pitching for his contract," Cashman said. "In the end Andy was important and wanted to be here. He got essentially his contract regardless. He just had to get it a different way."

CHAPTER 4

First Things First

The Yankees had addressed their rotation issues by adding CC Sabathia and A.J. Burnett, but despite claiming greats like Whitey Ford, Lefty Gomez, and Red Ruffing as their own, pitching had never been the franchise's identity. The Bombers were known for their bats. From Babe Ruth to Joe DiMaggio to Mickey Mantle, offensive prowess was their trademark.

A lineup that featured Alex Rodriguez, Derek Jeter, Jorge Posada, Hideki Matsui, and rising star Robinson Cano possessed more than enough talent to contend even with the departures of free-agent sluggers Jason Giambi and Bobby Abreu. It wasn't as prominent as the need for starting pitchers, but general manager Brian Cashman entered the offseason intending to address a hole at first base.

It had been less than three weeks since the Philadelphia Phillies won the World Series, defeating the upstart Tampa Bay Rays in a rain-soaked, five-game battle. While hot stove rumors began to swirl, the Yankees' pro scouting meetings set the course for the team's offseason plan. Landing Sabathia and Burnett was the top priority, but there was another name that intrigued Cashman and his lieutenants: Nick Swisher.

An emerging, slugger during his first three seasons with the Oakland A's, Swisher had hit 78 home runs between 2005 and '07. He was a prototypical A's player out of the Moneyball mold, possessing the power to hit the ball out of the park while displaying great patience at the plate.

The A's had locked up the switch-hitting slugger with an extension in the middle of the 2007 season, inking Swisher to a five-year, $26.75 million deal. It appeared that he would be a major part of Oakland's future, but less than eight months after signing the new deal, Swisher was traded to the Chicago White Sox for a three-player package headed by left-hander Gio Gonzalez.

In Chicago, Swisher clashed with manager Ozzie Guillen and the coaching staff. Swisher hit 24 home runs, but his .219 batting average and .743 OPS in 153 games represented dramatic drops from his numbers in Oakland. He seemed to be miscast—both as a leadoff hitter and a center fielder. When the 2008 season ended, Swisher got to work with his father, former big league catcher Steve Swisher. "Literally one day after the season ended, we were in batting cages grinding, working, trying to figure out what went wrong," Swisher said. "I feel like I got into a lot of bad habits in Chicago. I felt like I was trying to please a lot of people, and it just didn't work out for me."

Unbeknownst to Swisher, the silver lining in his White Sox tenure had been discovered in New York. The Yankees were in the early days of incorporating advanced analytics, and Michael Fishman had been appointed as the team's director of quantitative analysis. It was a fancy title that looked great on a business card, but Fishman's task was to unearth potential buy-low candidates for Cashman to pursue. "Fish walks in, and his exact words were: 'How would you like to acquire the second most unlucky player in baseball?'" Cashman said. "I was like, 'What?' He proceeded for the next half hour to an hour to talk to me about Nick Swisher."

The name was familiar to Cashman, who had tried to acquire Swisher from the A's, but Chicago's package blew away anything the Yankees were prepared to offer. Though Swisher's season in Chicago had been a disaster, Fishman's research suggested that it had more to do with bad luck than eroding skills or a change in approach. Swisher had the third lowest batting average on balls in play in the majors while his line drive and hard-hit percentages matched what he had done the previous three years in Oakland. "He proceeded to walk through every stat line that in his world proved this is the exact same player," Cashman said. "The only thing that happened was the balls he did hit went at defenders or got converted into outs. Bad luck."

Those numbers are more mainstream now, but a decade ago, Fishman was among the few investigating them regularly. Having graduated summa cum laude from Yale with a bachelor's degree in mathematics, Fishman was hired by the Yankees in 2005, two years after the release of Michael Lewis' deep dive into the Oakland front office challenged the rest of the league to catch up on the analytics front.

Fishman's introduction to baseball had come at age seven with Strat-O-Matic, a dice game that uses numbers to approximate players' skills. In his view there was nothing wrong with Swisher's card. He theorized that as long as Swisher stayed healthy, he would revert back into the same power threat he had been in Oakland. "I spent more time researching him than any other player," Fishman said. "When you have a mystery like why his performance was down, you had to dig deeper to get the answer. Was it randomness and bad luck, or was it change in his skill level and true talent level? All the research we did at the time concluded that it was more of a bad luck season, and his underlying skills hadn't changed. He still had the elite plate discipline and walk rate in Chicago. His strikeout rate was only up slightly, so it came down to: why did he not have as many hits? Why was his batting average of balls in play down? We looked at the studies on batted ball types, hit directions, ball distances; reviewed of all his batted balls; and just came to a conclusion that he was the same player that he was in Oakland. He just had bad stats."

Cashman knew that following the recommendation would require a leap of faith. The pro scouting department did not share Fishman's affinity for Swisher, but Fishman earned a gamble like this one. Cashman frequently referred to him as one of his "Knights of the Round Table." "I was like, 'Dude, that's a big bet to be placing,'" Cashman said. "But Fish kept climbing that credibility tree with suggestions he made. You're like, 'What does he see here?' I don't want to label myself as King Arthur, but he was one of my knights and he had earned a seat."

Cashman reached out to White Sox executive vice president Kenny Williams, who expressed no interest in keeping Swisher's escalating contract on their books. In Williams' view, there was also little reason to believe the relationship between Guillen and Swisher would improve in '09. "Personality-wise, it didn't fit," Cashman said. "Swish is a very strong personality in a positive way, but in a losing environment—as well as with bad production, which he had that particular year—that can definitely rub people the wrong way."

On November 13 the Yankees shipped utility infielder Wilson Betemit and pitchers Jeff Marquez and Jhonny Nunez to the White Sox for Swisher and pitcher Kanekoa Texeira, adding a powerful bat to the roster for a trio of expendable parts. Cashman dialed Swisher's telephone number and welcomed him to the club, telling him to expect duty as the everyday first baseman. Time in the outfield seemed unlikely, as outfielders Melky Cabrera, Johnny Damon, Hideki Matsui, and Xavier Nady were all in place. "Holy shit," Swisher said, recalling his thoughts at the time. "Why would these guys want me? I was literally going from having the worst season of my career professionally—and personally I had a tough year as well. He said, 'I don't care what kind of a season you had this past year. We know that you are going to have an amazing turnaround season. We know you are going to be successful.'"

In truth Cashman didn't know that for sure, but New York had taken advantage of a similar buy-low opportunity more than a decade earlier. Scott Brosius was traded from the A's to the Yankees following a subpar 1997 season in which he posted a woeful .576 OPS. At worst, Brosius would fill a utility infield role for the Yankees; at best, he would be their starting third baseman.

The Yankees sent right-hander Kenny Rogers to Oakland in exchange for Brosius, who produced an All-Star season in 1998, the team's historic 114-win campaign. Brosius saved his best for last, hitting .471 in the World Series sweep of the San Diego Padres to secure MVP honors. "It reminded me of the Brosius deal, which was buy-low; there was some upside," Cashman said. "In Swish's case everything Fish said was true. Everything he forecasted happened."

With a change of address, Swisher was about to have a new outlook on his baseball life. He had just gotten a new tattoo down the left side of his torso that read, "Persevere." Now here he was, reclaiming a promising career that had been temporarily derailed by his Windy City detour. "That was a major turning point in my professional career," Swisher said. "'I *am* pretty good and I *can* get over this hump.' To have the opportunity to come right over to the New York Yankees, to the team that everybody wants to play for, it completely changed my life from that day moving forward."

While the Yankees worked toward deals with Sabathia, Burnett, and Andy Pettitte, Cashman had agreed to meet with Mark Teixeira and his agent, Scott Boras, at the Four Seasons hotel in Washington, D.C. Considering the money that Cashman was preparing to throw at pitching, breaking bread with another first baseman seemed to be a courtesy. "He was not someone that was a realistic option," Cashman said. "But I know I was blown away with getting to know him in that environment, so it was impactful for me."

Even so, the Boston Red Sox were considered to be the overwhelming favorites to sign the 28-year-old switch-hitter. The Washington Nationals, Baltimore Orioles, and Los Angeles Angels of Anaheim were also in the mix. Was there room for the Yankees to get involved?

A product of Severna Park, Maryland, Teixeira was said to prefer a team on the East Coast, which was bad news for the Angels. Teixeira had enjoyed his two-month stint in Anaheim, but unless their offer was of *The Godfather* variety—one he couldn't refuse—it was going to be difficult for the SoCal team to sign him to a long-term deal.

Teixeira had grown up attending games at Baltimore's Camden Yards, counting Cal Ripken Jr. among his favorite players, and there was significant clamor from the fanbase to add Teixeira to an Orioles club that hadn't finished better than third in the American League East since 1997. The Orioles made Teixeira a seven-year offer in the $140-150 million range; it wasn't close to enough. "The Orioles basically made me an offer just to say, 'Hey, you're a hometown kid; we have to offer you something,'" Teixeira said. "But it wasn't competitive."

The other area team, the Nationals, extended an eight-year offer worth about $160 million. That was in line with what the Angels had offered, and while those stood as the most lucrative deals on the table, Teixeira continued to wait for a formal offer from the Red Sox.

He'd nearly landed in Boston once before, having been selected by the Red Sox in the ninth round of the 1998 draft before opting to attend Georgia Tech. Teixeira had no regrets about how that worked out. He had a great time on campus with the Yellow Jackets and then became a first-round pick in 2001. It seemed this second chance was preordained. Teixeira did list Boston among the best cities in the majors.

On the same day that the Yankees broke out the carving board to host the Burnett/Sabathia press conference in the Bronx, Red Sox owner John Henry, president Larry Lucchino, and GM Theo Epstein boarded flights to meet with Teixeira. They met at a hotel near Dallas/Fort Worth International Airport, and if Teixeira would accept eight years and $170 million, he'd be playing on Opening Day at Fenway Park. "We went to that meeting expecting to sign with the Red Sox," Teixeira said. "They told Scott, 'We're coming to close the deal,' which Scott assumed was going to be a better offer. Something happened, maybe on the flight down, but they didn't bring the deal that we thought they were going to bring."

Teixeira said that adding a ninth year or boosting the value of the contract closer to $200 million would have cinched it. Neither was offered. "Scott was very honest and said, 'Guys, that's what everyone else is offering. It's got to be a better deal, or we will continue to negotiate with other teams,'" Teixeira said. "At the time, we were negotiating with three or four other teams. It was very confusing. I was like, 'Well, this is just the business of baseball.' It didn't really bother me; it was just surprising."

The Red Sox had a history of not signing players for more than eight years and they were unwilling to establish a new precedent for Teixeira. After the meeting Henry sent an email to several media members, insinuating that the Red Sox were no longer in the Teixeira sweepstakes. "We met with Mr. Teixeira and were very much impressed with him," Henry wrote. "After hearing about his other offers, however, it seems clear that we are not going to be a factor."

The chain of events had Teixeira thinking more and more about the Yankees. Even though Teixeira had been an Orioles fan, Don Mattingly had been his favorite player, and there was allure in playing for the most successful team in history. His final at-bat in the old stadium was a grand slam off reliever Edwar Ramirez, who was moved to tears after the game. If the Red Sox would not go above and beyond, maybe Teixeira belonged on the other side of baseball's greatest rivalry. "I've always loved playing in New York; it suited me," Teixeira said. "I just knew that if I didn't go to the Yankees, I'd always wonder, *What if?* When you go to the best team, the most storied franchise, there's never going to be any regrets. No offense to the other 29 teams in baseball, but no one says, 'Man, I can't believe I never played for the Rays.' I always had this pull to the Yankees that if they wanted me, I was going to go there."

Teixeira's wife, Leigh, had expressed her preference for New York, which was no small factor. The couple, who first met while attending Georgia Tech, had two young children and were planning to set down roots wherever he signed. "She always enjoyed visiting New York. So if she was going to be happy, then I knew I would be happy," Teixeira said. "We were having dinner at home in Dallas one day, and I said, 'You make the choice; it's in your hands.' She said New York, and that helped. It wasn't the No. 1 factor, but again, all things being equal, everything kept bringing me back to the Yankees."

Cashman's initial pitch two weeks earlier, during which the GM touted him as the "missing link" to the Yankees' championship aspirations, also lingered in Teixeira's mind. "He sold me on, 'We have a good team and bad defense at first base, and I think you're going to make our pitchers better. You're going to make our infield better. You're going to make our team better defensively,'" Teixeira said. "No one ever sells you that. Everyone's like, 'Go hit 30 and 100.' With the pride I took in my defense, that mattered. He sold me on the new stadium and kind of the new wave of talent coming to New York. It was a great sales pitch."

After suffering through Giambi's substandard defense for much of the past decade, the Yankees were keen on the idea of adding a steady glove to anchor the right side of their infield. Derek Jeter would surely not complain about having a more talented defender to scoop his throws. "We learned the hard way that you can't just stick anybody over at first base," Cashman said. "When I started with the Yankees, we had Don Mattingly here, and he was obviously brilliant on the defensive side. There was a period of time where it was like, 'Well, we can sign a Giambi or we can put this guy or that guy over there, but the defensive side would hurt you.'"

Few took Henry's email missive to mean the Red Sox were out of the picture entirely, but with Boston no longer the clear-cut favorite, Cashman knew it was time to take a shot at Teixeira. "When the Red Sox were flying into Dallas, it sounded like they were going to be closing it out," Cashman said. "I had been having conversations with Hal that Tex could fit. After that meeting the reports were that it did not go as well as maybe the Red Sox and Teixeira had hoped. I was like, 'All right, there's a crack here.'"

The stalled negotiations with Pettitte left some financial wiggle room, but Cashman needed Steinbrenner's approval to push for Teixeira. He'd told Swisher to prepare as the starting first baseman, but if they could bring in a player of Teixeira's stature, Cashman would figure out what to do with Swisher later.

For 45 days the GM had been bending Steinbrenner's ear about Teixeira, explaining why he made perfect sense for the Yankees. As Cashman recalled, Steinbrenner's repeated response was "No, no, no," though that didn't stop Cashman from continuing to press the issue. "That was my job," Cashman said. "Hal is a lot like his dad in the fact that he wants to win. But unlike his dad, he wasn't impulsive. He's very methodical, he wants to make an informed decision, he wants to be walked through the process, educated, and then take time to think."

Cashman decided that Nady, not Swisher, would be the odd man out if they landed Teixeira. Swisher's plate discipline made him a more attractive right-field option. To gain Steinbrenner's approval, Cashman promised to move Nady's $6.5 million contract. Once that was settled, Cashman said that Steinbrenner signed on "rather quickly."

Washington had sweetened its offer to the nine-year, $180 million range, while various reports indicated Boston's eight-year, $170 million offer was still on the table. Teixeira had made up his mind. He instructed Boras to get a deal done with New York; on the afternoon of December 23, the agent delivered an eight-year, $180 million pact that included a full no-trade clause but no opt-out. "I told Scott, 'I'm going to the Yankees,'" Teixeira said. "He went to Brian and said, 'This is the deal. If you're willing to meet this deal, we'll sign with you.'"

Word began to spread to the Yankees' players and coaches, who were stunned. As recently as that morning, Hal Steinbrenner had told *Newsday* that the Yankees had no offers on the table to either Teixeira or Manny Ramirez (whom Hank Steinbrenner was said to prefer). With Sabathia, Burnett, and Swisher already in tow, the Teixeira signing was truly one that few saw coming. "We were golfing in Temecula, and my phone starts blowing up, 'You guys just signed Mark Teixeira,'" hitting coach Kevin Long said. "I was like, 'Oh my God, it's on!' That was huge. That was a big piece, and we knew it. We knew how valuable Tex was. You didn't realize how big of a piece Swish was going to be, but he was huge."

Sabathia's parting words with Cashman in the third and final meeting of their courtship had included a promise that the Yankees were about to spend more, but adding Teixeira was an outcome that Sabathia never considered. "When I signed, I might've already known that they were close to signing A.J., and Cashman said that they were going to look at Andy, but I had no idea that Tex was coming," Sabathia said. "That was crazy. That was awesome just finding that out. I don't think that was on anybody's radar."

On January 6, Teixeira was introduced in a press conference that turned out to be the final formal event at the old stadium. He was stunned by the crush of media documenting his arrival and, though he never complained, Teixeira revealed years later that a sinus infection had kept him from fully enjoying the event. "I had like a 105 fever, taking antibiotics, taking Tylenol every two hours to keep my fever down, doing the press conference," he said.

Teixeira might have been under the weather, but the Yankees felt great. When all was said and done, they had responded to a postseason miss by committing $423.5 million to Sabathia, Burnett, and Teixeira. For all the talk about how Hal Steinbrenner wouldn't operate the way his father did, the 2008 offseason sure read like a page out of The Boss' playbook. "Give

Hal credit," Alex Rodriguez said. "Everyone can say the Yankees have great resources, but the bottom line is you almost spent $2 billion on the stadium, we haven't sold a seat yet essentially, and now you've put close to another half of a billion dollars to work on three players. That takes a lot of fucking balls."

• CHAPTER 5 •

HOPE SPRINGS ETERNAL

Three years removed from his final big league at-bat, Alex Rodriguez glanced up from an oversized conference table on the 17th floor of a Manhattan luxury apartment building, acknowledged a pair of visitors, and extended his right hand. Dressed in a dapper Yankee blue suit, crisp white shirt, and silver tie, nine seasons had passed since he piled on his teammates at the center of the stadium infield, celebrating his one and only World Series championship.

A-Rod's routine might no longer revolve around batting practice and fielding drills, as it had in 2009, but retirement—much like his playing career—was anything but quiet. There were weekly trips to broadcast booths for ESPN's *Sunday Night Baseball*, appearances scouting business ventures alongside Mark Cuban and swapping celebrity gossip with Kelly Ripa, and a part-time advisor role that allowed re-entry into the Yankees universe whenever he felt the urge.

Rodriguez said that he'd delve into all of it, but as he checked his watch on this August afternoon in 2018, he was late for an appointment. "How much time do you guys have?" Rodriguez asked. "I've got to get to Fallon. Jennifer is on tonight. She wants me there when she gets in the [makeup] chair. We can talk on the way."

Jennifer, of course, is Jennifer Lopez, whom at that moment was being shuttled from a Brooklyn soundstage to Studio 6-B at 30 Rockefeller Plaza for *The Tonight Show* taping. Rodriguez whispered to an assistant, and a Mercedes-Benz van—outfitted with a leather interior that seemed more suited for a private jet than something on four wheels—appeared. As the tinted windows showcased Manhattan's shops and eateries at 25 mph, Rodriguez set the air conditioning on full blast, sunk into in a bucket seat, and returned to the spring of 2009. What turned out to be the most memorable year of his eventful life, Rodriguez said, had opened "like a bad dream; it was awful."

On February 7, a bombshell appeared on *Sports Illustrated*'s website. Selena Roberts and David Epstein reported that Rodriguez was one of 104 players who tested positive for banned substances in 2003, when he hit 47 homers and won his first MVP award. There were no penalties for positive tests at that time, but since 1991 Major League Baseball's drug policy had expressly prohibited the use of steroids without a valid prescription.

In 2003 MLB conducted survey tests to see if mandatory, random drug-testing was necessary; when more than 5 percent of players tested positive, penalties were instituted for 2004. Those results were supposed to remain anonymous, but a coded master list was seized in a 2004 federal raid on a drug testing facility in Long Beach, California, and the actual physical samples were seized in a related raid on a Quest Diagnostics lab in Las Vegas. As *SI*'s sources revealed, Rodriguez's urine showed traces of two anabolic steroids: testosterone and primobolan.

Four days after an irritated Rodriguez was challenged by Roberts with those developments in a University of Miami weight room, Rodriguez offered an admission in an interview with ESPN's Peter Gammons, telling the veteran reporter that he had "felt an enormous amount of pressure" to prove his value after leaving the Seattle Mariners to sign a record-setting $252 million contract with the Texas Rangers prior to the 2001 campaign.

Rangers owner Tom Hicks said that he felt "personally betrayed" and "deceived" by Rodriguez, who had flatly denied performance-enhancing drug use when pressed on the issue in 2007 by NBC's Katie Couric. Speaking to Gammons, Rodriguez explained that it had been "a loosey-goosey era" for baseball, which created a national ripple. President Barack Obama even addressed the situation in his first prime-time news conference. "It's depressing news on top of what's been a flurry of depressing items when it comes to Major League Baseball," Obama said. "And if you're a fan of Major League Baseball, I think it tarnishes an entire era, to some degree. And it's unfortunate because I think there are a lot of ballplayers who played it straight."

Rodriguez had spent most of his first six seasons with Seattle trying to escape the shadow of beloved center fielder Ken Griffey, Jr., and his February 2004 arrival in New York prompted perpetual (often unflattering) contrasts against Derek Jeter. The steroids admission earned a new parallel, as Brian Cashman likened his damaged superstar to Humpty Dumpty. Like the cracked character in the children's rhyme, Rodriguez had fallen. With nine years remaining on Rodriguez's contract, the Yankees had no choice but to put him back together again. "All the king's horses and all the king's men have to put Humpty Dumpty back together again," Cashman said. "I thought it was a perfect commentary. I spoke how I felt. I said, 'We have something right now that's broken. He's under attack mentally. We're invested heavily in him and we need him to be the player we invested in.' We're forced to walk through fire with him, and if we choose not to, then you're just actually making it worse."

Mark Teixeira thought he knew Rodriguez well from their lone season as teammates in Texas, but in a gym near his Dallas home, Teixeira halted his sets to absorb what he was hearing. "I was working out, and the gyms have TVs everywhere," Teixeira said. "I look up and I see the breaking news, and my first reaction was, 'What did I get myself into?' Everyone told me about the Bronx circus. It was going to be the Bronx Zoo."

Rodriguez and Teixeira were not particularly close during that 2003 season in Texas. Rodriguez was a superstar and carried himself with the presence of one, while Teixeira was a rookie in what he described as a "toxic clubhouse" of players who believed they belonged in better situations. Shortly after the admission, Teixeira spoke with Cashman, asking the general manager if he could be placed in all of Rodriguez's hitting and extra work groups. "It was the right thing to do," Teixeira said. "Plenty of people were going to turn their backs on him, but he was a teammate of mine in Texas while I was a rookie and he was the best player in the game. We weren't best friends, but I knew the guy had a good heart. I knew that obviously tons of players in that generation were mixed up in stuff. The fact of the matter was we needed him to be great for us to win a World Series."

Eight days after the Gammons interview, the Yankees hosted more than 200 reporters for a major press conference held in a picnic pavilion on the third-base side behind George M. Steinbrenner Field. Typically used during the summer for Florida State League sponsor parties, it was the same room where Andy Pettitte had apologized one year prior after his past use of human growth hormone was revealed.

Shuffling papers as he leaned into a microphone, an admittedly nervous Rodriguez expressed gratitude to those who had supported him over the previous weeks, including a 37-second pause when he referenced the dozens of teammates who had filled the room. Derek Jeter, Jorge Posada, Pettitte, and Mariano Rivera were seated in the front row; Jeter crossed his arms and slouched as Rodriguez told them, "I love you. It will be the best season of our lives."

"We are a group that is always going to pull for each other," Posada said. "It doesn't matter who needs the support, and obviously we wanted to be there during that conference. Alex had been through a lot, and we wanted him to feel comfortable and make sure that we were behind him and appreciated everything from the get-go that day. I think it got him closer to us. The team got closer that day. From Day One after that day, we were a tight unit."

"It's hard because we never went through situations like that before," Rivera said. "The team goes through a lot of things, but when this thing happened like that, everything exploded. It was a little tough, different, but again, we're family and we had to continue to do the same thing for family that we always do."

Saying that he was "here to take my medicine," Rodriguez spoke of his immaturity and stupidity. He detailed how a cousin—later revealed to be Yuri Sucart—suggested that the slugger could boost his energy by using a substance that could be purchased over the counter in the Dominican Republic. That was *boli*, a street name for primobolan.

Though Rodriguez said that he injected the drug twice a month for six months a year, he also said, "I knew we weren't taking Tic-Tacs," suggesting that there may have been an oral component. Rodriguez claimed that a 2003 neck injury halted his drug use, and that all of his seasons with the Yankees had been clean. His later ensnarement in the Biogenesis scandal, prompting Rodriguez's suspension for the entire 2014 season, suggested otherwise.

As Rodriguez continued to speak, Joe Girardi and Cashman were seated to his right, while Hank Steinbrenner watched from the back wall. Hal Steinbrenner monitored the developments on television from New York. Cashman remembers sitting quietly alongside Rodriguez, thinking how he would rather be anywhere else. Some of Rodriguez's teammates wondered if there could be a more productive use of their time. "It was a little bizarre, actually," Teixeira said, *"like I should be in the weight room right now, honestly. I should be taking ground balls. What is this?"*

"It was just packed. I just remember standing in that press conference like, 'Man, this is crazy,'" CC Sabathia said. "You're in New York now. This is what it is.'"

Almost universally, Rodriguez's teammates pledged their support. Years later, they'd recall that there had not been nearly as much fallout as feared. "I don't think it was a distraction for us," Johnny Damon said. "When we were asked about it by the reporters, it's kind of like, 'Well, it's not us. It's A-Rod who needs to answer these questions.' As much as you wanted to get some pressure off of him, there's nothing we could do. He's the guy who was doing the PEDs and he's the guy who has to talk about it."

"To be honest with you, it was like it hit and then it rolled over. It was gone," A.J. Burnett said. "It was nothing. He had a thing, and we supported him for it, and then it was baseball. It didn't linger. It wasn't like we're going on and going on. Alex said what he needed to say, manned up, and then played ball. I think it freed him."

Not all of the distractions were coming from Rodriguez's corner of the clubhouse. Damon and Xavier Nady had their financial assets frozen in late February when the federal government raided the offices of Houston-based financier R. Allen Stanford. Having been referred to Stanford through agent Scott Boras, the players were unaware of any wrongdoing.

Damon said that his Yankees paychecks were being deposited directly into Stanford's fund, which had been exposed as a massive Ponzi scheme. Nady's credit cards were frozen, preventing the outfielder from putting a deposit on a New York apartment despite his $6.55 million salary. Stanford would be sentenced to 110 years in prison and ordered to pay $5.9 billion in fines. "It stunk. I was building a house here in Orlando and I had to wait for every paycheck to come in to actually pay for it because every dime I had was frozen," said Damon, who was in the final season of a four-year, $52 million contract. "I knew it was going to be resolved. It was just a little distraction, but it was nice once the first checks started rolling in in April."

Because of the World Baseball Classic tournament, exhibition games were scheduled to begin on February 25, the earliest start to a Yankees spring training in at least seven decades. As Girardi settled into his second spring at the helm, he was aware that if the lights weren't flicked on at the new stadium come October, a new manager could be filling out the lineup cards in a year's time. "If you were around for the George Steinbrenner years, it was World Series or bust every year," Girardi said. "I didn't think the Yankees' slogan had changed, and Mr. Steinbrenner was still with us. I felt: Hey, that's why we put the uniform on. That's why we do all the work in the offseason, we do all the work in spring training. It's not to get to the playoffs; it's to win the World Series."

Sporting his No. 27 jersey while patrolling the practice fields, Girardi remembers being confident about the group in place, believing that Burnett, Sabathia, and Teixeira had the necessary qualities to succeed in New York. "I knew the offseason we had was an A-plus," Girardi said. "I watched from afar what CC did for Milwaukee. I mean, this is really, really impressive. I had heard so many good things of him inside the clubhouse. And I had watched A.J. stick it up our rear ends in Toronto and I was like, 'Okay, that's all right, too.' And I knew what a great player Tex was, so I was excited. I knew that we were going to be very good."

Early that spring Steinbrenner made a rare visit to the stadium that bore his name, riding an elevator to his fourth-floor office and accepting waves of visitors. Girardi and Jeter were first, followed by Rodriguez, who brought Burnett and Sabathia with him. Teixeira also attended, joined by Bernie Williams, who was in camp trying to get his body ready for at-bats with Puerto Rico in the World Baseball Classic. "[Steinbrenner] just said, 'Hey, hope you enjoy New York. Whatever your family needs, let anybody know,'" Sabathia said. "It was just one of those good talks like that. It was cool. I was nervous as hell. It was nerve-racking. I don't think I said too much."

Sabathia had been challenged to repair the fractured clubhouse, but Girardi wanted to help, attempting to shun the drill instructor perception that his first season at the helm painted. Some players had griped about a policy banning sweets and snacks that was implemented in 2008, though Girardi insisted that call was made by the organization. In truth, Girardi hadn't exactly been counting calories. He said that he had a soft spot for Hershey's Kisses and looked the other way one morning when Mike Mussina smuggled a box of jelly doughnuts into the visiting clubhouse at Detroit's Comerica Park.

That spring marked the first of the Yankees' off-site field trips, in which the club ditched their bats and balls in favor of a group bonding activity. It was a page borrowed from the playbook of New York Giants head coach Tom Coughlin, who took his players bowling during preseason camp in 2007 and was rewarded with a Super Bowl victory that season. The Coughlin connection was no coincidence; Cashman said that he provided Girardi with a magazine article about the adjustments that Coughlin had made to his leadership style. "Coughlin was very disciplined and strong, and I think there was an evolution that has been publicized," Cashman said. "I'm not going to say if it's valid or not, but he was very strict in a lot of different ways. With the communication with the new world order, some changes had to take place with the Giants for them to continue to move forward and have success. I remember providing him a copy of that article. I said, 'You've got to read this because I think it's a very similar circumstance.'"

Most of the players were preparing for a routine workout in late February when Girardi circled the clubhouse just before 9:30 AM, ordering the players back into their street clothes. They boarded a pair of waiting buses down the left-field line with drivers having been instructed to head toward Peabody's billiards hall on Tampa, Florida's Amberly Drive.

Due to injury concerns, Girardi couldn't have his players bowling or playing paintball, as he'd initially suggested. Girardi would eventually get to don paintball gear, suggesting to director of media relations Jason Zillo that the coaches and front-office executives should challenge the beat writers to weaponized games of capture the flag. Eight-ball was a solid compromise.

There were two rounds, and Rivera was a victor in both, winning the first while partnered with reliever Phil Coke, then joining Pettitte to defeat Nick Swisher and Hideki Matsui. The winners were rewarded with gift certificates to local restaurants, and players placed side bets as they competed on the nearby dartboards. "We specifically did it where we put an older player with a younger player because if they ever came up, we wanted a comfortable feeling," Girardi said. "Then the second round, you were with someone you would work with during the middle of the year, so second base and shortstop, third baseman and first baseman, that sort of thing. There was a method to our madness."

The impact of the bonding exercise waned in subsequent years. Chad Bohling, the team's director of mental conditioning, tried again with a field trip to a video arcade, a Texas Hold'em poker tournament, and the introduction of a bizarre motivational speaker who bent a frying pan with his bare hands. That first season, though, it was fun and new. Burnett said that the bonding exercises set the '09 Yankees apart from other teams that he had played on. "That was great," Burnett said. "You've got handfuls of new guys on the team that are impact guys. We need to all fit, and it wasn't like we had to try. That was the fun part; nobody really went out of their skin to try. Everybody just got along. Everybody has a goal in spring training to go to the World Series—no shit—but we had a locker room full of guys that were like, 'Man, we're going to be so good.' We just had fun."

Though Teixeira would criticize Girardi's clenched-jaw intensity following the Yankees' elimination in the 2017 playoffs, he said there were no such issues evident in 2009. "I saw a guy that was very comfortable," Teixeira said. "He wasn't trying too hard, which I kind of expected him to be, trying hard to figure out what went wrong [in 2008]. I think when we got CC and A.J. and then brought me in to sharpen the defense, he's like, 'Okay, this is the team that can win.' So I thought he was very relaxed. I thought he was calm. I thought he was very positive, and he was a very calming influence in the clubhouse…the first few years there, totally different guy. I think when he changed his number to 28 [after 2009], and as that pressure built, I told guys at ESPN, we were watching the playoffs [in 2017] and I was like, 'Look at Joe when a couple of guys get on. It looks like his head is going to pop off his shoulders.' That's new, that's the last few years. In '09 he did not show that at all. At least, I didn't see it."

If Girardi's personality seemed more relaxed, his camp was still no Club Med, as you'd expect from a man whose credit card bill includes an email service that directs his workout plan for each morning. When thunderstorms passed through the area, Damon said that Girardi would occasionally force the team to remain on the practice fields, which Damon believes inspired toughness. "His reasoning was: 'We're going to have to play in bad weather throughout the course of the season, so why don't we get some work in and be ready for Opening Day?'" Damon said. "[He'd say,] 'You guys aren't in trouble, but we're in this business to win a championship.' Everybody bought into it. Guys would run into walls for Girardi. That's why Girardi, to me, to this day, is the best manager in baseball."

Hired in 2005, Bohling was a driving force behind the billiards activity, and his mental conditioning exercises were as much a part of the camp atmosphere as running on the warning track or playing long toss. Players could request personalized highlight DVDs to pump themselves up for games or workouts, and several times each week, a projector was set up in the center of the clubhouse for a motivational video or speech. Bohling created an internal slogan, 'Mission 27,' that appeared on all of the team's documents and on signs in the clubhouse and weight room. "You talk about it in every spring training clubhouse, but okay, this is really our mission," Burnett said. "It seemed like every little thing we did was reminded of that. Whether somebody had it on a T-shirt or somebody said it or it was written somewhere, it always came back to 'Mission 27.' It put a statement in our minds that we're going to go through some bumps, we're going to lose some games, but Mission 27, man, that's the end goal."

Mission 27 was about the whole process from spring training on, the grind of it all. If you have success, you keep moving forward. If you have adversity, failure, injuries, you keep moving forward. We held more team meetings than we probably ever had, going from when I first started in 2005. A lot of times, you hear team meetings are called when things are going wrong. We would still have a team meeting when things were going right, just to understand why. How do we keep pushing ourselves? How do we not become complacent? That was important for us to have consistency and develop that kind of mentality as a team."

Swisher said that he believes Bohling was "a humongous part" of the Yankees' success that year. "You're taking a whole bunch of new guys, bringing them into a new organization, a strict organization," Swisher said. "These guys are like wild horses, and all of a sudden, you have to wrangle these guys and get everybody on the same page. That's not an easy thing to do. He did such an amazing job. That was the first time in my life that I even knew what a mental conditioning coach was. When things went tough, that was the stuff you fell back on."

With the press conference past him, Rodriguez attempted to subscribe to something approaching his normal routine. Rodriguez was received more warmly than anticipated at home games, but he was booed and taunted in his spring debut against the Toronto Blue Jays in Dunedin, Florida, when he belted a long fourth-inning homer off Ricky Romero in front of 5,014 customers.

Joking that he thought the fans were "pretty nice" and that he'd like to invite some of them to Fenway Park in the summer time, Rodriguez seemed to be in a jovial mood. The evening prior, he had broken bread with Reggie Jackson, and Mr. October was entrusted to pass along a message from Hank Steinbrenner. "You deliver this message," Steinbrenner told Jackson. "You tell him to hit the ball—and hit it when it counts."

If only it was that simple. Days after Rodriguez zoomed off in his Maybach luxury sedan to spend two and a half hours delving into his past

PED use for MLB investigators, there would be another significant revelation. Rodriguez's right hip had been an issue since at least the previous May, when the Yankees catalogued an underlying bone deformity while Rodriguez spent time on the disabled list with a strained right quadriceps.

Though he complained of occasional stiffness through the 2008 season, Rodriguez became aware that the issue might be more severe that winter while messing around on a basketball court. "The first time I could feel something was when I went up to dunk the basketball and I couldn't," Rodriguez said. "I remember one particular time where I was like, 'Okay, I've got to go get checked.' I could dunk any way I want and I had fun doing it. I'd be in jeans. I'm like, 'Holy shit, I can't reach the fucking net,' like Latino men can't jump? So that was alarming."

The Yankees were already planning to be without Rodriguez that spring, as he intended to play for the Dominican Republic in the World Baseball Classic. Born in Miami, Rodriguez had represented the United States in the 2006 tournament, drawing criticism from fans in Latin America. Rodriguez's parents, Victor and Lourdes, are both of Dominican descent. "My mom told me if I don't use the Dominican uniform, she would disown me," Rodriguez said. "I had so much pride that I was one of the leaders on the U.S. team, then three years later I'm one of the leaders on the Dominican team. I was playing for my mother and my other country that I love."

Managed by Felipe Alou, the Dominicans boasted a stacked squad that featured Pedro Martinez, David Ortiz, Robinson Cano, Miguel Tejada, and Hanley Ramirez, among others. Because of the troublesome hip, Rodriguez never made it past his initial workouts with the Dominicans. "I was taking batting practice and I could barely hit the ball to the warning track and then I would crush one, and it was at the warning track," Rodriguez said. "I realized then I had to go see a doctor."

Rodriguez boarded a private jet to meet with Dr. Marc Philippon, one of the nation's foremost hip specialists, at the Steadman-Hawkins Clinic in Vail, Colorado. Philippon drained a cyst and diagnosed Rodriguez with a tear of his labrum and a femoroacetabular impingement, which causes friction in the hip joint.

Philippon suggested that Rodriguez could return to a big league lineup in six to nine weeks with a hybrid procedure, in which two small incisions would be made on the side of Rodriguez's hip. The labrum would be repaired with some bone shaved away. Rodriguez was told that a decade of deterioration had made his hip more square-shaped, whereas a normal hip is round. The doctor had treated hockey legend Mario Lemieux, figure skater Tara Lipinski, and golfer Greg Norman, but those stars hadn't required anything exactly like what Rodriguez faced.

"I said, 'Great, Doc. Hybrid. That sounds great, sounds cutting-edge. Maybe they started this in Silicon Valley. How many have you done?'" Rodriguez said. "He goes, 'None.' I go, 'What?' He goes, 'Yeah, but I think I can pull the string; I haven't done it before, but if I get this one machine, I think I can jab it in there.' I was like, 'Whoa.' So I mean, if I thought I was nervous, now I was shitting bricks. I'm like, *I'm going to fucking die. I'm never waking up.*"

The Philadelphia Phillies' Chase Utley and Mike Lowell of the Boston Red Sox had returned from similar injuries in previous seasons, and, though Philippon told Rodriguez that the surgery had an 85 to 90 percent chance of getting him through 2009, another day under the knife would probably be necessary in the near future. Rodriguez approved the 80-minute procedure, crashing at a friend's home in the resort town so Philippon could oversee his recovery. "The idea was that we would do it and go back as soon as we can in the next two or three years when the thing exploded," Rodriguez said. "They were injecting me with PRP [platelet-rich plasma] and spinning my blood, being a guinea pig to speed up everything. I'd wake up at 6:00 AM and work out four times. Basically wake up, go to the track, then bike, rehab, train. It was literally like 24 hours a day of ice, pool, injections. I was a mess."

Cashman said that Rodriguez's decision to stay in Colorado had to be approved by Hal Steinbrenner and team president Randy Levine. At least one member of the team's medical staff wondered why Rodriguez was 1,950 miles away when he could be receiving similar treatment at the team's Tampa complex or at the stadium. "The cost associated with him being out there was significant, but we're dealing with an injury that none of us had ever dealt with," Cashman said. "It was a whole educational component, and then Alex—it would be different just because it's Alex. We were dealing with a lot of extra billing because of the Vail stay and the rehab clinic and specific physical therapists that I'm not sure were any different than our physical therapist here."

While Rodriguez worked to re-join his teammates, the Yankees were the darlings of the Grapefruit League. Though a good spring training guarantees little other than perhaps a strong Triple A team, the Bombers coasted to a 24–10 record, winning each of their last 10 games and outscoring opponents by 74 runs. "When I walked in in '09 in spring training and I saw the team we had, I'm like, 'Dude, we're winning the World Series,'" Pettitte said. "I mean, it's hard to do, but I expected it for sure."

Though most positions were locked, Girardi toyed with his crowded outfield. Behind Sabathia the rotation was set to feature Chien-Ming Wang, Burnett, and Pettitte, and Joba Chamberlain was granted a chance to serve as the fifth starter. There was hope that Wang could return to form and log 200 innings, though that seemed less crucial because Sabathia and Burnett had dislodged Wang atop the starting five. One year after being promised spots in the rotation, Phil Hughes and Ian Kennedy were assured of nothing.

With Rodriguez no longer available, Girardi planned on having Cody Ransom serve as the Opening Day third baseman. Matsui appeared to be running well following left knee surgery, and Rivera looked dominant following an October procedure to shave the AC joint atop up his right shoulder. "My first month, it was painful," Rivera said. "Even though they cleaned it up and everything, a surgery is a surgery. The first month, oh my God, it was painful. Then as the year was going, it was better and better."

Posada was brought along slowly as he recovered from right rotator cuff surgery, and there was some concern when the catcher's first throws behaved like a ping-pong ball meeting a stiff breeze. Posada's strength gradually returned, and there was optimism that Posada would be behind the plate for 100 games. That health was crucial; Cashman believed that Posada's absence had been a major reason why the Yankees missed the postseason in 2008. "Once we got to spring training, I wanted to catch every bullpen, I wanted to catch every start, and that's what I was able to do," Posada said. "Coming out of spring training, I thought we were in the right place and right frame of mind. Everybody was on the right page."

They were not completely whole—not while Rodriguez was still riding a stationary bike in view of Vail's ski slopes—but they were close enough. After seven and a half weeks in the Florida sunshine, these Yankees seemed ready to head north and show what they were made of.

CHAPTER 6

THE BIG MAN JOINS THE BAND

CC Sabathia kept thinking about what he was walking into. General manager Brian Cashman's words echoed in his thoughts: *The clubhouse is broken, and we need you to fix it.*

As a member of the Cleveland Indians, Sabathia had watched the Yankees from the other side of the field for nearly a decade. Since Sabathia's big league debut in 2001, the Yankees had reached the postseason seven times, winning six division titles and two league pennants. They were the winningest team in the game since the day he threw his first pitch, and the idea that they were some kind of dysfunctional group seemed implausible.

That's not to say that everything appeared perfect from afar. Sabathia's days with both the Indians and Milwaukee Brewers were filled with laughter, camaraderie, and more video games than any average person should play. The Yankees? They had the air of a Fortune 500 corporation, not a bunch of jocks playing a kids' game. Everyone was clean-shaven—a long-standing Steinbrenner rule—and they handled themselves with ruthless efficiency. "You just don't think they're having fun," Sabathia said. "They just come out and beat your ass."

Joba Chamberlain could understand why opponents viewed the Yankees that way. Chamberlain electrified New York as a rookie reliever in 2007 before struggling and injuring his shoulder during a transition to the rotation in 2008. For a young man with a boisterous, fun-loving personality, the room could take on the mundane atmosphere of Dunder Mifflin, the fictional paper company on NBC's *The Office*, which was in its fifth season. "Sometimes it felt like we were at a 9-to-5," Chamberlain said. "You came in, we talked to the media, we went to BP, we played the game, we talked to the media, and we went home. I don't necessarily know if 'broken' is the right word, but it became mundane."

"I pitched against them in Toronto, and it was business in the face, man," A.J. Burnett said. "They never even smiled when they dirt-rolled us. I didn't know what I was getting into."

Yet if celebrating a championship truly was the most important piece of the puzzle, as Sabathia and Burnett said, then they seemed to be in the right place. The hurlers were walking into a room occupied by some of the greatest players in history. Want to know how to win? Ask someone. Derek Jeter, Jorge Posada, Andy Pettitte, and Mariano Rivera had been through it all in New York, leading the Yankees to success at nearly every turn.

Reflecting upon Cashman's sales pitch, Sabathia wondered what was being expected of him. "That scared me more than anything," Sabathia said. "I'm like, 'You've got Jeter, you've got these guys; if they can't fix it, how can I fix it? When he was giving me that pitch, it kind of scared me off more than anything... *You want me to come into a broken clubhouse?* It was scary that he kept saying that."

That had been where Sabathia's wife, Amber, entered the picture. Just as Sabathia was the fun-loving rock of their family, she convinced him that he would have the same impact on his new team, no matter what the dynamics had been before he arrived. "I kept saying to Amber, 'He keeps saying that the clubhouse is broken.' What do you want me to do? And she's like, 'That's what you do.'" Sabathia said. "I've been in Cleveland for all those years and I hadn't seen myself in that light until she said: 'That's why he wants you to go there and fix that clubhouse.'"

Typically, spring training thrusts newcomers into the spotlight, when reporters cover bullpen sessions as though they were postseason starts. The spring of 2009 was different—thanks to A-Rod. Like a fire alarm pulled on the first day of class, Alex Rodriguez's performance-enhancing drug admission helped the team shake off its early jitters albeit amidst a circus unlike anything they had ever seen.

While the media hunted for morsels of gossip relating to Rodriguez, his mysterious cousin, and the hip injury, Sabathia used those early days to acclimate himself with Tampa, Florida; Steinbrenner Field; and his new teammates. He had competed for years against Jeter, Posada, and Rivera, but sharing a clubhouse gave him a fresh view on the icons. "They were way cooler than I thought," Sabathia said. "Playing against those guys for so long from the outside looking in, you don't know what to expect. They were great. It just seemed loose when I got there."

Whether he realized it or not, Sabathia contributed to that looseness. An avid basketball fan, Sabathia made the 90-mile trek to see several Orlando Magic games that spring, inviting teammates to join him each time. He also organized group dinners, uniting players away from the ballpark. Sabathia wasn't making a concentrated effort to bring his clubhouse together. As his wife had said, that's just what he did—and continues to do to this day. "I feel like everybody should be included," Sabathia said. "If I have tickets, let's all go sit in a suite and let's go hang out. I don't want guys just sitting in the hotel room."

Sabathia made special efforts to arrange outings that included all of the starting pitchers, believing in the value of a unified rotation. He and Burnett had become fast friends while Pettitte emerged as a mentor to both pitchers. Chamberlain, Chien-Ming Wang, Phil Hughes, and Ian Kennedy received invitations, as they would fill out the rest of the rotation, and relievers sometimes joined the fun. "The first time I ever sat courtside at a basketball game was with CC," reliever Brian Bruney said. "We got along really well. We had a lot of the same interests, but everybody was always invited. Just a big ol' teddy bear type of guy—everybody loved him. He brought everybody together."

When Sabathia took the pitchers to a Magic game at the Amway Arena, it was the first NBA game that Wang had attended. The Magic invited their celebrity guests onto the floor before the game, allowing them to shoot around. "It was cool," Sabathia said. "Joba hit a few in a row. Wanger, the first couple he airballed, then he hit one off the backboard. He had a good time. It was just fun stuff to do. I hadn't thought about the broken clubhouse thing. I was just trying to meet my new teammates. Alex had to do the press conference, and all of that stuff was going on, so it kind of let me like skate through spring training just because of everything that was going on."

Jeter and Posada were consummate professionals, but they didn't instill the type of free-wheeling culture Sabathia had experienced in his previous stops. He wasn't trying to commandeer the team from Jeter, the team's captain since 2003. Sabathia's goal was just to make everyone's time on the field as enjoyable as possible. "Guys like Derek, guys like Jorge that handle everything right and do things the right way, they aren't necessarily the rah-rah type of guys," Chamberlain said. "They'll make sure they put you in your place and do things the right way, but I think when CC came over, he could feel out what was going on."

Johnny Damon noticed that there were changes taking place. It hadn't been all that long ago that Damon had helped successfully infuse a fresh, fun attitude into the Boston Red Sox clubhouse, transforming a supposedly cursed franchise into the bunch of self-proclaimed "Idiots" who went on to win Boston's first World Series title in 86 years. Damon attempted to replicate that vibe when he signed with the Yankees after 2005, but with Joe Torre at the helm and much of that team seemingly set in its ways, he was unsuccessful. "I tried to change everything, but it gets tiring," Damon said. "Every day you have to try to motivate guys that it's great to play baseball. This is a kid's game; have some fun."

Tyler Kepner, *The New York Times*' national baseball writer, was in his eighth season on the Yankees beat in 2009. He sensed a push/pull between the old and new guard. "There was always that thing with Cashman. He knew that he needed the Core Four guys, but he also wanted to move beyond them," Kepner said. "That was the great bridge year because they were able to bring in new guys with a new voice and a fresh perspective who were younger before the old guys ran out of steam."

It was still Jeter's clubhouse, but the new guys were encouraged to make their presences felt. Distributing nearly a half-billion dollars of the Steinbrenner family fortune all but assured that. "There were fresh, respected voices from different teams that were able to able to infuse another layer in the clubhouse," said Jason Zillo, the Yankees' media relations director. "It's like when you put a fresh set of eyes on a term paper that you've been looking at over and over. You almost get double vision you've been looking at it so much."

The continuity created by the Core Four provided stability, but Sabathia added a powerful presence to the veteran council. "Some people just have it, you know?" first-base coach Mick Kelleher said. "When I first went to the big leagues on September 1, 1972 with the St. Louis Cardinals, I was a young player, and on that team was Bob Gibson, Joe Torre, and Tim McCarver. With these guys, you just fall in line."

Sabathia wasn't the only one causing culture change. Nick Swisher was impossible to ignore. With no volume control to be found, his presence stood out from the moment he arrived. "Swish was huge, his energy every day," Sabathia said. "The combination of us three together changed the dynamic into a lighter mood and more of a summer-time-baseball-team-hanging-out kind of feel rather than the corporate way it seemed from the outside."

Burnett had that same perception, but like Swisher, the pitcher had no plans to change who he was. Nobody busted balls like Burnett, and whether you were a rookie or a future Hall of Famer, you were susceptible to the pitcher's hijinks. "I'm going to mess with you whether you're Derek Jeter, whether you're Alex or Mo," Burnett said. "I don't know if anybody ever did it or attempted to do it or were scared to do it, but we messed with Al, with Jeet and Jorge, and were just laughing 24/7. I never thought the New York Yankees locker room could be like that. I thought it was like business, business, business; no one is going to ever smile. No, no, no, man. It was great. The way Cash brought in guys to mesh and to loosen up that locker room was a genius move on his part. We definitely lightened things up."

Burnett didn't come across as lovable to all. On the top shelf of his locker rested a bronze paperweight depicting four faces of Buddha. It was a gift from former Toronto Blue Jays teammate Jesse Litsch, who'd marveled at Burnett's mercurial nature. Hours before a start, Burnett pointed the angry face toward the room, a warning to not even try speaking to him. Some other days, Buddha might be smiling, but Burnett's persona remained gruff.

"I thought A.J. was a little bit of a dick just based on first impressions of being a tough guy," said Dana Cavalea, the team's strength and conditioning coach. "He felt that he had to have a tough exterior to be a competitive pitcher that people feared. But when you got him in the back and you were training with him, he was actually a sweetheart of a guy."

While Sabathia, Swisher, and Burnett were transforming the personality of the clubhouse, the other new star probably would've appreciated the status quo. Mark Teixeira saw the so-called "Yankee Way" as polished rather than formal and proper. It was exactly the type of atmosphere he had longed for; unlike Sabathia, Burnett, and Swisher, Teixeira didn't even have facial hair to shave. The old guard exemplified the world he wanted to live in. "None of them were flashy or flipping bats," Teixeira said. "Mo saved dozens of games against teams I've played with, never once pumped his chest, or threw his glove, or some of the stuff you see nowadays. That's what I always prided myself on being: a professional, and that's why I think I fit. I like seeing guys have fun and enjoy themselves, but our job is to win games. Seeing guys laugh it up and joke around on a team that's in last place rubs me the wrong way. The first thing I noticed, which I saw from afar, was those guys—Derek and Mo and Jorge and Andy—are all business. Not that they don't have fun while they win, but it's all about winning."

On his first day in camp, Teixeira walked to his assigned locker in a back corner of the clubhouse with a bag slung over his shoulder that bore the Angels' halo logo. Shaking the hands of every minor league coach, media member, or clubhouse attendant within sight, Teixeira promised that he would soon be able to recite every name in the room. "You know what I remember first about meeting Mark Teixeira?" said Yankees color commentator Suzyn Waldman. "He repeated your name and he never forgot it. He said, 'Nice to meet you, Suzyn,' and he never forgot it ever. And he was always smiling."

Teixeira viewed himself as a leader during his three previous stops and, as the recipient of a mega-contract, he assumed that he would hold the same status with the Yankees. "I always wanted to lead by example, doing the early work," Teixeira said. "I thought I was the best first baseman defensively in the game. I was out there for early work almost every day, and coaches told me, 'Hey, thank you, because it shows all these guys that have been here a while they've got to keep working.'"

To some in the clubhouse, however, Teixeira's approach rubbed them the wrong way. "Tex was a real pain in the ass when he first got to spring training because he didn't know the culture," Cavalea said. "He came from teams where he was the guy that was getting on everybody, and I don't think that he knew his place initially. He simmered it down pretty quickly because I think he realized that the clubhouse already had its police officers."

Teixeira's veteran status was soon deployed effectively. Joe Girardi was cognizant of the impact that he could have on younger players. After Teixeira rounded the bases to commemorate his first homer in a Yankees uniform, Girardi nudged Teixeira to take a more active role in Robinson Cano's preparation. "He points to Robinson Cano and says, 'You need to work on his work ethic,'" Teixeira said. "He goes, 'Alex has been working with him, but now Alex is having surgery. You need to work on him.' It wasn't me getting in Robbie's face; it was, 'Hey, Robbie, come out to early work with me. Hey, let's go take some extra swings.' That's the type of leader I always wanted to be."

Teixeira had wondered from afar how a player with Cano's supreme gifts could struggle and now he had a better idea of the situation. In 2007 Cano posted an .841 OPS that ranked fourth among all second basemen who qualified for the batting title. That fell to .715 in 2008, 15th among the 17 players in the same statistical group. Cano was receptive to the suggestions and followed the first baseman to take extra ground balls or perform extra sets in the weight room. "I knew the type of player he could be because he had been that player," Teixeira said. "It's not like he never had success. I think because Alex was gone he was probably even more receptive to working with guys like me or hanging out with Gardy and Swish. We're grinders. Alex is so smooth; he worked hard and he was talented and smooth. That's why he was so great. But grinding it out works as well."

Upon entering his free-agent period, Teixeira had heard the same rumblings that Cashman had revealed in Sabathia's living room. The clubhouse needed an injection of personality, and though Teixeira might not have wanted to take that upon himself, he knew Sabathia, Burnett, and Swisher had more than enough gusto to slap fresh paint on those walls. "It just had gotten stale there," Teixeira said. "Their hearts got ripped out in '04, then in '05: disappointment, '06: disappointment, '07: disappointment, '08: didn't even make the playoffs. You don't bring back Joe Torre, who is a God in New York. It was just not a great clubhouse to be in. So you bring in a larger-than-life personality in CC, who can back it up on the field, who just brings in new energy, brings in new life. You add Swish to the mix. As crazy as A.J. is sometimes, I thought he was great for the clubhouse, too. Sometimes you want to see somebody break a lamp or throw a trash can in the dugout. It's like that Paul O'Neill energy. Everybody brought something different to the table, and that was healthy for that team."

From hoops games to fantasy football drafts and NCAA Tournament watch parties to backyard barbecues, the clubhouse was feeling the winds of change, just as Cashman had hoped it would. Hitting coach Kevin Long said that Sabathia was widely regarded as "the dad that everybody wants around" and emerging as the team's social chairman. "You always went to CC with any issue or any problem or anything that you needed to do off the field," Long said. "Amber was a big part of it; she would bring the wives, and they'd have pajama parties, and CC was getting the guys together. The value of that, when you bring the team together, I think it's something that's missing in this day and age."

• CHAPTER 7 •

SWISHALICIOUS

Nick Swisher embodies eternal optimism. A colorful, energetic soul who refers to nearly everyone he meets—man or woman—as "bro," Swisher's resting face advertises enthusiasm, vigor, and positivity. He's a human can of Red Bull. Every day looks, feels, and sounds like his 10th birthday.

Want a perfect glimpse into Swisher's psyche? Following a stellar April, Swisher fell into a deep slump once the calendar flipped to May. He was completely lost, looking far more like the player who had struggled the previous season with the Chicago White Sox than the one who had carried the Yankees' lineup through the season's opening month. The Yankees had gone 14–9 over that span, which made the slump easier to stomach, but it was still grinding at Swisher's soul. He was thrilled that the team was playing well, but Swisher knew if he could get his bat going, things could really take off.

Rinsing off yet another hitless night against the Texas Rangers, Swisher zipped his bags and arrived at The Ballpark in Arlington, entering what is perhaps the quirkiest visiting clubhouse in baseball. An enormous set of steer horns stand guard over the entryway, a saloon door leads to the players' shower area, and a large sign on another wall reads: "What you see here, what you say here, let it stay here." Not exactly the most welcoming environment.

Given his woeful performance over the previous three weeks, few would have blamed Swisher for being salty. Instead, as he strolled toward his locker, Swisher fist bumped one of the beat reporters and flashed his customary ear-to-ear grin. "Swish, can I ask you something?" the reporter said. "You're in this horrific slump; I think it's like 8-for-70. How are you in such a good mood?"

Swisher paused for a moment. "Let me ask you this. If I come in here like a grumpy asshole and act like a dick to everybody, will that guarantee me three hits tonight? Because if it will, I'll do that," he said. "I'm just gonna be me instead. What do I have to be miserable about?...I play for the fuckin' New York Yankees, the best team in all of professional sports. I live in New York, an absolutely amazing city. I get to go out in front of the best fans in baseball every day. My life is pretty damn good. I'm pretty sure I'll get another hit or two before the season is over."

And with that, Swisher disappeared into the back of the clubhouse to begin his daily preparation for that night's game. He finished with a hit, a walk, and a run scored in the Yankees' 9–2 victory, beginning a five-game hitting streak. Over the next two weeks, Swisher would go 13-for-31 (.419) with a 1.375 OPS, hitting three home runs.

Swisher's attitude served him well given the streakiness that occasionally accompanied his game, but that over-the-top personality was one the Yankees may never have seen prior. Before Swisher, who was the last player to sport a faux-hawk, use his fingers to flash heavy metal horns while sticking his tongue out, and generally step up as the life of the party every night? "If it works, it's all good. If it doesn't work, then it's a whole other story," said Suzyn Waldman, the Yankees' longtime radio analyst. "I believe that I've never seen anyone who played baseball and enjoyed everything about being a New York Yankee as much as Nick Swisher."

Even the most free-spirited players of that pinstriped era had some subtlety to their daily disposition. Jason Giambi grew up in the raucous Oakland A's clubhouse, arrived in the Bronx carrying a $120 million contract, and eventually endured a performance-enhancing drug scandal that humbled the slugger. After jumping from the Boston Red Sox to the Yankees in 2006, Johnny Damon remained an outspoken player albeit one who rarely raised the volume of his voice.

Swisher was different. Like Giambi, Swisher had been a product of Oakland's frat house environment, so walking into Steinbrenner Field was an odd experience. "It was stuffy, bro," Swisher said. "It made me feel like I had a suit and tie on, and the tie was so tight that I couldn't even breathe. It was just so much different from what I came up in. I came up idolizing Jason Giambi with the long hair, the tattoos, and the party-like atmosphere. The music is so loud in the locker room you can't even hear yourself think."

That wasn't the case before Swisher's arrival. In fact, there hadn't been much music at all, especially not before games. Swisher remembers the first two or three days of spring training being very quiet, but with an assist from Damon, the role of clubhouse DJ was created. "Johnny Damon rolls into the locker room with this humongous speaker," Swisher said. "I said to him, 'Johnny, how does this thing work? Can I borrow that?' I brought it over to my locker, plugged it in, and was just literally throwing some jams on. It was crazy because I think everyone was like, 'What's going on here? What is that?'"

A less outgoing personality might have recognized the vibe and turned down the music. Not Swisher, who proudly showed off an eclectic iPod that shuffled the Black Eyed Peas, John Legend, Kings of Leon, Tim McGraw, and everything in between. At times, he'd grab a bat, pretend it was a microphone, and sing along. Swisher was also known to flick the lights on and off, like the Yankees had been transported to a rave. All that was missing was the glow sticks. "I'm in my own world, having a good time," Swisher said. "I was like, 'Oh my God, I'm in the Yankees locker room, bro, having a blast!' All of a sudden, A-Rod walks back and gives me the nod, like, 'Yeah, man. I like that.' Jeter, same thing. You're kind of like, 'Oh, okay.' It was kind of like the king comes in and says, 'Hey man, what you're doing is right.' I remember a lot of guys saying, 'If The Boss was still here in charge, he would've done this to you, he would've done that to you.' And my response was, 'Well, I guess I'm lucky he's not in charge right now. I guess I'm super lucky that the guys in charge actually enjoy this.'"

With that early spring stamp of approval, the Yankees world was getting a whole lot louder. The old guard of Derek Jeter, Andy Pettitte, Jorge Posada, and Mariano Rivera might not have been accustomed to the changing atmosphere, but they didn't oppose it. "Let's be honest, we know who ran that locker room," Swisher said. "If those guys didn't want music, there would've been no music. It felt good. For me, that is where I think the locker room started to change."

Maybe the only person who had reason to complain about the introduction of Damon's karaoke machine as a valued member of the roster was Brett Gardner, as it added a task to the 25-year-old's workload. Because Gardner tallied only 127 at-bats during his 42-game stint with the Yankees in '08, he retained his rookie status going into 2009. Damon and Swisher made sure that Gardner knew his place. "Back then, my job as a rookie was to carry around his big karaoke machine, and that thing weighed about 80 pounds," Gardner said. "It was the size of a small suitcase, and I had to carry it on and off the bus and on and off the planes. We put a lot of miles on that karaoke machine, a lot of songs. It was worth it."

Swisher and Gardner became fast friends, and given the amount of crap the two fired at each other on a daily basis, the relationship had a big brother/little brother quality to it. "It was a fun clubhouse to be around when those two would start going at each other," Phil Hughes said. "It kept things light. If you can't make fun of each other, it's really not a fun environment. Swish brought a different dynamic that the team didn't have before; we realized that it's okay to have these big personalities in the room. Everybody can still be themselves, close, and striving toward one goal. Not everybody has to be robots."

Still, with no off switch to be found, some began to roll their eyes with every passing "bro." Was Swisher's act sincere or was he trying to stand out among some of the game's biggest stars? Posada indicated that there was a learning curve to handle his enthusiasm. "Swisher was a guy that was outspoken, and you had to get used to having Swisher around," Posada said. "In the beginning we thought he was too much, but once we knew what he was all about and what he meant, we were all in favor of the things that he was doing."

"It was a personality that we hadn't seen come along, that I can remember," Pettitte said. "It amazed me sometimes how he could always be so upbeat and have so much joy all the time."

Early in camp, it was apparent that Swisher was who he was. Like it or not, he wasn't going to change. "A week into spring training I'm like, 'This is him every day. He's going to show up every day like this. This is how he is,'" CC Sabathia said. "I think it took people a couple months into the season where everybody got comfortable with him. I felt his voice right away. That's just Swish, man."

Michael Kay, the Yankees' play-by-play broadcaster on the YES Network, wondered if Swisher's entire persona was an act. "Nick and I didn't have the greatest start," Kay said. "He hit a double and he was acting 'Swishalicious' on second base, so I said something on YES like, 'Well, that's part of the package with Nick. That's what you get.'"

Jason Zillo, the team's director of media relations, approached Kay a day or two later and told him that Swisher wanted to speak with him. Kay agreed. "Swisher said, 'Dude, do you have a problem with me?'" Kay said. "I said, 'I don't have a problem; it just seems really contrived.' He goes, 'Dude, it's not contrived. This is the way I am. I'm not putting on an act.' I grew to like him a lot because that is him. Whether you like it or not, he's *not* putting on an act, he's *not* being that guy. I thought this was all for the cameras, but he's just this bubbly, loving-life sort of guy. He probably came the furthest for me in terms of how I felt about him from the beginning of the year to the end of his Yankee career."

Swisher also helped let Damon's wild side out again. Having felt pressure to hold back during his first three years in New York, Damon thought that finally he wouldn't stand out so much if he let his hair down a little.

Of course, that was just a figure of speech. Still enforced, George Steinbrenner's 1973-era grooming policy prohibits players from having beards or long hair, both of which had been Damon's trademarks in Boston. The Boss might not have approved of how his club was behaving behind closed doors, but Hal Steinbrenner and Joe Girardi had no complaints. "Sometimes I like guys that come in and turn a clubhouse upside down and bring energy," Girardi said. "Johnny Damon and Swish brought a loudness to the clubhouse that I thought was really good. It should be a place where they feel safe and it's loud, and they can do what they want, laugh, joke, and prepare for the game. Those two, I thought, were really important."

In turn, Swisher appreciated the opportunity to learn from some of the game's greatest players. His White Sox team the previous season included future Hall of Famers Jim Thome and Ken Griffey Jr., though both were at the tail end of their respective careers and, despite all of their success, had never raised the World Series trophy. These Yankees were different. "I'll never forget walking into the locker room at spring training and noticing the names on the walls, man: Jeter, Posada, Rivera, Pettitte, Rodriguez," Swisher said. "I'm like, 'Holy shit, man, where am I?' This is unbelievable. I've never been surrounded by this many stars in my life. I did the best I could to learn from them, watch how they worked."

Swisher didn't try to emulate his iconic teammates, but he noted the way they worked before, during, and after games. Swisher always worked hard, but now he was learning how to be smarter about his preparation. "Maybe it's not all about being in the cage for two hours trying to figure something out. Maybe you're only in there for 20 minutes," Swisher said. "Your swing is kind of like a knife. If you don't sharpen it by doing your drills and it goes dull, it's no good. But you can keep that swing sharp throughout your tee work, from flips, your net drills. I learned how to work like a true professional when I went to New York in the spring of '09."

When Brian Cashman welcomed Swisher to the team in November, he'd been told that he was replacing Giambi, the player whose footsteps he envisioned following in when he was drafted by Oakland in the first round of the 2002 draft. Six weeks after the trade, Teixeira had signed his deal and Swisher's days as the Yanks' first baseman were over before they began. "I was so pumped and so excited about the opportunity to be the first baseman for the New York Yankees," Swisher said. "That's an iconic position. Think about it—Lou Gehrig, Tino Martinez, Donnie Baseball. The list can go on and on, the names that have played there. I was geeked. Then all of a sudden, the Yankees sign Mark Teixeira for $180 million. Who do you think is going to play first base at that point?"

Swisher said that he knew there was still a great opportunity in New York and he needed that fresh start after the forgettable year in Chicago. As he had promised Hal Steinbrenner in advance of the Teixeira signing, Cashman attempted to trade Xavier Nady, but no match could be found. Girardi decided that Nady and Swisher would compete in right field, while Melky Cabrera and Gardner would share time in center field. Damon was being phased out of center field and would man left field full time.

Nady was coming off of a successful 2008 campaign, having batted .305 with 25 home runs and 97 RBIs with the Pittsburgh Pirates and Yankees, who had acquired him prior to the July 31 trade deadline. The Yankees had a road game against the Philadelphia Phillies in Clearwater, Florida, on the afternoon of March 23, and before the team headed for the bus, Girardi asked Swisher to step into his office.

The steel door slammed shut, and Girardi began to speak. Swisher had hit .231 during the spring, and, while he showed the ability to drive in runs, the Yanks' coaches and evaluators decided that it had not been enough to wrest the job from Nady's grasp. Since neither player had outdone the other on the field that spring, Nady's '08 performance served as the deciding factor. "I remember having a discussion with Swish about playing time and how we were going to play him," Girardi said. "Nady was going to start, but he was going to play a lot, and his time was going to come. Be patient, let things work their way out."

Swisher wanted to blast Girardi and unload his frustration into every microphone within the 813 area code, but he knew better. In the visitors' clubhouse of the Phillies' spring home, Swisher remained muted as he attempted to travel the high road, saying, "The door's not closed for me. There will be plenty of at-bats out there."

Swisher's father, Steve, had played in the majors from 1974 to 1982, making an All-Star Game with the Chicago Cubs in 1976 before continuing on to a respectable minor league managerial career. He taught his son how to handle himself like a man, and blasting the skipper wouldn't get you anywhere other than the bench or on the next plane out of town.

Privately, however, Swisher was fuming. "He was pissed," Teixeira said. "I told him, 'You should be pissed. But the only way you can do it is go out and prove it on the field.' I knew Swish from Oakland playing against him in the West for so long; he was a stud. It didn't work out in Chicago, but I knew the kind of player he could be. I told him, 'Earn your at-bats. You should be pissed. I'm glad you're pissed.' If I see a guy who loses his job and he's not upset, that's a red flag to me. The GM, the manager wants that guy to be mad about not being the guy and not getting the at-bats or not being the starter because that shows that he has that competitive fire. But he wasn't going to be a distraction. We had plenty of distractions; he wanted to be a positive."

Nearly a decade later, Swisher admitted that losing the job to Nady ranked among the biggest disappointments of his career. "Crushed, bro. Bummed. Super crushed. Super bummed," Swisher said, reliving that day in his mind. "All I wanted to do was run out on that field on Opening Day at Yankee Stadium."

What made it even more difficult for Swisher was his genuine fondness for Nady, who had become a friend that spring. While Swisher searched for a New York apartment, Nady and his wife, Meredith, invited him to stay as long as he needed with the couple and their nine-month-old son. (The child was named Xavier Henry Nady VII, the latest in a line of Xs that traced back to the 1500s and the French hamlet of Auxelles-Base.) "They were gracious enough to bring me into their home," Swisher said. "I mean, how awesome is that? What an amazing family, what an amazing man. So for him to get that nod, I was excited for him, but on the other side, I was bummed. As a competitor, you want to be out there. I'll never forget, man, it was the first time in my career that I did not start on Opening Day."

Swisher and Cabrera opened the season as the fourth and fifth outfielders. Though he doubled as the backup first baseman, Swisher knew that Teixeira had a reputation as an iron man, playing at least 157 games in three of the previous four years, including a pair of seasons in which he played in all 162. The chances of spending much time there were slim. "At that point in time, I knew what my role was. That doesn't mean you have to like it,"

Swisher said. "I got a late pinch-hit in the first game and I walked and then I got a pinch-hit in the second game and ended up hitting a late double."

Swisher got his first start in the third game of the season, going 3-for-5 with a home run, a double, and five RBIs, leading the Yankees to an 11–2 win against the Baltimore Orioles for their first victory of 2009. He knew that he was going to have to produce big numbers to muscle into the lineup, making it such a difficult decision that Girardi had no choice but to write his name down.

That's precisely what Swisher did, hitting .407 (11-for-27) with four home runs and 11 RBIs in his first seven starts. Take him out of the lineup? Heck, with Alex Rodriguez still rehabbing his hip, Swisher was the Yankees' best hitter. Swisher started three games at first base while Teixeira dealt with left wrist tendinitis, but that was going to be the exception, not the norm. His path to extended playing time was in right field—or, perhaps, he could pitch.

On April 13 after starting at first base for the third straight game and hitting a home run against Tampa Bay Rays left-hander Scott Kazmir, Swisher and his team landed on the wrong side of a blowout. Chien-Ming Wang gave up eight runs while recording only three outs, watching Tampa Bay take a 10–0 lead after three innings. Wang was miserable. "I badly wanted to get back to my original performance level," Wang said. "Every day I'd go all in, doing everything that my trainer and physical therapist told me to do, no matter how much pain I felt. Mentally, I wanted to get back quickly; however, the results of my performance indicated I was rushing the process and I was not ready."

The Yankees scored a pair of runs in the eighth to draw within 15–5, but with his team only halfway through an early-season stretch of 12 consecutive games without a day off, Girardi desperately wanted to avoid burning out the bullpen. Swisher was standing by the bat rack in the visiting dugout when Girardi approached, asking, "Swish, have you ever pitched?"

"I'm like, 'Oh, hell yeah,'" Swisher said. "I'm not going to let him know that the last time I pitched was like my freshman year in high school. I was like, 'Oh yeah, man, I got that. No problem.' He's like, 'Good. You're going in next inning, but if I catch you throwing hard, I'm going to take your ass out of there.' I was like, 'No problem, Skip, I got this.'"

Before Swisher could head to the mound, he needed to remove what he referred to as his "flair," including a gold chain, wristbands, and the assorted tape he used to keep himself wrapped together. He ripped it all off and strutted to the mound—eager to try his hand at something his ninth-grade teammates in Parkersburg, West Virginia, probably never dreamed that they would see him do again. "I've always been like a two-feet-in kind of guy," Swisher said. "Let's be honest, bro; when are you ever going to have the opportunity to pitch—and on top of that, pitch for the New York Yankees? I mean, come on!"

Swisher thinks back to that day and begins to rattle off the pitches he threw—much in the same way a pro golfer can recite his shots following a winning round on the PGA Tour. No Yankees position player had pitched since August 19, 1997, when Wade Boggs broke out a decent knuckleball in a blowout loss to the Angels in Anaheim. "That was kind of a lowlight for a pitching coach, having to have a position player pitch," said pitching coach Dave Eiland. "As embarrassing as it was, it's like, 'Okay, it's one loss, it's one game. It doesn't matter if we got beat 1–0 or if it was 15–5.' It's a long season; crazy things happen."

A walk to B.J. Upton, who later changed his name to Melvin Upton Jr., on a high 3–2 fastball opened the inning, and Willy Aybar singled to left field, putting a pair of runners on base. Swisher, a left-handed thrower, started off Gabe Kapler with two straight balls, taking a deep breath on the mound. "I was like, 'Oh my gosh,'" Swisher said. "I'm standing on the bump at Tropicana Field for the New York Yankees, like how did that even happen?"

Swisher dropped a pitch in for strike one, and Kapler fouled the next pitch to the backstop, evening the count. Swisher playfully shook off catcher Jose Molina—it's doubtful Molina was putting down anything other than a "1" for a fastball—and side-armed a 2–2 pitch to Kapler, who fouled off another one. The next pitch was fired past an overanxious Kapler, who swung through the 79-mph "heater" for strike three. *A strikeout?* Swisher gestured for Molina to roll the ball into the dugout as a keepsake. There's nothing like your first.

That brought up Carlos Pena, who had hit a grand slam earlier in the game and would go on to tie Teixeira for the American League lead with 39 home runs that year. Swisher got Pena to pop up to second base and then retired Pat Burrell on a flyout to left-center field. It was a scoreless inning, and, though the Yankees would head back to their hotel having absorbed a lopsided defeat, Swisher couldn't stop smiling about his 0.00 career ERA. "I remember getting through that inning and going into the locker room after the game," Swisher said. "I had six ice bags on like a journeyman, dude."

The postgame routine is pretty standard in baseball. About 10 minutes after the game is over, print, radio, and TV reporters enter the clubhouse to speak with the manager and any key players from the game. Girardi met with reporters, as did Wang. Jeter performed his duties as team captain, speaking with the media after the humiliating loss. "It's one of those days," Jeter said, standing at his locker. He would turn the page on the loss before he walked out of the room, something he had been conditioned to do since he entered the league as a rookie.

Swisher wasn't as ready to forget this one. "I had fun with it. When am I ever going to have a chance to do that again? Probably never," Swisher said that night. "We know we didn't play very well, got to find something to laugh about in that moment. I just happened to be the guy."

About 20 feet away, Posada stood at his locker, watching Swisher yuk it up with the reporters. If nothing else, Swisher was providing good color. "I remember Swisher having fun with it and thinking that it broke the tension of a really bad game," said Tyler Kepner, who covered the team for *The New York Times*.

Posada found no humor in the situation and, based on the scathing scowl he shot toward Swisher, the catcher was in no mood to hide his feelings. "You just can't be laughing when you're getting your ass kicked," Posada said nearly a decade later. "I know he took it as a fun time being on the mound, but I felt like even after that, he was doing interviews and he was laughing and stuff like that. It just doesn't sit well when you're losing and people are laughing. That's not our nature."

Swisher thought he was making the best of a bad situation, but as soon as he saw Posada, he knew he wasn't in Oakland anymore. This wasn't even Chicago. "I remember doing the interview. I was so excited," Swisher said. "I was like, 'Wow, to have the opportunity to do something like this, it was amazing. I can't even believe this happened.' Then I remember looking over to my right, and Jorge Posada was pissed. He's like, 'No. This isn't a funny thing.' Normally when a position player pitches, it takes away the sting of the loss and it makes it a little more funny. But no, not for Jorgie, man. Posada is staring daggers through me like, *That's not how we do things around here.* It was like, *Man, I'm kind of scared.* I'm like, *Dude, holy shit! I just pitched a scoreless inning in the major leagues for the New York Yankees!* How many position players can say that? But I do remember those daggers, bro. I still feel them."

It was never mentioned again between the teammates. Posada was satisfied that he had delivered a message. "We had to make sure that he understood the things we wanted to do and how we did things," Posada said. "We wanted him to have fun. The more fun he had, the better he hit. So we wanted him to still have fun but also understand the way we did things."

Eiland said that he thought Posada's non-verbal rebuke served as a good lesson for Swisher, saying that his joyful antics after the lopsided loss "made all of us raise an eyebrow." But Teixeira, who shared the same general attitude as his Core Four teammates, didn't mind Swisher's laugh-it-up approach that night. "I knew Swish and I loved Swish for who he was," Teixeira said. "You're not going to change him, so it did not bother me because that's Swish being Swish. He took a lot of pressure off the rest of us because we could be who we were. He could go be a clown, and the YES Network or whoever could be like, 'Look at what Swish is doing. Isn't this funny?' They didn't need me to be funny or Derek to be funny or Mo because that's not what we were going to give you."

Swisher was in left field the day after his one and only pitching appearance, going 2-for-4 with a home run in a 7–2 win against the Rays. The most consequential moment in the game did not involve Swisher, but it would wind up changing the course of his entire career.

With the Yankees clinging to a two-run lead in the bottom of the seventh, Nady fielded a Pena single to right field and looked up to see Evan Longoria attempting to advance two bases on the hit. Nady unleashed a throw to third base and felt a familiar sharp pain in his elbow. He had undergone Tommy John surgery in 2001 and immediately feared the worst. "As I threw it, it just popped," Nady said. "It just blew out again. Longoria is on third, and I'm like, 'Please just don't hit me another ball where I have to throw it.' Then of course, a sac fly gets hit to me [by Pat Burrell], and I think it was deep enough where I could barely throw it. I think that might've raised some eyebrows."

Nady wasn't due to hit in the eighth, so he disappeared into the tunnel behind the clubhouse, testing his arm. "I took a ball and was throwing a couple against the wall, and Girardi came down for some reason and goes, 'What are you doing?'" Nady said. "I said, 'I think I just tore my elbow again.' And he goes, 'You've got to be kidding me.' I said, 'No, unfortunately I'm not.'"

Nady landed on the disabled list, trying to rehab his elbow before ultimately resorting to season-ending surgery, but Swisher would help the Yankees not miss a beat in right field. "It was tough losing Nady because he's a great team guy," third-base coach Rob Thomson said. "Swish was on base a lot, he slugged, and he played a decent enough outfield that you knew playing in the smaller confines of right field of Yankee Stadium he's going to be able to do that. He had this energy that he brought to the ballpark every day that I thought was important for the other guys to kind of gravitate to. He did calm down a little bit once he got the lay of the land and understood what we're all about, but he's never going to be that solemn, lunch-pail guy who goes to work, does his job, and goes home. He's never going to be that, and we didn't want him to. We wanted him to be himself."

It was not the way that Swisher would have hoped to earn an everyday job, but he was ready to seize the opportunity. "I don't know if it was meant to be, but that's how it ended up happening," Swisher said. "You never want to be happy when you have success because of someone else's failures. I was bummed that my buddy X went down with Tommy John but also juiced and super excited about the opportunity that was in front of me. I always remember people saying, 'If the fans fall in love with you, Swish, you'll never leave.' So that's what I tried to do."

Nady and Swisher had become such good friends during the previous two months that they continued their arrangement as temporary roommates while the Yankees were at home. "In the morning he'd be sitting on the couch in just his boxers—no shirt, just his underwear," Nady said. "Every day I'd walk out and be like, 'Hey dude.' I mean, I've got my wife and nine-month-old here, but that's how our relationship was. I'd just wake up and I'd be dying laughing. This guy is just sitting in his underwear watching TV. He thought it was normal, like, 'Hey, what's up?' It's typical Swish. I just said, 'All right, I guess that's how he's going to roll around the house. Make yourself at home.' As awkward as it ended up turning out, me getting hurt, I always said, 'Things are going to happen. One of us is going to win this spot, and someone's going to get hurt, or an opportunity is going to happen somewhere else.' Little did we know I was going to blow out seven games in. The rest is history."

• CHAPTER 8 •

GRAND OPENING

CC Sabathia's assignment as the Opening Day starter had been a formality, one Joe Girardi made official as he entered the Steinbrenner Field weight room in the spring of 2009. Grunting between sets, the ace was told that he had drawn not only the April 6 season opener, but also the Yankee Stadium home opener 10 days later.

Breathing heavily, Sabathia offered his approval and returned to his preseason preparation, leaving his manager to wonder if his message had stirred any excitement in the newcomer. The significance of that chat would hit Sabathia weeks later, as he laced his spikes in a corner of the visiting clubhouse at Baltimore's Camden Yards. Years later, the image of seeing his teammates in full uniform for the first time remains vivid in his mind. "That was crazy. That was nerve-racking, man," Sabathia said. "That whole first 10 days I was nervous and I remember sitting in the clubhouse in Baltimore. Jeet walked by, Mo walked by. We didn't even have pinstripes on. It was the gray uni, and I'm like, *Damn! This is for real.* The uniforms looked different, you know what I mean? I had goose bumps."

Sabathia was new, but all of the Yankees needed to get acclimated to unfamiliar surroundings that month. Before opening the season with a nine-game road trip that saw Sabathia surrender six runs in his debut, the new Yankee Stadium received a two-game dress rehearsal with a pair of exhibitions against Lou Piniella and his Chicago Cubs. For many of the players, coaches, and staff, those games represented their first extended look at the facility.

Throughout the spring they had seen photographs of what was rising within the limestone exterior walls, but actually exploring their new surroundings was breathtaking. On the evening the team flew north from Florida, they peered through rain-streaked bus windows and were thrilled to see that the stadium lights had been flicked on. They hurried through the cold, raw tunnels, touring a place that the Yankees would be calling home for decades to come. "It should've been part of a movie," Nick Swisher said. "It's New York City and it's a brand new stadium, so you know it's going to have the best of everything. Let's be honest, nobody does things the way the New York Yankees do. So to be able to be part of all that and to walk out of that dugout and to be standing there with all the lights on, everything lit up, 'New York Yankees, Mission 27' on the scoreboard, it was by far one of the coolest things I've ever seen."

The stadium promised to exponentially increase the players' level of comfort. At the old building, they had to make a right turn out of the clubhouse and follow a long hallway to antiquated batting cages located under the seats in right field, an area that had been scarcely updated since Don Mattingly and Dave Winfield used it to battle for the 1984 batting title.

Now the cages were contained within the clubhouse, steps from the video room. Within the span of about 15 feet, a batter could shove his bat into the dugout rack and then break down his at-bat on a computer screen frame by frame. "Amazing," Jorge Posada said. "It was another level. They said they needed another month for little tweaks here and there. I remember just everybody's faces in the clubhouse, the locker room, just so many things that we took for granted that we didn't have at the stadium. It was unbelievable. It still is. That stadium is ridiculous."

Beyond the players' dressing area, the off-limits areas of the clubhouse extended to the right-field corner. General manager Brian Cashman boasted that if a player ducked into head athletic trainer Gene Monahan's office, the media would never know about it. A SwimEx underwater treadmill and multiple hot tanks awaited use, as the players were granted a spacious treatment area that Reggie Jackson said his Bronx Zoo Yankees could have only fantasized about. "You went out there with a roll of tape on your wrist and a pair of sweatbands, a Snickers bar, and a cup of coffee," Jackson said. "You swung, you grimaced, you got back in the batter's box. If you swung and missed and made an out, it hurt. If you hit a homer, it felt good. There wasn't a whirlpool that you can put a horse in."

The aquatic pool was a game-changer, according to strength and conditioning coach Dana Cavalea, who said that the technology greatly benefited starting pitchers and heavy-legged position players. "It was like talking to a seven-year-old at a Florida resort: 'Hey, do you want to go in the pool?'" Cavalea said. "They're like, 'Yeah, let's do it.' I used it as a selling technique to take a lazy day and turn it into a something day. We did a ton of aquatic work, especially with our starters."

The manager's office was a three-room suite. One served as Girardi's office, another received visitors, and there also was a toilet and shower. Even the visiting digs were cushy. Piniella's only complaint during the two-day visit was being unable to figure out how to use the Keurig single-serve coffee machine. "It is a beautiful ballpark," Yogi Berra said. "But you need a road map to get through it."

As the Twitter era dawned, each locker in the home clubhouse was outfitted with a laptop computer, though few logged on regularly. Derek Jeter did but not for the intended purpose of communicating with coaches or teammates; Jeter would frequently lock his screen onto a weather radar of the stadium, monitoring for green or yellow blobs. In later years the laptops were ditched in favor of iPads, which permitted players to summon game video on demand.

"It was magical," Andy Pettitte said. "I'll never forget walking out there the first day. You go out there and you check the field out. You're just looking around going, 'Wow.' Everything was so new. It was as nice as you ever could imagine. We had great chairs to sit in, we had couches, we had a kitchen. They had a cook in there for us. My first impressions were, 'Man, we are spoiled rotten.' It was like a hotel."

Pettitte's analogy was apt. The Yankees had hired top training executives from the Ritz-Carlton chain to school the dozens of blue-vested waiters and white-hatted chefs who were now employed at the stadium, intending to replicate the state-of-the-art customer service of a five-star hotel. It was a drastic change from the gritty, mom-and-pop feel of the old place.

Babe Ruth probably wouldn't have complained if his original home had been constructed with a steakhouse and martini bar, which were accessible underneath the translucent ceiling of a 31,000-foot Great Hall. "I see it as classy," Hal Steinbrenner said. "We did our best to bring all the tradition this great franchise has had the last century into this ballpark. At the same time, we made it as nice as we can for our fans. It's going to be here a long, long time, and I think we did a great job. Everybody in the organization is proud of it."

The first exhibition game was played on April 3. To match the prices of the April 18, 1923, opener at the original stadium, grandstand seats sold for $1.10, and bleacher tickets went for 25 cents. Jackson one-hopped the ceremonial first toss, and Chien-Ming Wang threw the first unofficial pitch to Aaron Miles, who singled to left field for the first hit in the facility. As he observed the Yankees' 7–4 victory, Mr. October said that he could see The Boss' influence everywhere. "It's done in George Steinbrenner style: forget the cost, do it right," Jackson said. "Spend the money, build it right. If the one you have doesn't work, get rid of it, get another one, and get rid of the guy that built that one. I'm a car collector, so I pay attention to restoration and detail. There were no corners cut. I notice the wallpaper, the hardware, the conveniences. It's well done."

Jeter had some trouble finding the balls and strikes on the 59' x 101' digital screen in center field, but he notched the first Yankees hit, a double down the third-base line off former Bomber Ted Lilly. Robinson Cano slugged the first homer, a two-run shot to right-center field.

There were long lines at the martini bar one level up from home plate, and the sports bar in center field swelled with a curious crowd peering through smoked glass. The atmosphere was big league all the way, but fans were reminded that it was still a Grapefruit League test drive when Mariano Rivera entered in the fifth inning. "That was a beautiful stadium," Cano said. "Coming from an old one that has a lot of memories and legends and to see everything new and modern—the seats and everything—you've got a nice gym, big weight room, nice kitchen. Everything was good in there.

To be able to come and play in that spring training game, I hit a homer. That was amazing."

To Mark Teixeira those first two exhibitions felt like the sensation of driving a new car or breaking in a glove. "I knew I was going to be there for eight years, so it felt like home," Teixeira said. "When I was in Atlanta and L.A., I didn't know if I was going to be there forever, so I felt like I was passing through. You sign an eight-year contract, you're in. Knowing I was going to spend the next eight years at this beautiful new stadium was a great feeling."

They could settle in more after returning from the road, having visited the timeless Camden Yards in Baltimore, newly renovated Kauffman Stadium in Kansas City, and perpetually drab Tropicana Field in St. Petersburg, Florida. While the team was away, engineers, electricians, handymen, and plumbers put the final touches on the stadium, while the stadium operations team pulled all-nighters in anticipation of the April 16 home opener. "We had a lot of punch list items to finish up," said Doug Behar, the Yankees' senior vice president of stadium operations. "Many were small, like, 'Hey, my door-knob turns the wrong way,' or they forgot to touch up paint somewhere. If there was a stray piece of paper, we picked it up. We were up in the suites cleaning drinkware, doing whatever we could to make sure this building was what everybody expected. Next thing you knew, the sun was coming up, and we were like, 'All right, I guess we're not going home.'"

Sabathia might not have been painting walls or tightening screws, but he was also trying to iron out a few wrinkles. His Yankees debut had been spoiled in a season-opening 10–5 loss at Baltimore, but he rebounded to pitch scoreless ball into the eighth inning in his second road start, leading the Yanks to a 6–1 win against the Kansas City Royals. He played it cool at the time, but as he tugged on his pinstriped size 56 jersey and pants with a 44-inch waist, the pressure of the stadium opener jangled his nerves.

It didn't help that Sabathia needed to face the Cleveland Indians so soon after they had traded him to the Milwaukee Brewers. Though he enjoyed a close friendship with the opposing starter, the excellent Cliff Lee, Sabathia was not jazzed about the added emotion of going against the team that wrote his first big league checks. "That was not fun, man," Sabathia said. "Opening Day, new stadium, Yankees, and then you've got to pitch against your old team. I didn't sleep for 10 days. That was the worst 10 days ever."

With multi-colored flags flapping on the stadium's roof on a sunny, 56-degree Thursday afternoon, Berra was entrusted with lobbing the first pitch to catcher Jose Molina. Hall of Famers Whitey Ford, Goose Gossage, Rickey Henderson, Jackson, and Dave Winfield headlined more than 40 former Yankees who ringed the infield. Ford and Don Larsen scooped dirt from the mound, as they had at the old building.

George Steinbrenner watched from his box to the left of home plate and was joined by commissioner Bud Selig and the real estate magnate-turned-reality TV star Donald Trump 23 years after his attempt to move the Yankees to Manhattan's West Side and just seven-and-a-half years before an improbable ascent to the presidency. Jay-Z was in the building, John Fogerty played "Centerfield," and Bernie Williams strummed an acoustic version of "Take Me Out to the Ball Game."

Swisher said that the hair stood up at the back of his neck when Kelly Clarkson belted out a terrific rendition of the national anthem, as the *American Idol*'s high notes were drowned out by the roar of four F-16C Falcons. Bob Sheppard's voice was heard only via recording; in March the 99-year-old was replaced at the public-address microphone by Paul Olden. Though he didn't know it at the time, Sheppard's final game was a September 5, 2007, contest against the Seattle Mariners. "Bob physically couldn't make it to the ballpark," said Olden, who broadcast Yankees games on WPIX-TV in the mid-1990s. "From what I was told, a couple of times he got in his car and started the journey to the stadium but didn't feel well and then turned around. It was not for lack of trying. They wanted me to do the lineups pretty much how Bob did, repeating the numbers in the Sheppard way. I had no problem with that."

Finally, it was time to play. Home-plate umpire Tom Hallion signaled to Sabathia, who inaugurated the stadium with a 94-mph fastball to Grady Sizemore that missed the strike zone. Sizemore grounded out to first base, as Baltimore's Brian Roberts had done in the final at-bat at the old building.

Mark DeRosa grounded out, and Victor Martinez's whiff accompanied the first in-game playing of the five-note strikeout whistle—an advertisement for electronics retailer P.C. Richard & Son—that would become ubiquitous. This new place was off to a perfect start.

A wink was offered to the old place in the bottom of the first inning. As Jeter strapped on his batting gloves, the bat that Ruth had used to homer in the original stadium's first game was laid across home plate. Jeter hoisted the treasure and playfully acted as though he wanted to use it, offering his black Louisville Slugger P72 to a bat boy. When Ruth's bat returned to the dugout, Posada and Hideki Matsui were among those who took turns trying to swing the massive hunk of lumber to the sheer terror of those entrusted to keep it intact. "It was fun, a nice gesture on the part of the organization to have his bat out there," Jeter said. "It was heavy. I know that."

Ruth's 36-inch solid ash stick had sold at a Sotheby's auction in December 2004 for $1.265 million and was on loan from collector Richard Angrist with arrangements made to have it displayed in the Yankees Museum. Jeter flied out to center field, and Johnny Damon followed with the building's first official hit, a clean single to center. "It means a lot," Damon said. "A lot of people don't remember the amazing things I did on the baseball field, and it's crazy. It's like, 'Eh, Johnny was all right.' People kind of forget how good I was and how I got offenses going. But yeah, getting that first hit at the new Yankee Stadium, I know everyone was hoping Jeter would do it, but you know what? That's where I stand."

Posada blasted the stadium's first homer, a solo shot off Lee with two outs in the fifth inning. The ball rattled in front of the retired numbers of Monument Park, which is now located underneath the glassed-in center-field restaurant, and Posada was summoned for a curtain call by the crowd of 48,271. It was one of just 10 hits that Posada would notch off Lee in 46 career at-bats (.217), including their showdowns to come that October. Though Posada didn't realize the historic nature of the homer until he reached the dugout, he kept the bat, which resides in a glass display case alongside other notable keepsakes in the movie theater of his Florida home. "I hit a home run off a guy that gave me trouble my whole career," Posada said.

"My numbers are not good against Cliff Lee, and to have a home run at the new stadium, I'm pretty happy about that. Later on, when you get older, you can talk about it a little bit more. For me that was big because of the way that I felt toward the end of '08. I felt like I had no power, like the ball was dying. That was big for me going into that season."

The fun soon stopped for the Yankees, as Sabathia walked five and burned through 122 pitches in five-and-two-thirds innings. His team absorbed a 10–2 defeat as the new Yankee Stadium's first victory was credited to Lee, who escaped most of his jams through six innings. "I didn't have fun," Sabathia said. "I've never liked starting Opening Day any time, but that one was just really, really nerve-racking. I just wanted to pitch good, trying to do well. I just wanted to get that over with and try to settle in."

The wheels came off in the seventh inning, as the Cleveland Indians blew open a 1–1 tie with nine runs. Jose Veras couldn't retire any of the three men he faced, surrendering a two-run double to Jhonny Peralta. Damaso Marte could not stop the bleeding; Kelly Shoppach lined a run-scoring single, and Trevor Crowe worked a bases-loaded walk before Sizemore belted the first grand slam in the stadium's history. Sizemore's bat wound up in Cooperstown. "Everything leading up to the game, I appreciated the heck out of," Teixeira said. "Once the game started, it's like, 'All right, it's baseball again. Don't start daydreaming about your new stadium and stuff. You've got to perform.' So that wore off pretty quickly. The cool factor of being in a new stadium wears off pretty quickly when you're down big to Cliff Lee."

By the time Victor Martinez added a solo homer, some fans were heard chanting, "We want Swisher!" Having tossed a scoreless inning against the Tampa Bay Rays three days earlier, Swisher was in no hurry to risk spoiling his perfect ERA. "That was when the relationship between myself and the Bleacher Creatures really took off," Swisher said.

The Yanks answered with a run in the seventh to cut the deficit, but the stadium's first official contest went into the books as a loss for the home team. "We got smoked," Girardi said. "Just how bad it was, how poorly we played, it was frustrating because you wanted to open up your stadium with a bang, but when I thought about the silver lining, one of the Core Four hit the first home run at Yankee Stadium…That was the silver lining in that day."

Sabathia shrugged off the defeat quickly. In fact, he invited Lee to cross the George Washington Bridge and check out his new digs that evening. "My wife cooked, and he came over and hung out," Sabathia said. "That's just how we are. We've always been pretty cool. The conversations are really never about baseball."

The Yankees slugged five homers to take the second game of the series 6–5 but were trounced 22–4 in the finale when Wang and rookie Anthony Claggett were each hammered for eight runs. The pitching quality clearly left something to be desired, but with hitters buzzing about how well the ball carried during batting practice, it was carrying over to game action.

"We saw that against the Cubs the first two games," Girardi said. "I was thinking, *Oh my gosh, the ball is flying out of this ballpark more than the other one.* I was concerned. I wondered, *Is it because the old stadium hasn't been torn down? Is it going to play like this all the time?* I remember thinking, *We're going to see a lot of runs in this ballpark,* and we did."

A few conspiracy theories popped up amongst the fanbase; one blog showed a satellite overlay of the old stadium compared to the new, which suggested that the dimensions were not exactly the same. Most notably, the auxiliary scoreboard in right field created more of a straight line toward the foul pole. Years later, hitting coach Kevin Long said that he believes the surge should have been credited to the Bombers' muscle rather than the ballpark. "There was so much noise about, 'This stadium's a joke,' and 'It's a bandbox,' and I'm thinking to myself, *Wait a minute. We have home-run hitters,*" Long said. "We were hitting home runs on the road that year, too; it wasn't just at home. It was short to right, and the ball did carry significantly better, but every team had the chance to do the same thing. We had better players and we had guys that could knock the ball out of the park."

Jeter insisted that the eight-foot high fences were slightly lower than they had been in the old park, as he recalled not being able to touch the area where 12-year-old Jeffrey Maier had reached over the wall to gift his favorite team a homer in the 1996 American League Championship Series.

Jeter now could reach that, and the 6'3" shortstop hadn't experienced a growth spurt in the years since that memorable drive carried over the head of Orioles outfielder Tony Tarasco. "I understand everyone is making a big deal out of home runs, but there's a lot of balls that were hit good," Jeter said at the time. "It's not like there's a bunch of cheap home runs being hit. I think people are swinging the bats well and hitting home runs. It's not like they're blowing out for one particular team, so I think people are jumping the gun with how the ball is carrying here."

Pitchers and catchers immediately noticed that the new stadium featured less foul ground behind home plate and down the baselines, reducing their chances of notching an easy out. That difference of a few feet was negligible, however, because of the suspicion that a wind tunnel was offering assistance to hitters by sucking balls out to right field. "There was a lot of talk amongst the pitchers, but it was just like the old Yankee Stadium," pitching coach Dave Eiland said. "Get beat in the big part of the ballpark, get beat in left-center, you still have to go out and execute pitches. You can't worry about the short porch in right field. If you're pitching to avoid that, it's going to do more harm than good. It's just like when you go into Fenway; you can't worry too much about the wall in left field. Complaining and bitching about the short porch in right field did us no good. It took a little time for me to get that message across. After a couple of weeks or maybe a month or so, the guys came to, 'Okay, it is what it is. We still have to go out and execute pitches.'"

Yankees brass went so far as to hire aeronautical engineers with NASA backgrounds to explore the home-run surge. Those commissioned reports offered the unsatisfying explanation that it was probably just weather-related. Although Yankee Stadium remains a homer haven, those first days of 2009 were historic. There were 28 homers hit through the first seven games at the stadium, a big league record for any new venue. Nineteen were hit to right field. "I knew from Texas that wind patterns were huge in stadiums," Teixeira said. "Depending on the wind in Arlington, the ball could jet out to right, or any ball you hit to center or left-center would come straight back at you. I figured that we had some wind blowing out to right because there were balls that shouldn't have been home runs. Still to this day, you see balls that should not be home runs. They get up into a wind pattern that goes out in right field. I think we were just figuring that out that first month."

Years before Aaron Judge's 2017 emergence prompted the construction of "The Judge's Chambers" seating area in right field, Swisher recalled that another Bombers outfielder sparked talk of a catchy nickname early in '09. "Johnny Damon was hitting balls into the second deck in right field like it was going out of style," Swisher said. "They were going to call it like, 'Damon's Deck,' and I was all pissed off because I was the right fielder and I was like, 'No! This is my area over here.'"

Even if they had, would the seats be occupied? The images of vacant cushioned chairs with teak armrests, many of which were in the expensive Legends area, created fodder for those who wondered if the efforts to engage a more affluent fanbase had reduced the stadium's intimidation factor. Terry Francona, then the manager of the Boston Red Sox, noted that his players were no longer berated during the national anthem like they once had been. "I was a big fan of the old one," Francona said. "You swallow a little asbestos; that's not the end of the world, is it? Now you look sometimes in the lower bowl, and people aren't really there. It's a gorgeous stadium, and the clubhouses are wonderful. I just thought the other place had an unbelievable amount of personality."

Though the Yankees repeatedly said that the empty seats belonged to fans who were enjoying the high life in the Legends restaurant or wandering the ballpark, adjustments were made in late April. The most expensive of the Stadium's 52,235 seats had been priced at $2,625, ranging down to obstructed-view bleacher areas that went for $5. In light of the economy still staggering from Wall Street's collapse the year prior, the Yankees slashed some top-tier seats by 50 percent. "If anybody in any business had known where this economy was going to go, they would have done things differently," Hal Steinbrenner said at the time.

That did not extend to the Yankees' free-agent spending spree, for which they expected to be rewarded handsomely. On the day of Teixeira's press conference, he had walked on the playing field with agent Scott Boras, who elbowed his client and pointed toward the 314-foot marker in right field. Teixeira nodded, fully expecting that he'd be among the biggest beneficiaries.

Teixeira would hammer plenty of balls over that wall in the years to follow, but they didn't materialize immediately. He had been a notorious slow starter in his other big league stops, so it did not panic Teixeira when his production lagged in his first month as a Yankee. That included an 0-for-4 debut, and Teixeira batted .200 with just six extra-base hits in April, collecting three doubles and three homers with 10 RBIs. "Not many people know this, but I hurt my wrist in Baltimore [in the] second game of the season," Teixeira said. "I actually missed a game or two in Kansas City that year [with what the Yankees said at the time was left wrist tendinitis]. My wrist was killing me the first two or three weeks of the season. I've got a hurt wrist, I can barely swing right-handed, so as excited as I was, I was like, 'Oh, gosh.' The anxiety of knowing I didn't have all my bullets was tough. It wasn't as fun as it could've been. Of course, I wanted to get off to a good start, but I didn't panic because I knew my history. I knew who I was. It was my seventh year in the big leagues. My first six years were as successful as I could ever imagine, so there was no panic. The fact that we got off to a bad start as a team was more worrisome for me. I knew I was going to be fine."

Thanks in part to Melky Cabrera, who produced the first of the Yankees' walk-off wins with a 14th-inning drive to topple the Oakland A's on April 22, the Yankees completed their first month with a 12–10 record. They did so while weathering a four-game losing streak that began with a Mariano Rivera blown save on April 24 in Boston—part of a series sweep by the Red Sox that included an embarrassing straight steal of home plate off Pettitte by Jacoby Ellsbury.

The Yankees had allowed more runs (136) than they had scored (128). Among other pressing issues, they'd lost Xavier Nady, while Wang seemed to be completely out of whack. After he allowed eight, seven, and seven runs to the Baltimore Orioles, Rays, and Indians, Wang and his 34.50 ERA were shipped to the team's minor league complex in Tampa, Florida, for the team's extended spring training games. Phil Hughes was promoted from Triple A to fill the rotation vacancy. "We were giving up runs left and right," Teixeira said. "Wang was our No. 2 pitcher and he was giving up seven runs every outing. We couldn't figure out what was going on. We were trying to figure out what our bullpen looked like. Is Joba a starter? Is Phil Hughes a starter? So there was a lot of stuff going on that first month."

Fortunately, Wang wasn't the only key Yankee occupying a near-vacant ballfield 1,200 miles from the Bronx. As Alex Rodriguez continued to slug batting practice homers in the Florida sunshine, help would soon be on the way.

• CHAPTER 9 •

A-ROD RETURNS

No athlete of the 1980s stirred the imagination quite like Bo Jackson. A combination of raw power and blazing speed, Jackson starred in both the National Football League and Major League Baseball, the only player in history ever to be selected to both an MLB All-Star Game and an NFL Pro Bowl.

Jackson's signature poster—the one in which he's resting a bat on his shoulder pads—hung on the wall of countless children, reminding them that anything is possible (as long as they wear Nike shoes). Jackson was the ultimate athlete, representing not only the Los Angeles Raiders and Kansas City Royals, but also the embodiment of every dream on Little League and Pop Warner fields around the country.

In a January 1991 playoff game against the Cincinnati Bengals, Jackson suffered a serious hip injury on a seemingly routine tackle that derailed his brilliant career. He never played in the NFL again, and, although Jackson appeared in 160 major league games between the 1993 and '94 seasons, the explosiveness that had made him the object of the sports world's affection was gone. He retired from baseball before his 32nd birthday.

When Alex Rodriguez learned he would need major hip surgery during spring training, the first thought that entered his mind was Jackson's truncated career. "Hip surgery to me was synonymous with Bo Jackson," Rodriguez said. "What do we do when we have an issue? We Google it. I Googled 'hip surgery baseball,' and every fucking article and picture is Bo Jackson, and then I saw the results. I didn't have enough education or information of data points to know it was going to be less than that."

A-Rod wasn't alone when it came to his lack of knowledge about the injury that threatened to disrupt his career. General manager Brian Cashman said that he had "no idea" what the team was dealing with, remarking, "I didn't even know hips had labrums at that time, to be honest." Rodriguez had undergone left knee surgery a decade earlier, but a hip injury represented the great unknown. "From my studies now, looking back, it said a lot of people retired in the '60s, '70s, and '80s because they would have hip surgeries and they called it 'aging,'" Rodriguez said. "I was like, 'Fuck. I hope I just get to be a father and get to walk around.' It was much greater than 'I hope I'm good this year.'"

At the age of 33, A-Rod wasn't contemplating retirement despite the ambiguity regarding his physical status. With nine years remaining on a 10-year, $275 million contract—not to mention 553 career home runs and a legitimate chance to break Barry Bonds' all-time record of 762—Rodriguez prepared to do whatever it took to get back on the field. "I felt like I had to give it a shot," Rodriguez said. "I have this responsibility of many more years on my contract. I'm young and I felt like I was strong and healthy. I was really hoping that I would not be disabled because I knew that was an option. I was hoping that I could get better."

Rodriguez underwent arthroscopic surgery on March 9, creating a slew of new questions. How long would his rehab program last? Would he have the same torque in his hips that had allowed him to drive the ball so well during the first 15 years of his career? Could he still handle everyday duty at third base? "There was concern," Joe Girardi said. "Any time you start talking about wrists or hips or backs for position players, there's a huge concern."

"We didn't know how long he was going to be gone," Jorge Posada said. "They told us he was going to be back, but we didn't know when. We were thinking more after the All-Star break."

Dana Cavalea, the team's strength and conditioning coach, played an integral role in structuring Rodriguez's rehab plan. With input from the doctors and team trainers, Cavalea designed a program that would help A-Rod build strength and regain his form. "He was definitely open to anything you gave him to get back on the field," Cavalea said. "That was his biggest thing: 'What do I have to do to get back on the field? Give me the program, give me the structure, and let's get going on it.'"

A month after surgery, Rodriguez returned to the team's facility in Tampa, Florida, to continue his rehab. There was one thought Rodriguez couldn't shake: Bo may have known greatness, but he was a mediocre baseball player after hip surgery, hitting .248 with 32 homers and 102 RBIs for the Chicago White Sox and California Angels.

Rodriguez's first week of rehab games in Tampa gave the Yankees and A-Rod hope that this would not be a reprise of that sad exit. With the big league team off to a sluggish start, the lineup needed his powerful bat. Hitting coach Kevin Long was among those getting daily updates from Tampa while poring over video and written reports. "As much as I had hoped he would be the monster he was, you don't know," Long said. "You kind of wait and see, go through his drills. I remember thinking, *Oh boy, he's not there*, then there becomes a point where you go, *Oh, he's back*. You could see his hip was responding, his body was responding, and he got through it. There was some uncertainty. There was a part of me that thought, *I hope this isn't the end*."

The Yankees won four straight as April turned to May, the last of which was a walk-off win against the Angels on Posada's two-run single. At 13–10 the Yankees seemed to be holding their own, but the team went into a tailspin, losing five in a row, including a pair of two-game sweeps at the Stadium at the hands of the division rival Boston Red Sox and Tampa Bay Rays. "I don't think it was just Alex, but missing Alex didn't help things," third-base coach Rob Thomson said. "With any team when you add a bunch of new players, there's a period where you've got to adjust to each other and get to know each other. It took a little bit."

At 13–15 they faced a five-and-a-half-game deficit behind the Toronto Blue Jays in the American League East. With a six-game road trip about to begin in Baltimore—and finishing in Toronto against the first-place Jays—the lineup needed a boost. The Yankees needed Rodriguez's bat in their lineup, not with their Class A team in the Florida State League.

The decision was made. It was time to get Rodriguez on a plane. He had gone 7-for-36 (.194) against minor league pitching with three homers. If capable of hitting the ball out of the park, it was better he do it in the big leagues. On May 8 Rodriguez joined his teammates in Baltimore, arriving at Oriole Park at Camden Yards for his first major league game in more than seven months. The national media descended upon the Inner Harbor to chronicle A-Rod's first game since *Sports Illustrated* had outed him as a former performance-enhancing drug user.

This wouldn't just be the biggest story in baseball. It would be the biggest story in sports. For some unbeknownst reason Rodriguez felt serene as he walked through the concrete corridor underneath the third-base grandstand, offering a smirk to a crush of photographers as he made the hard right turn into the visiting clubhouse. "I was oddly the calmest I've ever been in my entire career, walking into a storm," Rodriguez said. "I guess I'm used to that."

A-Rod's every move was chronicled. How did teammates react to his return? Was he favoring one leg over the other? Was the ball jumping off his bat during batting practice the way it once had? For a change Rodriguez intended to let his on-field performance do the talking.

For years he had a proclivity for putting his foot into his mouth, often saying something he believed to be innocuous only to see it explode into a headline—or several days of them. In the last calendar year, Rodriguez had endured a divorce, a high-profile dalliance with Madonna, and a steroid scandal. He was also only a few months removed from an ill-advised photo shoot for *Details* magazine, during which he'd agreed to kiss himself in a mirror, a decision that prompted snickers when bemused teammates passed the glossy publication around the Steinbrenner Field clubhouse.

Rodriguez also had to sidestep the noise accompanying an unauthorized biography. Selena Roberts, one of the *Sports Illustrated* reporters who broke the steroids story in February, scored a substantial advance from HarperCollins to publish *A-Rod: The Many of Lives of Alex Rodriguez.* The book said that Rodriguez used performance-enhancing drugs as early as high school and occasionally tipped pitches to friendly opponents in lopsided games; he denied both claims.

As Rodriguez prepared to return, the 33-year-old heeded the advice bestowed upon him by Jason Zillo, the team's director of media relations.

As Zillo told Rodriguez, most people wanted to hear more from the players on the Yankees. He had become an exception to that rule. "Talk less, play more—that was our thing," Zillo said. "He kept the outside noise at a bare minimum and stuck to the script. It's like compounding interest. He's like, 'Wait a second, this is working. Let's keep doing it.' That's what we did."

Wearing a plain white T-shirt and his road-gray uniform pants, A-Rod was all smiles as he sat on the dugout bench and said that he was where he belonged. He spoke of having nine years remaining on his contract, during which he intended to become a better player and a better person. "I've made a lot of mistakes in my career, and they have been well-documented," Rodriguez said that afternoon. "I think I've paid the price. I'm really excited about the present and the future. Those are the only things I can control from here on out."

For Rodriguez, watching his team scuffle through five weeks had been torture. He was a self-professed baseball junkie, frequently watching West Coast matchups after returning home from his own games. He was surprised to learn that not everyone was wired that way; Rodriguez was once taken aback when he learned that Derek Jeter hadn't sprung for the TV package that delivers out-of-town games.

Now, he would have another opportunity to make an impact, the way he had since reaching the majors in 1994 as an 18-year-old who—in his words—went from his high school prom to facing Roger Clemens at Fenway Park. It had been a weird ride, but as his eyes scanned the pregame activity in the Baltimore outfield, Rodriguez said, "I still have an opportunity to have a happy ending."

After the media gaggle began to dissipate, Rodriguez granted an interview to Kim Jones of the YES Network, the team-owned television outlet. Jones, who had witnessed her share of A-Rod drama since joining YES in 2005, sensed something different that day. "It was a contrite Alex," Jones said. "I remember thinking that he said a lot of the right things. It was a big moment overall—obviously in his life—but for that team and for the Yankees organization. It had a big feel to it, even though at that time of year those games never had big feels to them, necessarily. But that one did."

Girardi penciled Rodriguez into the lineup in his customary cleanup spot, playing third base. Cody Ransom's time as the starting third baseman had lasted 15 games before a strained quadriceps muscle forced him to the disabled list. Most recently, the Yankees had been giving starts to journeyman Angel Berroa—whose claim to fame was beating out Hideki Matsui for the 2003 AL Rookie of the Year Award—and light-hitting rookie Ramiro Pena. "We were whole as a team, and I think that's what every team wants to feel like," Girardi said. "There are so many days you go through a season that you're not whole, but it was the first time all year that I felt like we were whole and we looked different."

The manager cautioned against setting expectations too high for Rodriguez, though there was no hiding the fact that the Yankees' limping lineup needed an infusion. Jeter led off the game with a ground-out, and Johnny Damon and Mark Teixeira each drew walks against the Orioles' Jeremy Guthrie.

Rodriguez strolled to the plate accompanied by a loud chorus of boos, though that was hardly a novelty for him. Fans behind home plate waved rubber syringes, making the stands nearly as entertaining to watch as the action on the field. A 30-year-old right-hander who was beginning his third full big league season, Guthrie challenged A-Rod with a 98-mph fastball, the type of pitch Rodriguez admitted that his hip had not allowed him to handle down the stretch in 2008.

Rodriguez turned on the heater and launched it in the air to left-center field, sending Baltimore's Luis Montanez racing to the warning track with his glove outstretched. *Oh my God*, Rodriguez thought. *My superpower is back.*

The drive cleared the 364-foot marker and landed about six rows deep into the seats, delighting the hearty contingent of Yankees fans who had made the 200-mile trip from New York. Drama always seemed to have a way of following Rodriguez around, but this was almost too much—even for him. "I remember saying to John [Sterling], 'Well, so much for needing spring training,'" said Yankees radio analyst Suzyn Waldman.

The Yankees dugout erupted as Rodriguez's awestruck coaches and team-mates marveled at his flair for the dramatic. Nearly a decade later, they remain amazed at what they saw. "This ain't real life," A.J. Burnett said. "I'm like,

'There's no way I just witnessed this.' I mean, I've seen some cool things in my life, but are you kidding me? First swing? If you can tell me that swing didn't jolt our season, I don't even know what to tell you. I knew this guy was good, but are you kidding me? Really? I mean, come on. We all just loved it, like kids at Christmas, three years old with a bike under the tree."

"When he hit that ball, the dugout went absolutely apeshit," Long said. "We're like, 'He's back! He's back!' It was a big day for our team, knowing that we had No. 13 back. To hit a home run, it was just typical Alex Rodriguez fashion: the spotlight, his first game back, and it wasn't a single or a double, but a home run. It was big for us to know that he still had that in him."

To nobody's surprise, Nick Swisher was more excited than anybody else. Had someone asked at that moment, Swisher would have given the okay for the Yankees to print postseason tickets. "There's no stage that's too big for a guy like that," Swisher said. "There was an explosion. I was kind of like, 'Oh, by the way, we've got this guy, too. He's been lying in the weeds for the last five weeks, but we've got this motherfucker, too!' It was just like, 'Oh my God, this is it.' Things started to feel really, really good at that point in time."

The Yankees had three quick runs on the scoreboard, but the advantage seemed larger, especially because it was their first lead in six days. "It felt like it was a fucking 13-run homer," CC Sabathia said. "I don't think we were playing that good; we hadn't been scoring any runs. He hit the homer, and I just remember the dugout was going crazy. First pitch off Jeremy Guthrie. I mean, we went nuts. I felt like we had won it in that moment. It was just so much excitement."

As encouraging as A-Rod's big swing had been, there was an even bigger reason for the Yankees to be confident. A 6'6", 300-pound reason, to be specific. Sabathia's Yankees career hadn't begun well; the key signing of their winter was 1–3 with a 4.85 ERA through six starts for his new employer. "We felt like CC was going according to script," Girardi said. "He always struggled in April. I still don't know why he struggles in April. I don't get it."

New York lost four of those six games—hardly the result the club expected when sending its new ace to the hill. Sabathia said he wasn't worried, but he needed the losing to stop. "I didn't want it to get out of control, I guess, where it started compiling and I started thinking that I can't pitch in New York," Sabathia said. "I think that's where guys get in trouble."

For one night, at least, Sabathia wasn't going to be the story. Once Rodriguez hit the first-inning home run, it was difficult to focus on anything else. "A lot of people don't even remember 'C' from that game," Burnett said. "But he dealt."

Still feeling the adrenaline from Rodriguez's big swing, Sabathia gave up hits to the first two Orioles hitters he faced, though neither came around to score. With rookie Francisco Cervelli flashing fingers behind the plate, Baltimore wouldn't have another hit until the ninth inning. "I remember I was nervous; it was Cervelli's first start, Alex coming back," Sabathia said. "I just remember once Cervy got back there and was calling a good game, I was like, 'Oh, we're going to be good.' Then Al got me hyped hitting the homer, so I just wanted to finish."

Cervelli had been in Double A less than a week earlier, but with both Posada and Jose Molina on the disabled list, the 23-year-old catcher was asked to get the league's highest-paid pitcher on track. It was Cervelli's first start of the season and only the second of his career. "I remember everybody talking, 'Oh, it's CC,' and I was scared," Cervelli said. "He was the No. 1 guy in the rotation."

Cesar Izturis and Brian Roberts opened the ninth with singles, and with the tying run on deck, Girardi could have brought in Mariano Rivera for what had rapidly become a save opportunity. But neither Girardi nor pitching coach Dave Eiland budged from the third-base dugout. Sabathia, who had thrown only 98 pitches to that point, would have a chance to finish the job. He responded by striking out Adam Jones, Nick Markakis, and Melvin Mora— Baltimore's 2–3–4 hitters—to complete his masterpiece. "He needed to come out and make sure everybody knew why they signed him," Burnett said. "'Don't forget who I am and what I do.'"

Sabathia's final line: nine innings, four hits, one walk, eight strikeouts. The Yankees had their cleanup hitter back and they finally saw the Sabathia they had been waiting for. As they returned to their hotel in Baltimore's

Inner Harbor, the buzz was back. "It seemed like from that moment on, you were expecting seven, eight, nine [innings] every night," Thomson said. "He was just dominant. That was an incredible night all the way around."

For the record, Rodriguez struck out in his next two plate appearances after the homer and grounded out in the seventh inning—not that anyone would remember. It would be referred to as The A-Rod Game and while he recognized the significance of his return he also knew that his contribution paled in comparison to what Sabathia delivered. "One swing," Rodriguez said, "and the rest was CC."

· CHAPTER 10 ·

PIE IN THE SKY

The Yankees had been largely amused by the four-faced Buddha that A.J. Burnett refused to travel without, and occasionally someone would ask about his many tattoos, particularly the ones of Bruce Lee or the bloody Spartan warrior from the movie *300*. That was fine, but he had more to add to the universe than frequent scowls and excessive ink.

While with the Florida Marlins and Toronto Blue Jays, Burnett established a reputation as the "pie guy," anointing himself with the task of sneaking behind the heroes of exciting victories and smashing them in the face with a towel full of goop, preferably during a television interview. To Burnett's recollection the practice began with shaving cream in Miami, but teammates complained when they were blinded by the frothy foam.

Burnett made a wise shift to whipped cream, instructing clubhouse attendants to keep a canister of Reddiwip handy near the dugout runway. It was some good-natured, not-so-clean fun, the type that the buttoned-up Yankees had never experienced. "I've got a great picture where Jeff Conine has got it dripping off his face, whipped cream all over," Burnett said. "In Toronto I did it to a bunch of guys. I honestly didn't know if I should do it when I got to New York. I didn't want to disrespect this organization by going out there and throwing whipped cream on somebody, but I was like, 'I've got to do it.'"

All Burnett had to do was wait for the right opportunity, and it seemed to be coming. Alex Rodriguez's return spurred the team back to the .500 mark following its early May slide. With Derek Jeter and Hideki

115

Matsui hampered by injuries and Jorge Posada on the disabled list during a series in Toronto, the offense received contributions from unlikely sources.

Brett Gardner hit his first major league homer on May 13, while rookies Ramiro Pena and Francisco Cervelli delivered big hits against the first-place Blue Jays. Jeter and Matsui returned to collect key knocks as the Yanks finished off a series win, ending the trip on a high note. CC Sabathia followed his gem in Baltimore with eight innings of two-run ball, winning back-to-back starts for the first time as a Yankee.

Though A-Rod had struggled through his first week back—his dramatic home run in Baltimore serving as one of the few highlights during a 3-for-21 stretch over his first six games—he was all smiles as his teammates prepared to head home. He had missed the fun when the Yankees christened their new ballpark, and the series opener against the Minnesota Twins would be his first opportunity to step on the field for a game at the new Yankee Stadium. "All the guys have been telling me about our new home," Rodriguez said then. "For me, it's like Opening Day all over again."

The Twins carried a 4–2 lead into the ninth inning, handing the ball to closer Joe Nathan for the final three outs. The Yankees had already recorded a pair of walk-off victories through the season's first four weeks with Melky Cabrera and Posada delivering the deciding hits. Those types of wins breed confidence. As they came to bat, the feeling in the dugout was anything but defeated. "We were starting to play the way we were capable of," Joe Girardi said. "When you win games late, there's a feeling inside that clubhouse, in the dugout, and on the field that night that no lead is big enough for you not to come back. Once you start to get that feeling as a team, I think you're really dangerous."

Gardner had raked a ball past left fielder Denard Span for an inside-the-park home run in the seventh inning—the first in the stadium's history—to pull the Yankees within two runs. Entering the game after Johnny Damon's third-inning ejection for arguing balls and strikes, Gardner hadn't even been in the lineup, but there was magic in his hit.

Earlier that day, Gardner visited the children's hospital at New York Presbyterian, where an ailing teenager had offered him a yellow bracelet for good luck. If he wore it, 18-year-old Alyssa Esposito promised that Gardner would hit a home run that night. After the scrappy South Carolinian completed his 14-second dash around the bases, he remembered the girl in the wheelchair. "I didn't want to say anything when she gave it to me," Gardner said, "but I'm not really a home-run hitter."

Incredibly, the same night that Gardner rounded the bases, Esposito was being wheeled from her seventh-floor room into surgery. A donor heart had been found, and the Staten Island resident was about to receive the heart transplant that she had been waiting for since January. When she woke up and her breathing tube had been removed, Esposito's parents told her that she should watch the replay of the game. "He's running for me," Esposito had said, drawing tears from her mother, Laura. "The way that day turned out was not like I expected and better than anything that I expected."

After the homer Gardner delivered again, leading off the ninth with a triple and scoring on Mark Teixeira's infield single. Now the deficit was at one run. A-Rod drew a walk, but Matsui fanned, and Nick Swisher grounded out. Minnesota intentionally walked Robinson Cano to load the bases for Cabrera, who had belted a 14th-inning game-winner against the Oakland A's on April 22.

Still recovering from the disappointment of losing his spring battle with Gardner and attempting to find a role as a valued fourth outfielder, Cabrera jumped on Nathan's first pitch, looping a single into left-center field. Teixeira and pinch-runner Ramiro Pena scored as players spilled out of the dugout, mobbing Cabrera near second base. "That was kind of symbolic of not just the veteran players playing well, but even the new players, the younger players coming in and displaying what they're capable of doing," Matsui said. "That game was symbolic of what was to come."

While the Yankees celebrated, Burnett emerged from the clubhouse holding a towel layered with shaving cream, having forgotten to explain to the clubhouse attendants why he might need to quickly access whipped cream. Cabrera was speaking to Kim Jones of the YES Network as Burnett raced out of the dugout, smashing the goop into his teammate's face. Cabrera laughed with delight, wiping it from his eyes. "It may not have been a

Yankee thing, but it was an A.J. thing," Burnett said. "I felt like if I didn't do it, I wasn't being me. One thing I promised Joe and Cash and people in New York is that I was going to be me. Whether I did good or whether I did bad, I was going to be A.J. Burnett."

About 14 hours later, the teams were back at it for a Saturday matinee. This time, the Twins were the ones to mount a late-inning comeback, scoring twice against left-hander Phil Coke in the eighth inning, turning a one-run deficit into a lead. Teixeira drove in a run in the bottom of the inning to tie the game at 4–4, and the contest went into extra innings. These Yankees didn't die. "Somewhere in that series I thought, *Okay, there's something kind of cool going on in this building,*" Alex Rodriguez said. "We just knew that we were going to win no matter what and we had this arrogance about it."

Teixeira opened the 11th inning by drawing a walk against left-hander Craig Breslow, bringing up A-Rod, who was searching for his first hit at the new stadium. Rodriguez looked at a strike on the first pitch before crushing Breslow's next offering into the left-field seats to send the crowd into a frenzy. Rodriguez raised his arms as he rounded first base, high-fiving third-base coach Rob Thomson before flinging his helmet and jumping into a mob of teammates at home plate. As he spoke with Jones on YES, Rodriguez became Burnett's second victim in as many days. Apparently, this wasn't a one-time thing. "I loved it," Rodriguez said. "I loved every part of it because in many ways we were starving to just have fun. 2008 was so difficult, then we had the challenges of spring training. All of this was just like, 'Man, we are just having so much fun.' We were all like loving each other like brothers."

Jones continued her interview with A-Rod after Burnett's pie smash, but distracted by the whipped cream hanging off of Rodriguez's right ear, she was having trouble concentrating on his responses. "My instinct was to wipe the whipped cream that was dangling off Alex Rodriguez's face," Jones said. "I did it, and after I did it, I was like, 'What are you doing?' Sometimes postgame interviews can be a little stilted; they could be repetitive. The pies made it a lot more fun. I would never walk up to a player in the postgame locker room interview where he had eye black where it didn't belong and wipe it off. But it was whipped cream and it seemed like the thing to do."

Minnesota tried to shake off the two difficult defeats on Sunday afternoon, marking Burnett's turn to take the ball. Though his postgame antics had been largely well-received, he was being paid handsomely to pitch, not throw pies. Through seven starts, his 5.36 ERA was not what the team expected; if Burnett couldn't deliver on the mound, the pie-throwing act might get tired in a hurry.

Through six innings, Burnett and Kevin Slowey were locked in a scoreless duel. In the seventh Burnett allowed two hits and three walks, unleashing two wild pitches. Minnesota led 2–0, though the Yankees had proven they could come back. A-Rod led off the bottom of the seventh with a solo shot off Slowey, cutting the deficit in half. Matsui doubled, moved to third base on Swisher's sacrifice bunt, and scored on Cabrera's sac fly to knot the game at 2–2. More late-inning luck resulted in further Twins misery. "We never quit. We never gave up even when we were scuffling," Burnett said. "Sometimes it's hard to see that; sometimes it's hard to see that we're fighting until the end. We kept fighting and fighting and fighting, and then that weekend came. It showed we have so many weapons to beat people with. It showed us we just need to keep our team in the game."

With Burnett off the hook, the teams traded zeros over the next two frames, moving to extra innings for a second straight day. Alfredo Aceves, a versatile right-hander who could start or pitch out of the bullpen, threw a scoreless top of the 10th inning. Damon stepped to the plate with one out, working the count full against righty Jesse Crain before crushing a 95-mph fastball into the right-field seats.

Nobody could believe what had just happened. It had been nearly 37 years since the Yankees had won three straight games in walk-off fashion, but it took only one month in their new ballpark for them to accomplish the feat. The Yankees celebrated with the unabashed glee of Little Leaguers, and Girardi remarked that, though he had more gray hairs as a result of the series, "They have things that take care of that."

And yet, as Jones prepared to interview the star of the game in front of the home dugout, she wondered: would A.J. strike again? Having exited the game in the seventh, there was a good chance that Burnett was still in the trainers' room, icing his arm or receiving other treatment. He was, but it could wait. As Damon stood on the field waiting to speak live to homes throughout the tri-state area, his stealthy teammate smacked him in the face with whipped cream.

Damon loved it. He had seen some crazy things during his four years with the Boston Red Sox, and now Burnett was changing the conservative tone of the Yankees' demeanor one pie at a time. "[Jason] Giambi brought a lot of fun to us the years before, but some people were always trying to keep it down," Damon said. "It's like, man, if you can't have fun playing baseball, then there's something wrong with you."

Burnett's baked goods weren't the only new tradition infiltrating the clubhouse. The pitcher's sons had gifted a replica WWE championship belt to Damon earlier in the month, which was being passed around to the star of each day's game. Later it was replaced by the real deal. After learning of the practice, wrestling legend Jerry "The King" Lawler (a Cleveland Indians fan) shipped a 10-pound replacement to CC Sabathia, delighting the players.

The Yankees were still using the plastic replica on that afternoon against the Twins when Damon proudly showed it off in recognition of his game-winning blast. "Everyone wanted to hoist that belt; everyone wanted to be the star," Damon said. "We were having a bunch of on-field celebrations at the end of the game. Burnett was the mastermind behind that. We didn't only get a great pitcher coming from Toronto; we got a great human being."

The Yankees finished off the four-game sweep on Monday, improving to 23–3 at home against Minnesota since the start of the 2002 season. In the visiting clubhouse, the Twins' Span glumly said, "I can't wait to get out of here. Not just the stadium, but the whole city."

The series had been a reminder of the Yankees' dominance against Minnesota and marked the beginning of a trend that would come to define their season. In their minds, as Swisher recalled, they truly believed that they were going to win every game. Almost as important, the pies were here to stay. "That's what I remember the most about it," Swisher said. "All of a sudden, A.J.'s coming out and he's hammering people with pies. People in New York were probably like, *What the fuck is going on?* It was definitely not a Yankee thing, bro, and it ended up becoming a Yankee thing. For A.J. to have the balls to do something like that, that was walking out on a limb because you don't know how it's going to be taken."

The Yankees swept the Baltimore Orioles in a three-game series, extending their winning streak to nine. The defending World Series champion Philadelphia Phillies ended the streak with a May 22 win in the Bronx, but the Yankees bounced back the next day—with a walk-off win, of course. "That weekend flipped the switch to understand that we're never out of these games," Joba Chamberlain said. "It became typical for us, like, 'Okay, we're down one run. Here we go.' We know we're going to walk it off, and then A.J.'s going to smoke you in the face."

Down 4–2 in the ninth, Rodriguez belted a game-tying, two-run home run against the Phillies' All-Star closer, Brad Lidge, a blast that Rodriguez would call upon for research come November. Cano singled and stole second base, setting up Cabrera's game-winning single—already the 24-year-old Dominican's third walk-off hit of the season and the Yankees' sixth.

"Passing the baton was a big statement that you heard throughout the year," hitting coach Kevin Long said. "If they don't want to pitch to a certain guy, it's the next guy in line. We started getting that feel; we were never out of it. We'd talked about 'Mission 27,' but this was about playing 27 outs regardless of the score."

With four walk-off wins in a nine-day stretch, Burnett's new tradition became the talk of the town. Even though the players seemed to be enjoying it, there were a few purists who believed it was beneath the Yankees. "I remember watching on ESPN and people making a big deal of it and I was like, 'Why is it such a big deal?'" Sabathia said. "We won, we should be able to do what we want. But it's the Yankees, so I remember that being a big story and I'm like, 'Why is that such a big story?'"

There was a belief that the Steinbrenner front office wouldn't stand for such shenanigans. Brian Cashman had heard rumblings that some in the organization "weren't all that geeked for it because it wasn't our way," but the general manager defended the fun. "I loved it," Cashman said. "I love letting personalities come out. I love people showing passion and positive emotion and even negative emotion if they're frustrated by not having success. Show me who you really are. Show our fans who you are. You don't have to be stoic and robotic and boring. If that's your personality, that's fine, but I don't want people showing up here and having to tone themselves down because they're like, 'Oh, I'm not going to be accepted.' I thought the pies in the face were fun-loving and unique and different because it's not something that existed here prior. The fans responded to it, for the most part the team responded to it, and I think it was always an exclamation point to this being a new world order. The players I brought in, I told them, 'I need you to change this clubhouse. I need you to take over,' and they did."

Music in the clubhouse was one thing. Once the whipped cream was flying, the personality of the team began to reveal itself. That same month the Yankees had resuscitated an old-school baseball tradition with Mariano Rivera serving as the judge in their kangaroo court. Burnett, Damon, and Jeter were selected for jury duty, and players filled a cardboard box at the center of the clubhouse to report their teammates for various infractions—real or imagined.

It was a practice that had ended in 1995, when Wade Boggs presided over the court. With Xavier Nady scribbling down all of Rivera's rulings in 2009, Coke was banged with a $30 fine for serving up a homer to Minnesota's Joe Mauer. Swisher parted with $20, his penance for talking to the TV cameras without a shirt on. The most laughs were heard when Rivera banged a wooden gavel and fined A-Rod for missing the first five weeks of the regular season. "I'm definitely a traditionalist, and things are done a certain way, but I also realize that things change, and you've got to be able to adapt and change," Andy Pettitte said. "We had some new guys on the club that we brought in, and that's something that they enjoyed doing; I thought it was great. It was fun to see guys excited and happy who enjoyed playing the game."

Speaking specifically about Burnett's pie-throwing, Posada said that he started to look forward to the act, scanning the dugout to see where the hurler might come running from. Even Jeter and Rivera said that they saw no harm in Burnett's ritual. "We never did things like that, but at the same time we were okay with it," Rivera said. "We celebrated, we were happy. As long as we were winning, it was fine."

"The pies in the face," Jeter said, "I have no problem with it because it only happens after we win."

Most surprisingly to some, Girardi found himself enjoying the fresh act. "The Yankees have always been very businesslike, which I like," Girardi said. "But I also like creativity and players having fun. I think that's really important. People look at me and don't necessarily see that, but I love it. I think it's hilarious, I think it's fun, I think it's enjoyable, and I thought it was great. And if I didn't, I would've told them not to do it."

It got to the point where Girardi would see a late rally beginning to form and think to himself, *Where is A.J.?* The manager preferred the pies to seeing his players risk injury by hoisting heavy water coolers. As they ticked off 15 walk-off wins in all, Girardi and the Yankees would have many more chances to revel in Burnett's tomfoolery over the next five-plus months.

"You started seeing cracks in that kind of no-fun armor," Teixeira said. "I bought into: 'We're being professional here.' But when the game's over and you won in a walk-off, why not celebrate? It's almost like you stole a game."

On July 4 it was Posada coming through against the Blue Jays. Matsui was the hero on July 20 against the Orioles, while A-Rod launched a game-winning home run in the 15th inning of a scoreless game against the Red Sox on August 7. Each time, Burnett was ready. "We had the whipped cream in the video room; it was sitting in there, and you'd kind of look at it like, 'Who's going to get the pie today?'" Long said. "A.J. embraced it; everybody looked to him to do that, and he loved it. He loved every minute of it. He had all his tools ready to go and he was ready to give the guy the next pie."

Cano joined the fun on August 12 against the Blue Jays and did it again with a home run to beat the Chicago White Sox on August 28. On September 8 Swisher went deep to beat the Tampa Bay Rays, picking up his first walk-off hit of the year. When Burnett ran down the tunnel to prepare for Swisher's hit, he found shaving cream where the whipped cream was supposed to be. "I'm like, 'Are you kidding me? I can't put this in his face; what am I going to do?'" Burnett said. "So I did it anyway. But before I did it, I said, 'Close your eyes; don't open them until you wipe it off. It's shaving cream.' And he's like, 'Okay, just do it!' He was so excited. We actually ran out of whipped cream we were hitting so many walk-offs. It was fully stocked the next day, though."

"After I got hit with the pie, the crowd was so excited that I just turned around and gave them a big pump with both hands up in the air," Swisher said. "That was just kind of one of those things you never forget, man. That doesn't happen every day."

It did happen two more times during the final month, though. On September 16 Cervelli became the third Yankees player to deal the Blue Jays a walk-off loss, while rookie Juan Miranda—who had nine at-bats in the big leagues that year—delivered the 15th walk-off hit of the season for the Yankees, beating the Kansas City Royals on September 29.

By the end of the regular season, a total of nine players had delivered walk-off hits. Players weren't the only ones that had become prepared for Burnett. Jones, the YES Network reporter who was usually conducting an interview with that day's hero, found herself constantly on the lookout. "There was no longer a sense of surprise, which almost got to be more fun," Jones said. "In some cases, like Posada, they definitely wanted to dodge it. Players like Cervelli, I think the first thing he said to me on-air was, 'Where's Burnett?' So the anticipation became part of the postgame."

People would ask Burnett if he was prepared to smash a cream pie in the faces of the team's biggest names—especially Jeter. Michael Kay, the Yankees' longtime broadcaster, said that he wishes Jeter had produced a walk-off hit just to see if Burnett would have followed through. "They would've had to do it to him because they did it to everybody else," Kay said. "Because everything with Derek works out the way it should, he was never put in that situation. I think Derek would've accepted it; I don't think he would've loved it."

Burnett's stock response was that he didn't care who got the hit; if you delivered a walk-off, you were up next. He even promised Girardi that if the Yankees won the World Series, there would be a pie with the manager's name on it. "I told Jeter every day of the year, 'I can't wait to get you, man,'" Burnett said. "He was on deck for so many of them, too. There were so many times that we he had a chance to get him. He was the only one I didn't get."

• CHAPTER 11 •

RIVALRIES RENEWED

The Yankees trudged away from the Fenway Park diamond in the late evening hours of June 11 through an ancient corridor with peeling white paint—where the likes of Mickey Mantle or Yogi Berra might have once stopped to tie their cleats—and toward the cramped confines of the visiting clubhouse. They honestly believed they were better than the Boston Red Sox, but as Hall of Fame NFL coach Bill Parcells, who had coached teams in both regions, was fond of saying, "You are what your record says you are." At that point, they'd played eight games against Boston and had absorbed eight losses. This team needed to catch a break or two, and Joe Girardi felt that the time was right to call a meeting. "I said, 'Look, guys, we're a good team,'" Girardi said. "'Things just haven't went our way in this series. It's going to turn around, and when it does, it's going to turn around big.' I was really confident in that team. I just felt like this team is really good. It's talented and it's going to take off. And we did."

Boston swept the Yankees in a three-game set at Fenway from April 24–26 and won its first two games at the new Stadium on May 4–5, so the Yankees arrived in Beantown seeking payback. Instead, the midweek visit was a complete wash for the Bombers, who dropped the contests by scores of 7–0, 6–5, and 4–3, falling two games behind in the American League East.

In the series opener, Josh Beckett limited the Yankees to an infield hit through six innings, offering an olive branch of sorts by noting that since Alex Rodriguez was recovering from hip surgery and had missed the first five losses, "We'll start counting after that." The gesture was of no consolation to A.J. Burnett, who'd allowed three runs and five hits, walked five, and recorded just eight outs before taking his frustrations out on a dugout water cooler. "Considering that's all you hear and that's all you see every Sunday, those series mean more for some reason. They just do," Burnett said. "It's been a thing since baseball started and it's a different series than any other series. It's different than the Subway Series; it's different when you play Boston home or away. They dirt-rolled us early. I couldn't get the ball anywhere in Jorge [Posada's] mitt when I pitched in Fenway. Nothing ever got to him."

The next night, Chien-Ming Wang's miserable season continued with a third-inning exit, having served up a Mike Lowell homer. Kevin Youkilis also went deep against Phil Hughes as Mark Teixeira's four hits went to waste, including the slugger's American League-leading 19th homer. "It was like, 'We can't beat these guys. What's going on? Why can't we beat these guys?'" Teixeira said.

In the finale CC Sabathia held the Red Sox to one run through seven innings and was permitted to begin the eighth after Francisco Cervelli and Rodriguez slugged doubles in the top of the eighth, providing a 3–1 lead. The advantage evaporated as J.D. Drew sparked a rally with an RBI single that chased Sabathia, scoring the go-ahead run on Lowell's sacrifice fly off Alfredo Aceves. Despite the final scores that were posted on the hand-operated Green Monster, Sabathia said, "I never really thought they were good at that point back then. I knew we were better than them."

Sabathia was but one of 25 men in the room, and, as Girardi ditched his lineup card, he was concerned that some other corners of the roster were taking on a downtrodden mind-set. "I wasn't down on them because I loved the effort," Girardi said. "I just thought some screwy things happened that kept us from winning some games. The park can play funny, and the dimensions are weird. I just said, 'This is going to change, guys. We are too good for this not to change.'"

The last time the Red Sox had dominated their blood rivals so thoroughly was 1912, when they'd helped christen brand-new Fenway by pasting a team known as the Highlanders through their first 14 meetings. The Yankees would not see the Red Sox again until August 6, when they'd follow through on Girardi's urging to produce a better outcome. "You remember every meeting in that [Fenway visiting] clubhouse," Burnett said. "It's so little. I do remember that one. It was the same type of thing. 'Hey, let's not get too caught up in what the hell's going on here.' Of course, Joe would never say that. 'Let's think about the mission, let's get back on track. They're going to come to us, and we're going to kick their butts, so let's just stay even-keeled and Mission 27.' It was planted in us."

Andy Pettitte said that while Girardi's speech may have helped improve the Yanks' performance, it just as easily could have been a matter of good timing. "Look, I'm not a big believer in a whole lot of meetings," Pettitte said. "You've got a team filled with veteran players, and we know what to expect. Sometimes you've got to ride some stuff out, and things go bad. I definitely remember that we had struggled early against them in the year and then I felt like we had turned it around. Maybe we were playing a little uptight or a little stressed. A lot of times, you've got to relax a little bit and stop thinking so much about things."

Years later, some of the Yankees had all but forgotten that they struggled so mightily against the Red Sox, against whom they finished the year 9–9. "We were? Wow, that's pretty amazing," Damon said. "Yeah, obviously that puts pressure on us. A good way to think of it is if you lose to a team all year long, you're bound to beat them sometime. Going 0-for-8, I know our fans couldn't have been too happy about that, especially with the matchups. That's not good. We played great against everybody else but the Red Sox. *They had our number and nobody else's? That's a crazy stat.*"

Reliever Brian Bruney had also forgotten that the Yankees opened so poorly against Boston, but the reminder triggered a lesson that he'd learned from Derek Jeter early in his Yankees tenure. "Throughout a season, you don't look at any of that stuff," Bruney said. "I remember early in my career looking at numbers. Jeet was like, 'Hey, why do you look at that?' And I said, 'I don't know. I need to know where I'm at.' I remember him saying, 'Are you going to try harder if they're not any good?' I said, 'No,' and he said, 'Well, then don't look at them. They'll be there at the end of the year. Look at them then.'"

Anyway, there was precious little time for the Yankees to lick their Sox-inflicted wounds, having to return home to meet the New York Mets for the first Subway Series game played at the new Stadium. After birthday boy Hideki Matsui hit one of five home runs in the game, David Wright snapped a 7–7 tie with an eighth-inning RBI double off Mariano Rivera, and the Mets called upon closer Francisco Rodriguez—known as "K-Rod"—for the final three outs.

Brett Gardner fouled out, but Jeter singled and stole second base as Damon struck out. Teixeira was granted an intentional walk to bring up Alex Rodriguez, who slammed his bat on home plate in frustration after lifting a 3–1 pitch into shallow right field. K-Rod pointed toward the sky, pumping his fist in celebration. A Mets win had been secured, or so it appeared.

Near the lip of the infield dirt, second baseman Luis Castillo attempted to camp under the ball, backpedaling and shuffling a few feet to his left. Castillo realized that he was in trouble as Alex Rodriguez's sky-high pop-up had more top-spin than expected. "I remember dropping my head, thinking, *Damn, like we missed an opportunity,*" Girardi said. "And then hearing screaming and looking up. I was thinking, *You've got to be kidding me. This just happened?*"

The ball smacked into the palm of Castillo's glove and fell safely to the outfield grass. Castillo dropped to his knees and lobbed the ball to shortstop Alex Cora, who whipped a throw to catcher Omir Santos. It was too late, as Teixeira slid home with the winning run of a wild 9–8 Yankees victory. As the Yanks celebrated, a stunned K-Rod stood on the field with his hands on his head. "It's almost like a microcosm of the Yankees and Mets history," Teixeira said. "The Yankees are always the team with the talent and they win. And the Mets are always the team of 'How can this happen?'"

To Teixeira's credit, he had been running hard immediately on contact, making the play possible. "I'm as proud of that play as any play in my career because I always thought of myself as a grinder," Teixeira said. "Obviously, with the way my body broke down the last four years of my time in New York, I kind of proved to everybody this is not easy. I played through broken bones, I've played through torn wrists, I played through all these things. That grinder in me was proud that people appreciated that because New York's a kind of grind-it-out, blue-collar city. That ball went up, and I just said, 'I'm going to bust it. You never know. Why not hustle?' When I heard the crowd cheer, I didn't have to look. I knew what had happened. When Rob Thomson was sending me home, I was like, *I'm scoring here.* I knew I was going to score."

A relieved Alex Rodriguez was mobbed by his teammates at first base with Robinson Cano repeatedly slapping his teammate on the helmet before enveloping him in a hug. Alex Rodriguez said that events like the dropped pop-up are the breaks that make the difference in championship seasons. "Honestly, when things like that happen, you're just like, 'We don't need that type of luck. We're good. We don't deserve that break,'" A-Rod said. "But when things like that happen, you're seeing more signs like, 'Maybe this is supposed to be the year.' When weird shit starts happening and Tex is hustling his ass all the way around, I think when you have great fundamentals and you play hard and you play the right way, great things are going to happen."

Billy Eppler never heard the ball drop. Then the Yankees' assistant general manager, Eppler vividly recalls listening to John Sterling and Suzyn Waldman's radio broadcast in a rental car outside a hotel in Rome, Georgia, having just watched the Yankees' Class A Charleston affiliate play against an Atlanta Braves farm team. "They go, 'Pop-up to second base,' and I turned the ignition off in the car," Eppler said. "I go and check into the hotel, put my bags down. There's a convenience store across the street, so I go walk over and get bottles of whatever stuff I wanted to pick up, walk back to the hotel room. I finally sit down, unpack, open up my laptop, connect to the WiFi, and I'm like, 'What? Oh my God, he dropped the pop-up.' Now I always listen all the way through."

The Mets responded with a 6–2 victory in the June 13 afternoon contest, but the Yankees unloaded in the series finale. Hours after Bruney and K-Rod had to be separated by teammates during batting practice in left field, the Yankees delivered a knockout by pounding Johan Santana in a 15–0 victory that marked the biggest blowout between the Big Apple rivals.

Jeter went 4-for-4, and the Yankees got two-run homers from Matsui and Cano in a nine-run fourth inning as they built a 13-run cushion for Burnett. "We basically had a bad series in Boston," Matsui said at the time. "So it was important to start fresh and clear."

The batting practice tiff between the relievers had stemmed from Bruney remarking that K-Rod's exuberant celebrations were a "tired act," and that the blown save on the Castillo pop-up "couldn't happen to a better guy on the mound." Having led the majors with 62 saves the year prior, Rodriguez fired back: "If it came from somebody big like Mariano [Rivera], somebody who has been around and who is good at what he does, I would respect that. But somebody like that, it doesn't bother me."

Backed by a tie-breaking Cano double, Sabathia continued the homestand by pitching into the eighth inning in a 5–3 victory against the woeful Washington Nationals shortly after A-Rod made an unannounced appearance in Monument Park to greet fans. Any hope of a soaring climb was doused as the last-place Nationals took the final two games of the series, handing New York a 3–0 loss on June 18 in front of about 10,000 people, following a five-and-a-half-hour rain delay. "The only problem that I think we had was in our lull times when things were bad, I think we literally just forgot who we were," Nick Swisher said. "And that's kind of half the battle."

It was a gray send-off for the Yanks, who zipped their bags for a nine-game trip to Miami, Atlanta, and back to New York for their first visit to the Mets' new Citi Field. They had no way of knowing that their season was about to take a dramatic turn.

After leaving the game in the ninth inning, Derek Jeter tips his hat to the crowd during the last game at the old Yankee Stadium on September 21, 2008, which capped the facility's 85-year history.

Newly-signed hurlers A.J. Burnett (left) and CC Sabathia (right) pose for photographers on the field of the new Yankee Stadium on December 18, 2008.

After the Yankees signed Mark Teixeira to an eight-year, $180 million contract, (from left to right) Joe Girardi, Teixeira (who was battling an illness during the press conference), Hal Steinbrenner, and Brian Cashman meet with the media in January 2009.

Yankees players, including Mariano Rivera, Andy Pettitte, Derek Jeter, and Jorge Posada, attend Alex Rodriguez's press conference
in February 2009 to support the Yankees star as he admits to having used performance-enhancing drugs.

Attending the first game at the new Yankee Stadium on April 16, 2009, George Steinbrenner—with his daughter, Jessica—makes a rare public appearance that season.

Alex Rodriguez drills the very first pitch for a three-run homer against the Baltimore Orioles in his first major league at-bat after coming back from a hip injury.

After a July victory against the Tampa Bay Rays, A.J. Burnett smashes a pie in the face of CC Sabathia. Burnett became known for this celebratory prank during the 2009 season.

After recording his 2,722nd hit to surpass Lou Gehrig as the all-time hits leader in Yankees history, Derek Jeter salutes the fans on September 11, 2009.

While celebrating Johnny Damon's walk-off home run in May, Nick Swisher (left) and Damon (right) show off a bit of the frat boy vibe they introduced to the typically buttoned-down Yankees franchise.

Catcher Jorge Posada and pitcher A.J. Burnett had trouble seeing eye to eye during the 2009 season, which led to Jose Molina becoming Burnett's full-time catcher.

Mark Teixeira celebrates his game-winning home run in the 11ᵗʰ inning of Game 2 of the ALDS against the Minnesota Twins.

Kendrys Morales and the rest of the Los Angeles Angels of Anaheim struggle to deal with New York's 45-degree temperature in Game 1 of the 2009 ALCS.

Jorge Posada and Mariano Rivera embrace after the closer saves Game 6 of the 2009 ALCS to send the Yankees to the World Series for the 40th time in franchise history.

Jay-Z, a regular presence in the Yankees' clubhouse, and Alicia Keys perform "Empire State of Mind" prior to Game 2 of the World Series at Yankee Stadium.

A signature moment in the 2009 World Series, Johnny Damon deftly rounds second base and heads to third to complete a double steal in Game 4.

Part of his six-RBI night, World Series MVP Hideki Matsui hits a two-run double during the fifth inning of Game 6.

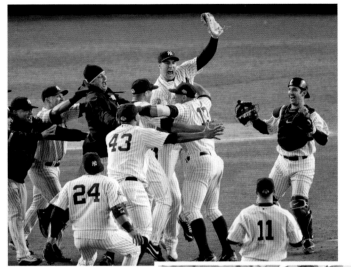

After first baseman Mark Teixeira catches the final out of the 2009 World Series, teammates envelop him in celebration.

Jay-Z, a fedora-adorned Alex Rodriguez, and a suit-wearing Francisco Cervelli celebrate as their championship float passes through Broadway.

Fans celebrate the Yankees' 27th championship as the floats carrying the team make their w through the Canyon of Heroes.

• CHAPTER 12 •

A Visit from the Principal

Traffic crawled at the corner of East 161st Street and River Avenue just outside the home-plate entrance of the gleaming new stadium. Four stories above, general manager Brian Cashman leaned back in his executive's chair as an all-too-familiar sensation of anxiety coursed through his 5'8" frame. Schooled in the win-or-else environment that George Steinbrenner had demanded from his employees, the longtime Yankees general manager frequently said that it was in his job description to never be satisfied with his team's performance. At this moment in time, Cashman assuredly was not.

He had done everything in his power to construct a contender during the offseason. There had been plenty of bumps along the way, but the Yankees had overcome their early-season malaise, climbing out of a six-and-a-half-game hole to gain sole possession of first place.

Yet their 4–9 stretch against the Boston Red Sox, New York Mets, Washington Nationals, and Florida Marlins had been punctuated by an offense that struggled to score runs. Boston surged past New York into first place in the American League East, making Cashman feel even worse. Consecutive series losses to the lowly Nationals and Marlins washed out the good vibes produced by Luis Castillo's gift error.

There were whispers that some players had enjoyed the Miami nightlife a little too much, and a few bleary-eyed hangovers would have explained their lackadaisical play. As the series against the Braves at Atlanta's Turner Field began on June 23, Cashman found himself cursing at a high-definition television screen as he observed another listless performance. A rookie named Tommy Hanson limited the Yankees to four hits over five-and-one-third

scoreless innings, and the vaunted lineup fared no better against three relievers, who combined to hold them hitless over the final three-and-two-thirds
frames. The No. 2–6 hitters—Nick Swisher, Mark Teixeira, Alex Rodriguez,
Robinson Cano, and Jorge Posada—finished a collective 1-for-19.

A-Rod, in particular, seemed to be lost, as his hitless night extended a
1-for-23 skid. They had scored 18 runs over their past nine losses, averaging
two runs per game. "We were losing to teams at the time we shouldn't be
losing to," Cashman said. "You can go on a bad stretch, but this started
to extend into a much longer stretch. Offensively, we were challenged for
some reason against subpar pitching."

At 38–32 the Yankees trailed the Red Sox by five games for the division lead. They wouldn't get another crack at their rivals for another six
weeks, but if they wanted those games to mean something, they needed to
get their groove back before the AL East race became a pipe dream. "We
just haven't been playing well; that's pretty much it," Derek Jeter said after
the series-opening loss in Atlanta. "People always try to dissect everything
and break it down, but we haven't hit. That's why we've been losing. It's
nothing deeper than that."

Cashman didn't know exactly what was going on, but he wasn't about
to sit in his office while the season was falling apart. Though Cashman
typically preferred to allow the clubhouse to be the domain of the manager,
coaches, and players, believing that he shouldn't usurp their authority, his
fingers dialed the numbers for traveling secretary Ben Tuliebitz.

Screw it. He needed a plane ticket to Atlanta.

"We were an elite team, at least on paper, and I didn't know what was
going on," Cashman said. "So I flew in to address all of it, to try to get
into the blood and guts. Your manager and your coaching staff and your
players are all there on a daily basis, trying to fight through this stuff. But
sometimes I do believe if you have to insert yourself, you can't be afraid
to do that."

The GM had planned to be at a ballpark on that date—just not a big
league venue. His initial itinerary involved a leisurely 90-mile trek to Moosic,
Pennsylvania, home of the Yankees' Triple A affiliate, where rehabbing

outfielder Xavier Nady and pitcher Sergio Mitre were slated to play in a minor league game against the Washington Nationals' top farm team.

Cashman's visits to parks in the sticks were usually social affairs, including hobnobbing with local executives and employees, a gentle reminder that the big league club was invested in what transpired on their soil. But Cashman didn't feel much like shaking hands and submitting to small-talk banter, not with his team having lost nine of 13 games—many to what he judged as inferior competition. He needed to speak to his team. "I don't do it much because I leave most of that stuff to our manager and our coaching staff, but I have always been the bad cop," Cashman said. "When the real bad stuff had to be dealt with, I wanted players running through the wall for Joe Torre. I wanted our players running through the wall for Joe Girardi and I want our guys running through the wall for Aaron Boone."

Within hours Cashman was airborne, touching down in the Peach State in the early afternoon. He walked into the visiting clubhouse, the room where Torre's Yankees had assembled before trouncing the Braves in Games 1 and 2 of the 1999 World Series while rolling to their third championship in four years. He planned to meet with the hitters, but first Cashman inspected the lineup posted for that night's game. He wasn't happy. "Swisher, who at the time was one of our best hitters, wasn't in the lineup," Cashman said. "So right away, we're offensively challenged. I grabbed Kevin Long and I grabbed Joe Girardi and I'm like, 'What's going on here? We're not scoring runs, and I already see you have Melky Cabrera in the lineup in right field and not Swish.'"

Cashman recalled that Girardi replied: "I'm just tired of him banging his helmet all the time after he makes an out."

"I'm like, 'He's our best player,' and he's like, 'Yeah, but I've got to send him a message,'" Cashman said. "I asked, 'Well, have you talked to him? Does he even know that bothers you?' And the answer was, 'No.' I was like, 'Get Nick Swisher in here right now.' He brought Swisher in. Joe told him, and Swish was like, 'I won't do it anymore, Skip.'"

Swisher was back in the lineup, batting sixth and playing right field. Girardi said at the time that the original lineup had been "a mistake."

Communication had not seemed to be an issue to that point, but the incident seemed alarming to Cashman. What else might Girardi have been doing based upon pet peeves or seemingly insignificant incidents? "That should define the relationship between Joe Girardi and myself. He wanted me to figure out things that I had no idea pissed him off," Swisher said. "I'm not the only dude on the planet that's ever kicked his helmet. Do you know me, bro? My heart is on my sleeve. You know exactly what I'm thinking all the time. He brought me in there and was like, 'Hey, I don't like you doing this.' I'm like, 'Okay, great. I won't do that anymore.'"

During much of George Steinbrenner's reign, a losing streak could result in a change in the manager's office, or at least the threat of one. An 0–8 start against the Red Sox would have surely placed any of The Boss' skippers on the hot seat. Despite his lineup issue, Cashman stressed at the time that he was not there to evaluate Girardi or his coaches. This was not about them. "He's not slumped over, he's not down and out, woe-is-me, depressed, on edge, or tight," Cashman said of Girardi. "He's keeping guys up, keeping them positive. I hear the messages he sends to them. He's doing everything he needs to do. The reason I'm here is I've got to be doing everything I need to be doing, and, ultimately, we believe that will translate onto the field."

Consider that a vote of confidence, but unlike many of his players, Girardi didn't have a long-term contract. He was in the second year of a three-year deal and said that he knew the drill: "You win or you go home." The players buzzed about Cashman's unexpected presence in the clubhouse. What did it mean? "Other than the Steinbrenners, he's the high man on the totem pole," Swisher said. "So for him to come down, I remember being a little nervous, a little scared because at that point in time you don't really know how it's going to shake down. Obviously, I had heard stories about The Boss and how he approached losing streaks. It just felt like, 'Oh man, what's going to happen?'"

Cashman gathered the hitters, and his missive cut straight to the point: You're better than this. Prove it. "I had a simple message: remember who you are," Cashman said. "I was like, I feel like you guys are giving these opponents too much credit. If you're any pitcher facing this lineup—and I mentioned everyone 1 through 9—I was like, those guys are on that rubber saying, 'How the hell am I going to navigate this lineup without getting my brains bashed in?' I said, 'I feel like you've forgotten who and what and how good you really are. Just do your thing.'"

Cashman never raised his voice from its usual peppy monotone during the meeting. There was no need to; the results spoke volumes. After the GM said his piece, several players stood up to deliver words of their own. Francisco Cervelli recalled Jeter standing up to answer Cashman's speech. "I remember after he talked, Jeter raised his hand and asked him about Washington: 'Is this a big league team?'" Cervelli said. "And [Cashman] said, 'Yes.' And Jeter said, 'Well, we lost against a big league team. We got this. Don't worry about it. Don't worry. We got it.' [Jeter] didn't talk too much. But when he said something—amen."

Johnny Damon added some encouraging words for the team, as did Teixeira, who compared the situation to a principal visiting an out-of-control classroom. "It wasn't a chew-out. Cash never gets loud and yells," Teixeira said. "He basically said, 'I put you guys together to be a lot better than you are. We have way too much talent in here' to be whatever the record was. If you go 2–6 to start a season and everyone starts panicking, you fire the manager and you change the rotation, that's just the panic button. That's not healthy for a team. You can say, 'Guys, it's early. Relax, we're going to get into a rhythm.' By June you've got to stop saying it's early. I think that was Cash's point. He said, 'I don't want to hear it's early anymore. It's not. It's June. We've got to start winning more games, and everyone needs to have a little more sense of urgency. Stop waiting for us to get healthy; we're healthy now.' So I just think that was a good reminder that this team was put together to win a World Series. You don't have to yell to get your point across. Some guys have just a look, a tone. Cash had both."

Swisher was inspired to speak up, adding colorful words of his own. "As much as I thought he was going to come in there and it was gonna be a full-fledged ass chewing, it was a reminder of who the fuck you guys are," Swisher said. "You're the New York Yankees and you guys need to remember who you are. I think for a minute we lost sight of who we were and really how good we were. All of us were like, 'He's right. We've got to remember who we are.'"

Though Cashman spoke only to the position players, his message quickly spread to the pitching staff. During his first decade as GM, Cashman had dealt with countless players for specific issues, but some of the veterans were caught off-guard by his impromptu arrival. "It was different, I will tell you that," Posada said. "I think that was the first time we ever had a meeting with him. The guys that were there for a long time were surprised that we're having the meeting, but it made sense. He put the team together—a hell of a team—and it was just one of those things that needed to be said."

"Very uncharacteristic of Cash, and I think that's why it had so much value," A-Rod said. "In all my years, in 15 years of being part of the organization, I think it's the only time he's ever done it. It was a really tiny coaches' room; I remember where he was sitting and I was sitting across, and we had the whole team there and we were all shoulder to shoulder. He fucking lit in to us, and I fucking loved it. That's why I loved playing in New York. I loved it because I thought it showed he cared so much, he had so much passion, he cared enough to fucking let us know how he felt."

Imagine Cashman's dismay when the team took the field that night and produced more of the same sluggish result. Braves rookie pitcher Kenshin Kawakami made quick work of the Yankees' lineup over the first three innings, retiring all nine batters he faced. Kawakami left the game after being hit in the neck by a Joba Chamberlain line drive on the final play of the third inning, but another rookie hurler, Kris Medlen, picked up where his teammate left off, retiring six straight batters. The Yankees didn't have a base runner through the first five frames, leaving them scoreless through the first 14 innings of the series.

One night after making Hanson look like Greg Maddux, the Yankees were making Kawakami and Medlen look like Tom Glavine and John Smoltz. Chamberlain was doing his best to give the Yankees a chance, but Jeff Francoeur's solo home run in the fifth gave the Braves a 1–0 lead. "There was a real positive vibe I felt coming out of that meeting," Cashman said.

"Then for five innings we're getting shut down, I think no-hit, and I'm like, 'What a fucking waste of time this was.'"

The way things were going, even the slimmest of deficits seemed insurmountable. Having scored only 13 runs over their previous six games, a week that included a pair of shutout losses, the idea of scoring two runs felt optimistic. First, the Yankees would need to get one runner on base. Baby steps. Brett Gardner drew a walk against Medlen to start the sixth, breaking up a perfect game. He didn't stay at first base long. Medlen whirled and fired a bullet to first baseman Casey Kotchman, who slapped a tag down as Gardner dove back to the bag. First-base umpire Bill Welke jabbed his fist, screaming, "Out!"

Convinced his team had been hosed, Girardi bolted from the dugout. Replay reviews for calls on the base paths were still five years away, and there would be old-school fireworks on this one. Girardi admits that he had made up his mind before his shoes touched the grass; no matter what, he was getting ejected. "He let me argue forever, and I'm thinking, *Would you just throw me out so I can leave?*" Girardi said. "I finally said, 'I'm not leaving until you throw me out.' And he threw me out. I just felt like we needed something. Try something different."

As Girardi's tirade continued, interrupting Cervelli's at-bat, the rookie catcher approached Chamberlain in the on-deck circle. "Cervy comes up to me and he goes, 'Watch this: I'm about to hit a homer,'" Chamberlain said.

"Joba was in the on-deck circle with me, and I said, 'Be ready to say hello,'" Cervelli said.

Different words, same sentiment. Four pitches later, Medlen grooved a pitch that the catcher swatted into the left-field seats for the first home run of his career. The no-hitter was gone, and the game was tied. The Yankees had new life. "I still can't believe he called that shit," Chamberlain said. "That shit was crazy."

Finally on the board, the Yankees loaded the bases against Medlen in the sixth before A-Rod broke the tie with a two-run single off Jeff Bennett. Swisher homered in the seventh, and then the team scored two more runs in both the eighth and ninth, rolling to an 8–4 win.

Would any of that have transpired had Girardi sat on his hands? There was no way to know for certain, but the storyline of Girardi's ejection sparking his team out of its doldrums was a lay-up for the team's beat reporters, who furiously hammered away at their laptops on deadline. "You'd like to think that you had a real big effect, but I'm not so sure if it was just that the guys were really good and they just came together and started playing," Girardi said. "Sometimes you have a meeting, and it doesn't take effect for a week, so I don't know. But I think the reminder of how good they were and the willingness to fight for your players can sometimes fire players up."

Girardi joked at the time that if he could guarantee they'd score eight runs, he'd get tossed bringing out the lineup card. He didn't even need to raise his voice the next day. Girardi hung around for all nine innings, enjoying the view as the Yankees teed off on Derek Lowe, scoring eight runs and dealing a fourth-inning knockout to the former All-Star.

A-Rod had homered only once in his previous 60 trips to the plate, but he went deep in the first inning against Lowe as part of a three-hit, four-RBI game. He would hit four homers over the next six games—all Yankees wins. The Yankees were learning what Rodriguez's body was capable of handling, less than four months removed from major hip surgery.

Days off would be necessary; he had been given a two-game break during the series in Miami, causing a mini-uproar. Then again, nearly everything A-Rod did had that effect, so why would this be any different? The respite turned out to be the perfect tonic for Rodriguez, who hit .355 (11-for-31) with four home runs and 15 RBIs over the nine games following his two-day vacation. "There's no question that once I got some rest, I was a different person," Rodriguez said. "What I had to remember was that I just basically finished my spring training and building that endurance. Atlanta was a wake-up moment. I got physically healthier, and Cashman woke us up. It was like a perfect storm. It was like *boom*. I took off, and we took off."

The Yankees were now winners of seven straight games, sweeping the New York Mets at Citi Field and taking the first two at home against the

Seattle Mariners. An offense that had looked so feeble now looked invincible, scoring nearly seven runs per game during the streak.

Had Cashman's visit to Atlanta, in Swisher's words, been the "kick in the ass" they desperately needed? Or did the appearance simply come at a time when a good team was getting ready to break out, regardless of the tongue-lashing? The chicken or the egg. "It was a turning point 100 percent," Burnett said. "You can get talked to in a bunch of different ways. It doesn't matter if you're 10 or 40. If you have a job and you're not doing it, you're going to get scolded, but it wasn't like that. He was in it, he was for us, he had our back."

• CHAPTER 13 •

THE MASTER'S APPRENTICES

For the better part of 19 seasons, the Yankees' gameplan adhered to a simple formula. Get the ball to Mariano Rivera, let the greatest closer in history do his job, and then shake hands. They were following that script on June 28 as Rivera was summoned to record the final four outs of the Subway Series sweep of the New York Mets with an opportunity to log his 500th regular-season save.

Rivera can recount some memories of that game, though the haze of having succeeded 652 times—plus 42 more in the postseason—tends to obscure some details. What Rivera remembers most about that night was logging the only RBI of his career, a bases-loaded walk in the eighth inning against Mets closer Francisco Rodriguez. "The RBI is the best," Rivera said. "It was my first RBI. It was my 500th save."

The free pass followed an intentional walk to Derek Jeter and forced home Melky Cabrera with an insurance run, giving the Yankees a 4–2 lead as they continued the hot streak of 13 wins in 15 games that followed Brian Cashman's address in Atlanta. It was the third regular-season plate appearance for Rivera and his second in five days; he'd ignored a take sign and lifted a fly ball to center field during the Braves series. "It was good," Rivera said. "At the same time, it was something special because I didn't do it alone. It was amazing. I liked it because everybody was involved, everybody. We did it winning."

Wearing Cody Ransom's batting helmet, Rivera grinned broadly as he trotted to first base and then returned to the mound in the home half of the ninth and dispatched the Mets quietly around a two-out single. The final out came as Alex Cora chopped a grounder to second baseman Robinson Cano.

Pitching coach Dave Eiland said he delighted in being the one to press the phone to his ear and ask Rivera to warm up for that historic appearance. "He wasn't able to do it at home at Yankee Stadium, but he was still able to do it in New York City, and that was special," Eiland said. "It was an honor to make that call."

Rivera was lauded two days later at the Stadium and invited to throw the ceremonial first pitch prior to a game against the Seattle Mariners, a rare honor for an active player. He also threw the last pitch of the day, hurling a perfect ninth inning to conclude an 8–5 win against Seattle. "There's something unbelievable about that guy," Jorge Posada said. "He could've pitched for two more years if he wanted to. I mean, he's blessed. The velocity wasn't there anymore, but he still had the cutter and he could put it wherever he wanted to. He can get people out. His mind, his mental toughness, was the No. 1 thing about Mariano."

The passage of time seemed to have no effect on the great Rivera, who was on his way to posting a 1.76 ERA, saving 44 games and finishing 55 in his age 39 campaign. His continuing success was a given, as the devastating knee injury that would impact Rivera's retirement plans was still more than three years into the future. "What was so incredible about it was I had a chance to catch him when he was a rookie and how dominant he was," Joe Girardi said, "then so many years later how good he still was. I was in awe. Mo was like a blankie. You could bring him in to clean up anyone's mess. It just seemed to pacify everybody when you brought Mo in. You never worried."

As much as anyone, Girardi understood the value of a good bullpen. He remembers the hopelessness of facing the Cincinnati Reds' "Nasty Boys" of Norm Charlton, Rob Dibble, and Randy Myers during the early years of his career as a Chicago Cubs catcher and then experienced its benefit firsthand in 1996, when the Yankees' dominant crew of Rivera, Graeme Lloyd, and Jeff Nelson set up for closer John Wetteland. "It was a five-inning game," Girardi said of the 1996 squad. "If you didn't get to us by the fifth inning, you were done. There were nights where Mo would go two-and-two-thirds. I never forgot those things. As far as the importance as having someone to bridge the gap, it's a necessity. And when you don't, you lose too many games that you shouldn't have lost. Those demoralize teams more than anything."

As the Yankees discovered in 2009, they possessed the makings of a formidable crew that could reliably deliver the ball to Rivera with Phil Hughes' emergence standing out in particular. The 23rd overall selection in the 2004 draft out of Foothill High School in Santa Ana, California, Hughes earned praise as a sophisticated, physically mature prospect and then conjured dreamy comparisons to another hard-throwing right-hander upon his arrival in big league spring training in 2006. After facing Hughes on a back diamond of the team's complex in Tampa, Florida, an impressed Jason Giambi exited the batting cage and dubbed Hughes "Pocket Rocket," saying the 6'4" hurler reminded him of a smaller Roger Clemens. Posada called Hughes "the best arm in camp," a group that at the time included future Hall of Famers Randy Johnson, Mike Mussina, and Rivera.

When Joe Torre and Alex Rodriguez also offered glowing praise—"Easy cheese," Rodriguez had remarked of the prospect's fastball—the bar had been set impossibly high.

"That's one of those things I've always tried to ignore because I knew who I was," Hughes said. "All that other stuff was kind of just noise to me, but I feel like for the most part the fanbase could never let that part go. So that was probably the most difficult part, just knowing that you were never going to live up to being Roger Clemens. That was a pretty tough ceiling to reach. You were kind of set up for disappointment from the get-go. For myself, I just wanted to be Phil Hughes, and that was what I strove to do. And I feel like that, regardless of how fans perceived me, it was still a great opportunity to be on the team with such high expectations and, ultimately, a team that was able to accomplish some pretty special things."

In April of 2007, Hughes made his big league debut 59 days shy of his 21st birthday. Summoned to assist an injury-depleted rotation that was lacking Mussina and Carl Pavano, Hughes' promotion came immediately after Chase Wright surrendered homers to four straight Boston Red Sox at Fenway Park, tying a major league record set in 1963.

Hughes was the youngest Yankee to start a game since 18-year-old Jose Rijo in 1984 and in his second start he gave the Yankees both a glimpse of what they hoped their future could be and a sobering reminder that stardom was anything but assured. Carrying a no-hitter into the seventh inning against the Texas Rangers in Arlington, Hughes felt a pop in his left hamstring. Instead of celebrating the Yanks' first hitless performance since David Cone's 1999 perfect game, the top prospect landed on the disabled list and didn't return to a big league mound until August.

Hughes' abbreviated performance for Torre's final Yankees club—5–3 with a 4.46 ERA in 13 starts, plus five-and-two-thirds innings of one-run relief in the playoffs—swayed the organization to guarantee his rotation spot in 2008. Then Hughes' 6.62 ERA in eight winless starts nudged the club toward spending big, and Hughes began '09 in Triple A. "For me being a young player, I had to figure out how I was going to get my feet back under me," Hughes said. "I was told that I wasn't going to make the team out of spring. That was the plan all along. I had a pretty good [Arizona] Fall League, I worked really hard in the offseason to get back to what I thought I could be. I actually had a good spring, but they're like, 'Hey, you know you're going to Triple A. Obviously, if something happens, we'll call you up.'"

Chien-Ming Wang's inconsistency earned Hughes an early-season return to the rotation, during which he'd gone 3–2 with a 5.45 ERA in seven starts. An eight-inning scoreless gem on May 25 in Texas stood out, but other efforts had been less convincing. As June dawned, Wang had returned from the disabled list, and Hughes was summoned to Girardi's office, believing he had been ticketed for a return to Triple A. Instead, Girardi and Eiland told the 23-year-old that they believed Hughes could help in a relief role. Hughes eagerly accepted the challenge, recognizing that it represented his ticket to avoiding a return assignment to the Waffle Houses of the International League. "To be honest, I thought I was getting sent back down," Hughes said. "When they told me that they were going to give me an opportunity in the bullpen, I was just ecstatic to stay there. I knew the team had a chance to do something special and I was really excited to be a part of that—and to not be riding buses for the next few months."

Relievers Brian Bruney and Damaso Marte were unable to remain healthy, so there were innings to be pitched. The day of Hughes' bullpen assignment, Brian Cashman participated in a meet-and-greet with fans at the stadium. He spotted a guest relations representative holding a cardboard sign that read, "How May I Help You?" "You can help me find an eighth-inning guy," Cashman quipped.

Little did Cashman know the answer was already in place. Hughes pitched a scoreless inning on June 8, allowed a pair of runs two days later to the Boston Red Sox, and then didn't permit another run until July 30. "Once I gained a bunch of confidence, I just rode that wave," Hughes said. "Our starters were giving us six, seven innings every night, and we were up by one to three runs. You knew the phone was going to ring for you, and I got ready and did my thing. It was one of those really, really good stretches. It was a lot of fun to be part of, and I think the team was also rolling around that time. Those good times always feel like they fly by."

Elevated to the seventh inning in July, Hughes took over as Rivera's primary set-up man in August with Bruney, Alfredo Aceves, Phil Coke, and David Robertson serving as important contributors. As a reliever that year, Hughes was 5–1 with a 1.40 ERA, striking out 65 against 13 walks in 51 ⅓ innings. Cashman likened that performance to Rivera's 1996 season and Chad Green in 2017, and Girardi said that there was a clear uptick in Hughes' velocity. "He was throwing 97, his location down and away to left-handed hitters was impeccable," Girardi said. "He was able to air it out and use his breaking ball, and his control was so good. He wasn't asked to go through a lineup two or three times. He was completely different as a reliever than as a starter. It was like they were seeing a new guy, and his stuff was dominant."

Generally speaking, a starting pitcher's velocity tends to jump out of the bullpen. He has the freedom to unload for an inning or two rather than budgeting exertion over 80 to 100 pitches. Out of the bullpen, Hughes threw his fastball more than 80 percent of the time, mixing in occasional curveballs and cutters. That aggressiveness was part of what had made Joba Chamberlain a phenomenon late in 2007, when the righty relied almost exclusively on his fastball and slider to fantastic results. "He was a great weapon," Rivera said of Hughes. "Knowing that he only had to go one, two innings, it was amazing. It was amazing because he could focus on that and give everything he had for just two, three innings, whatever he was throwing that day. He did a great job for us."

Johnny Damon said that Hughes also had discovered a secret fuel source: the players' dining area at the Stadium. "A bunch of us ended up spending a lot of time there that year, especially Phil Hughes," Damon said. "He kept putting on weight and he kept throwing harder and harder. Brian Bruney told him to keep eating if you're going to keep throwing harder."

Hughes agreed with Damon's recollection, saying that the food had been "amazing" that first year. CC Sabathia said that the Yankees' dinners were catered from New York restaurants, ranging from Shake Shack to TAO, and Hughes took full advantage of the culinary delights.

"Johnny was always really funny," Hughes said. "He was such a good dude to be around. He always had my back 100 percent even when I was super young coming up. He always kept things light and was funny. There were times where it seemed like I was throwing every single night, so he would joke that I was going to blow out by the end of the year, but it was all going to be worth it. It was good times."

The Yanks' relief crew was a melting pot of interesting characters. Then 26, Aceves hailed from San Luis Río Colorado, a Mexican border city near Yuma, Arizona. The Yankees had acquired Aceves from Sultanes de Monterrey in the Mexican League in 2008, purchasing his rights along with those of 18-year-old left-hander Manny Banuelos for $450,000. "[Aceves] took the ball every time we asked him to take the ball. He never said no," Eiland said. "He was a horse in various roles. This guy could pitch, and he wasn't afraid."

Enjoying an '09 season in which he would go 10–1 with a 3.54 ERA over 43 appearances (including one start), Aceves favored uniform No. 91, honoring eccentric NBA power forward Dennis Rodman. Unlike Rodman, Aceves preferred to shave his head. He sketched cartoons, sang, and played guitar in his spare time, belying a battle-hardened exterior. "He was a scary dude," Bruney said. "Not somebody that you would want to get in an altercation with, but he was awesome. He was really good that year, too. He was a little bit quirky but still a fun guy. Not somebody that you want to have any bad blood with for sure."

Then 27, Bruney was with his second big league team, having been acquired from the Arizona Diamondbacks prior to the 2006 season. A burly, hard-throwing right-hander who expressed his fondness for beer and ice cream, Bruney battled a lingering flexor strain early but recovered in time to go 5–0 with a 3.92 ERA in 44 regular-season appearances. "Everybody there was hungry," Bruney said. "We all wanted to provide a part in that recipe and that puzzle. We wanted to be that piece that fit in and bridge that gap to Mo. You get it to him, and it's over. That was just our goal. Whatever role it was, I don't think anybody cared. My name's called, I'm ready to go. That's the definition of a bullpen."

Marte had expected to be the top left-hander in the bullpen, but the 34-year-old struggled in seven April appearances before acknowledging that his shoulder hurt. Marte had compiled a 3.29 ERA over nine seasons when the Yankees rewarded him with a three-year, $12 million pact. They'd squeeze just 31 regular-season innings from that investment, though it would later be argued that the 12 outs Marte recorded in October 2009 justified the price tag.

Marte's extended absence benefited Coke, who spent the entire year on the roster and pitched to a 4.50 ERA in 72 appearances. The eccentric left-hander represented a throwback to the days when players held winter jobs, like when a young Yogi Berra found employment in Sears' hardware section. Coke spent one offseason as a chimney sweep in his hometown of Sonora, California, where he also replaced 500-pound stoves and installed in-ground fiberglass pools. "The hardest part was getting the soot off of you," Coke said. "You're getting pretty dirty, but I grew up messin' around in the mud anyway, so it wasn't a big deal. You smelled really funny; it was hard to get it all off your skin."

Robertson would go on to prominence as a big league closer, nailing down more than 30 saves in three consecutive years from 2014 to 2016, but in '09 he was a fresh-faced rookie trying to avoid a return to the minors.

Then 24, Robertson couldn't help but fret each time he permitted a run; Yankees color commentator Suzyn Waldman recalls him repeatedly asking her, "Are they going to send me down?"

To Robertson's relief, he was able to spend most of the season in New York, living out of the cheapest Manhattan hotel he could find to save most of his prorated $403,300 salary. In 45 appearances Robertson pitched to a 3.30 ERA and finished 20 games, including his first save on July 27 at Tampa Bay against the Rays. His greatest impact was still yet to come, but Robertson's personal expectations were soaring. "About halfway through the year I was like, 'We're going to win the World Series, and it's not even going to be a challenge,'" Robertson said. "We went on a West Coast road trip, we won five in a row, then lost a game to Seattle. I remember coming in the clubhouse, and everybody's looking around like, 'What just happened? We just lost a game?' I was like, 'We're going to win every game from now on. We've just got too many weapons.'"

Eiland said similar conversations about the bullpen's depth were taking place in Girardi's office. "Joe and I would talk about, 'So if the starter goes five, we've got this guy for this inning, this guy for this inning, and this guy for this inning,'" Eiland said. "We had weapons down there. Hughes came on, Aceves was doing his part, Robbie was coming on, Coke could get lefties out as well as righties, Marte. It's like what we had in Kansas City in '14 and '15. We didn't have to worry about matchups because our righties could get lefties out; our lefties could get righties out."

Joined by contributors like Sergio Mitre (51 ⅔ innings), Chad Gaudin (42 innings), Jonathan Albaladejo (34 ⅓ innings), and Jose Veras (25 ⅔ innings), the relievers were united in their fierce admiration for Rivera. "Everybody looked up to Mo," Hughes said. "We were just kind of role players in trying to get him the ball. Nobody wanted to screw that up, so that gave everybody extra motivation. We knew we had the starting rotation, we knew we had the closer. It was just a matter of who was going to fill in those other pieces."

As Robertson recalls, Rivera's pinpoint command extended beyond the strike zone. He'd use those gifts to pick on favored targets. Edwar Ramirez, whose skinny frame Torre had once compared to a thermometer, had been a regular recipient of Rivera's teasing; one occasion Rivera stuffed the young Dominican into a locker at the old Stadium, cracking a belt menacingly as though it were a whip. Robertson experienced his fair share of Rivera's playful side as well. "He'd throw gum constantly during batting practice," Robertson said. "He was a pretty good shot, too. He managed to throw a piece in my ear one time. We were sitting in the bullpen, and I was telling a story. He threw it from across the bullpen into my ear, and it stuck it in there. It was smushy and wet and gross."

Rivera's 10th All-Star selection came in 2009, and those who watched him work remain impressed by the marvelous consistency that earned him unanimous induction into the National Baseball Hall of Fame in 2019. Eiland said that Rivera's leadership was directly responsible for the success of that year's bullpen: "You can't put a price on that."

"What I tried to do was try to keep the boys relaxed and give all the knowledge and advice that I could to keep them together," Rivera said. "They were young and they were ambitious. They wanted to win. Me being there with them, it was kind of great in a sense that they were able to assert, listen, and execute."

CHAPTER 14

BIRTHDAY BASH

From his spring steroid scandal to a challenging recovery from hip surgery, Alex Rodriguez's season had been anything but normal—even for him. As the red-hot Yankees ripped off nine straight wins to start the second half of their schedule, it was telling that one of the steadiest aspects of his life seemed to be a relationship with a high-profile Hollywood actress.

Given the inordinate amount of drama he had endured, Rodriguez deserved a night to cut loose. His girlfriend, actress Kate Hudson, made plans to throw a large party on the final Saturday of July, two days before the slugger's actual birthday. The daughter of Academy Award-winning actress Goldie Hawn, Hudson rose to prominence for her performance in the 2000 film *Almost Famous* and then was a frequent box-office draw in romantic comedies. The bubbly blonde's relationship with Rodriguez had sparked in November 2008, when they were spotted together at the re-opening of the Fontainebleau Hotel in Miami. "She was really cool," A.J. Burnett said. "She was down to earth and she enjoyed having the wives around."

As the team continued to play well, Hudson and her stepfather, actor Kurt Russell, became fixtures at the Stadium. She was frequently seen in the front row down the third-base line, striking friendships with Karen Burnett, Michelle Damon, and Amber Sabathia, among others. "She was one of the most delightful famous people I'd ever met," said the YES Network's Michael Kay. "I never saw a famous person be that nice to people that had nothing to do that could help her. It seemed like she knew the groundskeepers by their first names, the ushers. She was just a complete sweetheart."

The Yankees' winning streak came to an end on July 25 with a 6–4 loss to the Oakland A's, but that didn't dampen the enthusiasm for the festivities. The team held its annual family picnic on the diamond at the Stadium, and, as youngsters ran the bases and played Wiffle Ball, shutterbugs clamored to capture the moment that Hudson and Rodriguez smooched on the grass behind home plate.

It was an appetizer for the main course to come. A-Rod was renting a swanky mansion in Rye, New York, a suburb approximately 20 miles northeast of the stadium. Virtually the entire team—players, coaches, support staff, wives, and girlfriends—made their way to the exclusive Milton Point neighborhood to toast Rodriguez's 34th year on the planet. Catering was provided by Nobu, the wildly popular Japanese restaurant, and most attendees were dressed in their finest garb as they explored the grounds of the Parsonage Point estate. The distant, twinkling lights of Manhattan were visible from across the Long Island Sound, and the guests were wowed by Hudson's decorative touches and attention to detail. "That party was huge for us," Sabathia said. "That was like the first time we had something where almost everybody on the roster came, and we had a blast. Just doing something together away from the field, I think it helps guys. You may not really bond with this guy or like this guy so much, but if you see him in a different light, different place, you might be able to. I think it just helped us get that much closer."

Hudson wasn't the only A-list entertainer at the party. Jay-Z, the Grammy Award-winning rapper, counted Sabathia as a close friend and would later ink him as a client for his Roc Nation Sports agency. In fact, Jay-Z was around so much that season, some referred to him as the 26th man on the roster. "He was a part of the team," hitting coach Kevin Long said. "I don't know if Jeet's going to take this the right way, but he might've been the team captain."

Some of the coaches left the party on the earlier side, as did a handful of players who wanted to zip home to see their kids before bedtime. "I'm not much of a party guy, so I made an appearance, said hello, and hit the road," Andy Pettitte said. "I definitely remember it was at an unbelievable house, a big ol' place out in Rye, right on the water. It was a pretty special event."

The party continued late into the evening, and as the music thumped and booze continued to flow, someone suggested that they should shoot around on the mansion impressive basketball court. That turned out to be a poor decision for Phil Hughes, who attempted to dunk over Jay-Z and fell to the hardcourt, an act that his teammates still chuckle about a decade later. "Hughesy was an epic fail on that one," Joba Chamberlain said, with a laugh. "He tried. I mean, the effort was there, but it just didn't happen. I don't know how to describe that other than it just didn't happen."

As the bash appeared to be winding down—Rodriguez remembers it as being "the seventh inning of the party"—Burnett and Sabathia were drawn toward the beautiful Olympic-sized swimming pool. "Me and CC had a plan from the first minute: we're ending up in the pool," Burnett said. "It was just a beautiful spread: tables lined up around the pool, food, awesome. I was like, 'You know we're going to end up in there,' and he's like, 'Oh, for sure.'"

The pitchers had mentioned their plan to A-Rod, expecting to receive some pushback. After all, he and Hudson had thrown an elegant party that by all accounts had been a smashing success. Would Rodriguez want to see it devolve into hijinks? "As the night's going on, we had a few [drinks] or whatever. We walked by Alex and mentioned to him, 'Hey, we're going in the pool later,'" Burnett said. "He said, 'Oh, yeah, I'm in. First one.' And we kind of just looked at each other like, 'This dude ain't gonna jump in. Come on, yeah right, Alex.'"

The smoke was still in the air from the extinguished candles on Rodriguez's cake when he backed up his words, making no effort to remove his expensive articles of designer clothing. *Cannonball!* "He blew out his candles and ran and jumped in that pool," Burnett said. "I looked at CC, CC looked at me, and we ran and jumped in. Then everybody runs and jumps in. It was wild. Phones, watches, everything on. It was just, 'Oh, he did it. We've got to go.'"

Rodriguez didn't remember being the first man into the pool, but he was not the last. "Somebody jumps in the pool, and then somebody else, and before you know it, you have 40 people inside a pool," Rodriguez said. "It's past midnight now, and you're going, 'Shit, we have a day game the next day. I hope we don't lose.' It was a blast."

No one had thought to pack trunks or bikinis, but in the wee hours of July 26, Rodriguez's celebration officially became a pool party. Burnett said that Hudson leapt into the pool after Rodriguez, followed by Amber Sabathia and Karen Burnett. Incredibly, Joe Girardi was right behind them. "It got to the point of, 'Why aren't any coaches in here?'" Burnett said. "So Joe jumps in and starts grabbing people, grabbing coaches, grabbing teammates, chucking people in left and right. It was awesome. It was great bonding. If you would've told me that was the way that birthday party was going to end up, I probably would've been like, 'You're crazy, no way.' It was like it was on the schedule: we're going to go there, we're going to mingle for a little bit, we're going to eat, we're gonna sing 'Happy Birthday,' and we're all going to jump in at the same time. That was what it seemed like. It was crazy."

Amid the splashing and laughter, one of the younger Yankees was opting to remain on the sidelines. "Dave Robertson was balking; he was actually upset," Long said. "He was very upset. It was almost to the point he was tearing up, he was so upset."

Robertson was an admittedly green rookie, having boarded the New York-Scranton shuttle multiple times throughout the 2008 campaign. He opened 2009 at Triple A, going up and down twice during the first two months of the season before sticking with the Yankees for good in late May. The young pitcher soaked in all he could by watching Mariano Rivera, but Rivera never prepared Robertson for an impromptu pool soiree. "I didn't want to get in the pool," Robertson said. "I didn't think I would be at a high school party. I was past college and past high school and just didn't think it warranted it. I was wearing a brand new suit because I had just been to an event with Johnny Damon. I had one suit and, yeah, I wasn't into it."

"He didn't have any money, and A-Rod bought him that, and it was an expensive-ass suit," Nick Swisher said. "I don't blame him for not jumping in."

With more than two decades of pro baseball experience as a player and coach, Long understood that bonding with teammates far exceeded the value of whatever designer threads Robertson had on his back. Robertson wasn't budging. "He's in front of the house, sitting on the steps, and I'm like, 'Listen, Dave, everyone's being thrown in. You need to go do that,'" Long said. "He was saying, 'I don't want to. Alex bought me this suit; I really like it.' I said, 'Dude, he'll buy you another one.'"

"He was about ready to fight somebody if they dragged him in the pool," Hughes said.

Burnett ultimately convinced Robertson to get into the pool—or threw him in, depending on which account you're inclined to believe. "I think A.J. pushed him in," Sabathia said. "He was pissed at somebody. A.J. would haze D-Rob at that point in his career, always giving D-Rob shit. To see D-Rob turn around and actually be pissed, I remember he was chasing A.J. down."

"I remember wanting to get out of there as quickly as possible," Robertson said.

Nearly a decade later, Robertson's amicable mood darkened when asked about the party. "There were some people that almost got some blows thrown at them that night," Robertson said. "It wasn't funny then and it isn't funny to me now."

Robertson's memories from that night may be unforgettable, but at least he can recall specific details. That is not the case for some of his teammates. "I don't remember a single thing, bro," Swisher said. "I do remember everybody having an awesome night."

And a horrible morning. The one aspect of the party that Hudson failed to consider was the Yankees' schedule. They had a 1:05 PM game against the A's the next day, and even with Girardi granting a late mandatory report time (no chance they were taking batting practice), the world was moving slowly for some of the overserved. "I threw up on the way home and had to pitch the next day, a day game against Oakland," Hughes said. "I was so hungover I didn't know if I was going to make it through. I felt absolutely miserable."

It is a testament to the quality of that team that at far less than 100 percent they were able to post a 7–5 win some 16 hours after Rodriguez's leap into the deep end. Protecting the two-run lead, the hungover Hughes worked a perfect seventh and then gave up a one-out double in the eighth. Brian Bruney bailed him out, recording two outs on four pitches to hand the ball to Rivera in the ninth.

There were other memorable shindigs that summer. Following the blueprint that he had established in his Cleveland Indians days, Sabathia invited the team to his Alpine, New Jersey, home for an Independence Day celebration, another epic night that stood out. Six years before the New York Giants' Jason Pierre-Paul mangled his right hand in a fireworks mishap, one prominent Yankees player nervously avoided a similar fate. "A.J. Burnett was a pyro and he wanted to light everything on fire," Chamberlain said. "It's like, 'Holy crap, I hope nobody blows their fingers off or anything.' It was fun. When you talk about the culture aspect, we wanted to be around each other. There are times when you're around somebody so much you're just like, 'Dude, I don't want to see your face, I don't want to talk to you,' but I never felt like that was our team in '09."

July was a busy month on the Yankees' social calendar. A few weeks later, Sabathia distributed invitations to a birthday party that was held at the 40/40 Club, a luxury sports bar and lounge owned by Jay-Z. Located steps from Madison Square Park in Manhattan, the establishment has huge plasma screens and multiple private lounges. For Sabathia's party, Jay-Z's people added a little more sizzle. "They had chicks sitting on the stairs and they had snakes on them," Chamberlain said. "I don't like snakes, but if you're a hot chick with a snake on you, I'm probably going to stare at you. I woke up the next day with one sock on and all the lights on in my house."

Hughes said that though team events can be overdone, the '09 squad seemed to find balance between business and pleasure. "Maybe once every other homestand, somebody would do something," he said. "It was more fun for the guys instead of an obligation, which was a good thing. We had a lot of fun, but it wasn't like we were going out to dinner with each other every single night either. It was a good balance of family time and having time together as well."

For Rodriguez, the acceptance that he felt on the night of his birthday party offered another indication that he was moving past his early-season drama. At least within the clubhouse, he had seemingly become baseball's equivalent of the Andy Dufresne character in *The Shawshank Redemption*, who crawled through a river of sewage and came out clean on the other side. "I never played with him before and I didn't know him, but I knew this wasn't the Alex I had heard about," Burnett said. "This guy's great; are you shitting me? If you would've told me he was going to jump in that pool, I would've said, 'No chance.' You just saw his personality coming out as that year kept going on. I think everybody enjoyed seeing Alex like that. He just kept opening up little by little that whole year, and that party really made us come together."

The Yankees held sole possession of first place, A-Rod was performing well on the field (he had a .917 OPS and 19 home runs in 67 games) and he was a part of a group that could help him fill the biggest void on his baseball résumé: a championship. "I had nothing to lose; I felt like I was in a happy place," Rodriguez said. "I felt very grateful to get the opportunity to come back and play because I just came back from what I thought could've been a Bo Jackson, career-ending injury. Here I am in the middle of the summer, playing with what I think is the best team in baseball—and playing well. Then we had the personalities. CC Sabathia was a game-changer for us not only in the clubhouse, but being the No. 1 horse that every championship team needs. We were starving for that. A.J. came with the pie stuff, and Johnny Damon was a guy that I always tell people took us from being the uptight Goldman Sachs executives to more of a kind of a college frat house."

As long as they could back it up on the field, these Yankees were free to indulge their *Animal House* impulses, and no one wanted to miss the next party. "I had been with them for five years, and we had never done that before," Rodriguez said. "We all let our hair down and gave in to the moment."

• CHAPTER 15 •

ANGELS AND DEMONS

The Yankees had been virtually unstoppable since Brian Cashman's unannounced visit to Atlanta, erasing a five-game deficit to pull into a first-place tie with the Boston Red Sox. How good did they feel about the situation? Not even the Rally Monkey scared them.

The Los Angeles Angels of Anaheim—who were battling with both the Texas Rangers and Seattle Mariners for the top spot in the American League West—had long been a thorn in the Yankees' side, winning each of the nine season series since 2000 while eliminating them from the postseason in 2002 and '05. Angel Stadium is a gorgeous place to watch a game, but it had been a house of horrors for the Yankees. Joe Torre's 2002 team coughed up a 6–1 lead in Game 3 of the American League Division Series and then watched David Wells get blown up during an eight-run fifth inning in Game 4 that ended the Yankees' season. Three years later the Yankees returned to Anaheim for a decisive ALDS Game 5 that saw outfielders Bubba Crosby and Gary Sheffield collide on an Adam Kennedy fly ball, allowing two runs to score. The miscue gave the Angels a second-inning lead, one they would never relinquish, sending the Yankees home in the first round for the second time in four seasons.

Jose Molina, the backup catcher who spent parts of seven seasons with the Angels before being traded to the Yankees in 2007, thought the discrepancy in payrolls served as inspiration for him and his fellow Halos. New York outspent its West Coast foe by a 2-to-1 margin in those years. "It wasn't about being jealous of them or anything like that," Molina said. "We just took it that way so we could play a little bit harder. I think that worked very well because we [beat them] quite a bit."

161

The Angels won seven of 10 meetings during Joe Girardi's first season as manager, though the retooled 2009 squad was in peak form after taking three of four from the Toronto Blue Jays—including yet another walk-off, a July 4 holiday special courtesy of Jorge Posada—and sweeping a three-game series at the Metrodome against the Minnesota Twins.

Mariano Rivera, Derek Jeter, and Mark Teixeira—the latter of whom had snapped his career-long 94-at-bat homerless streak in the series finale against the Twins—were named to the American League All-Star team. Alex Rodriguez had his first midseason break since 1999, and the rest of the players would scatter to enjoy a few days off but not before closing their first-half schedule with a three-game set in Southern California. "I remember everybody saying this was a big series," CC Sabathia said. "They said, 'Anaheim's always given us trouble, so we need to come in here and play good.'"

Joba Chamberlain had allowed eight runs over three and two-thirds innings in his previous start and, though the offense bailed him out with a 10-run outburst, he was 4–2 with a 4.04 ERA through 16 starts as he pre-pared to start the first game in Anaheim. The Yankees handed the 23-year-old a 5–1 lead by the fifth inning, but, as was often the case in that ballpark, the Angels stormed back with a vengeance. Perhaps inspired by their Rally Monkey mascot, they knocked Chamberlain out in the fifth and posted a 10–6 victory.

Chased during a seven-run inning, Andy Pettitte went out the next afternoon and gave away a three-run lead in the fifth inning. "It's like a merry-go-round," Rodriguez said that day. "They just keep coming at you."

The 14–8 loss marked the first consecutive defeats for the Yankees since Cashman had spoken with the team in Atlanta, but they had one more game to right the ship before the break—and Sabathia was on the mound. The Angels scored five runs in six and two-thirds innings against Sabathia, including four in the fourth inning. The Yankees dropped the finale by a 5–4 score. "It was a wake-up call because that was the first time I thought we could get beat," Sabathia said. "Before that, I felt like we were going to roll everybody. To go in there against the team we always had trouble with, even though me and Tex we didn't know that…and to get swept, that was a big deal. They beat our ass that series. I remember thinking to myself, *Shit, it's going to be hard to win the World Series.* That was the first time feeling mortal."

Their first-place tie had lasted all of one day. The Yankees went into the break trailing the Red Sox by three games, having lost all eight meetings with their division rivals. "That series definitely concerned me," Rodriguez said, "because I was thinking, *We've done all these great things, all the walk-offs, all the wonderful stuff; but at the end of the day, the road is going to have to come through here. If we don't handle our business, we're going to come up short.* It was an 'Oh shit' moment. We'd better figure this shit out."

Girardi knew this series would stick in his craw during the four-day hiatus and, though he didn't want his players to let it ruin what had been a successful first half, he made sure to use the sweep as a motivator. "After the last game, Joe got everyone in the clubhouse," third-base coach Rob Thomson said. "He said, 'Fellas, it's a tough weekend. I hope you guys have a great All-Star break. Remember this: we will play these guys again and the next time we play them we're going to beat them. Just remember that.'"

"I said, 'Look guys, we're a good team,'" Girardi said. "'Things just haven't went our way in this series. It's going to turn around and when it does it's going to turn around big.'"

Assistant general manager Billy Eppler would become the Angels' general manager in October 2015, trying on different colors after 11 years as Brian Cashman's understudy. Eppler was in Anaheim for that series and said that he forecast an October clash to come. "That was a phenomenal Angels team and a phenomenal Yankees team," Eppler said. "I remember coming out of there against them and thinking to myself, *We are going to face them again.*"

While players enjoyed their break, Cashman, Eppler, and the baseball operations group worked to improve the roster. They had less than three weeks to go until the July 31 trade deadline. The Yankees' retooling began on July 1 with the acquisition of infielder/outfielder Eric Hinske from the Pittsburgh Pirates for a pair of low-level minor leaguers.

The trade deadline was the final day of the month, and while rumors swirled around pitchers Roy Halladay, Jarrod Washburn, and Bronson Arroyo, the starting pitcher the Yankees were targeting was the Mariners' Felix Hernandez, a 23-year-old ace who would finish second in AL Cy Young voting that year before winning the award in 2010. That interest wasn't a new development; the Yanks had scouted King Felix extensively in Venezuela and actually offered him a larger signing bonus than Seattle.

Seattle ultimately decided not to trade Hernandez, and even as Chien-Ming Wang headed for surgery to repair the capsule in his shoulder joint, it was by no means a certainty that the Yankees would deal for a starter. Cashman was comfortable with his pitching staff; Sabathia, A.J. Burnett, and Pettitte would lead the rotation, while Chamberlain was locked in as the No. 4 starter—at least until his innings limit (believed to be between 140 and 150) expired. Sergio Mitre had a shot to take Wang's spot, though Alfredo Aceves remained an option, as did Phil Hughes, who had been electric in a late-inning relief role. Cashman even mentioned Kei Igawa, though it was difficult to believe that the $46 million bust would set foot in the new Stadium without a ticket.

The Yankees rattled off eight straight wins after the All-Star break, which had apparently arrived at the perfect time. "It really lit a fire under us when we came back, and everyone was talking about how we had lost three games to Anaheim," Nick Swisher said. "We had won nine out of 10 and then lost three and for some reason we were the worst team in baseball."

The starting pitchers were rolling, particularly Burnett, who was on an eight-start run during which he went 6–1 with a 1.68 ERA. Pies weren't the only thing he could throw exceptionally well. Burnett said that he wouldn't be satisfied until the Yankees got to October, but July was looking pretty darn good. "A.J. is one of those guys you dream about at night—not in a good way, but in a bad way," Johnny Damon said. "I compare him to Pedro [Martinez] because I remember facing Pedro when he was the best in the game, and you don't sleep well at night. You go to the ballpark knowing you better have your A-game on."

Hal Steinbrenner had given an indication that no major trade was in the works, hailing the work of the team's young players during a late July visit to the stadium. "We've been really pleased with what we've seen out of the Cervellis, the Penas, the Gardners," Steinbrenner said. "We've always believed that you have to have a good balance of veterans, mentors, and young kids. I would consider myself to be pretty balanced in that respect. If we need something, there are only certain ways sometimes that you're going to be able to get it. Everybody trades away young talent at some point for a trade they deem absolutely necessary. I don't like doing it, but we look at all possibilities and alternatives."

The Cleveland Indians dealt reigning Cy Young winner Cliff Lee to the Philadelphia Phillies, removing a potential suitor for Halladay, the Blue Jays' ace. To deliver Doc to the Bronx, Toronto was asking the Yankees for a package headlined by either Hughes or Chamberlain with top prospects Austin Jackson and Jesus Montero also on the Jays' wish list.

Cashman held firm, Halladay remained in Toronto, and Washburn was traded to the Detroit Tigers. The Red Sox made a big move by adding designated hitter Victor Martinez, and the Chicago White Sox dealt for right-hander Jake Peavy. The Yankees had contemplated deals for White Sox reliever Octavio Dotel, Nationals outfielder Josh Willingham, and pinch-runner types like the Washington Nationals' Corey Patterson and Willie Harris, but their lone move was to acquire utility infielder/outfielder Jerry Hairston Jr. from the Cincinnati Reds for a low-level minor leaguer. "Any move we've made has been to fill a need, and there's a need for a Jerry Hairston with the loss of Brett Gardner," Cashman said after the deadline, referring to a fractured thumb that would keep the outfielder shelved until the first week of September. "I tried to address and upgrade the pitching side, made what I felt were strong and reasonable offers. My interest just didn't match up with other teams' demands. Beauty is in the eye of the beholder."

Every contender in the American League had improved with at least one major acquisition, but the Yankees had added only a pair of bench players in Hinske and Hairston. The heavy lifting had been done during the off-season, and Girardi believed that he already had everything that was needed to chase a championship. "We've gotten to first place with this group of guys and we're still in first place," Girardi said. "I believe in the guys we've got in the room."

CHAPTER 16

JOBA RULES

There is a crisp in the air on an autumn afternoon, and, as usual, Joba Chamberlain is transfixed upon a ballgame being played before him. After a decade in the big leagues spent mostly peering through bullpen windows, his vantage point is now a television screen. The Houston Astros and Cleveland Indians are on the field for Game 1 of the 2018 American League Division Series with the Yankees and Boston Red Sox scheduled to open their series later that afternoon at Fenway Park.

Chamberlain's attention is diverted as someone pushes through the glass door of the high-end casual sports pub that bears his last name in his hometown of Lincoln, Nebraska, and is wedged into a strip mall between a rotisserie chicken joint and a fast-food sandwich shop. The yellow and gray of the bar's lettering mimics the cursive font used in the long-running NBC sitcom *Cheers*. It is an appropriate choice. Around these parts, everyone knows the proprietor's name. "Not yet. Thank you," Chamberlain calls to a would-be customer. "We'll be open here in about another hour or so."

Chamberlain looks past the red vinyl chairs and tabletops fashioned out of bourbon barrels, and his thoughts return to his Yankees years, a period of time that remains unforgettable to anyone who experienced it firsthand. Still a young man at 33, Chamberlain reveals that his first invitation to Old-Timers' Day arrived in the mail a few weeks prior. He had laughed, politely declining to attend. "It feels like it was so long ago, but yet it feels like it was yesterday," Chamberlain said. "My heart races more now watching it than it ever did pitching because I could dictate what happens, I could dictate the pace. But now just watching these playoff games and watching certain things, it's like you can't control anything."

He is watching Houston's Justin Verlander and Cleveland's Corey Kluber battle, and Chamberlain knows that at one time he could have gone toe-to-toe with those aces. Blessed with an explosive fastball and a biting slider, Chamberlain had led the University of Nebraska to victory in the 2005 College World Series, prompting the Yankees to draft the burly right-hander with the 41st overall selection a year later.

Big league hitters did not have to wait long to test their mettle against Chamberlain. He was promoted to the majors in August 2007, gifting manager Joe Torre with a virtually unhittable late-inning weapon for the postseason push. The 21-year-old admittedly had no idea what he was doing, but he was dominant, fashioning a 0.38 ERA while striking out 34 against six walks in 24 regular-season innings. "I had never pitched in the bullpen before, so I didn't know what to expect," Chamberlain said. "I literally just tried to watch people. *Okay, you're taking some Advil, and you're taking a Red Bull.* So I would just try to copy that because I had never done it before."

Like most fun toys under a Christmas tree, Chamberlain came packaged with instructions. The "Joba Rules," which intended to protect him from overuse, soon took on dual meaning. The actual guidelines were hazy, though it was generally accepted that Chamberlain would not pitch on consecutive days and would get an additional day of rest for any inning pitched in an outing.

A decade later, Brian Cashman said that he had no regrets. "It doesn't guarantee pure health, but I'm proud of the fact that we were strong enough to do what we thought was right by the athlete," Cashman said. "I know there are veterans that are like, 'Who cares? Let him throw 300 innings, as long as we win because I'm going to retire in a year or two.' No, this guy hopefully had a long career ahead of him. We didn't want to jeopardize that for us and for him."

Scores of frustrated opponents could attest that the flame-throwing rookie was indeed exceptional. Navy blue T-shirts with the "Joba Rules" slogan became fashionable choices for any Yankees fan, cheering on the team as they secured 94 wins, two games behind the Red Sox but good enough to secure the American League's wild-card berth. "I wish I would've made a dollar off those 'Joba Rules' shirts, but I didn't make a cent," Chamberlain said. "Shoot, a year before that, I was living at home with my dad and going to college in Lincoln, Nebraska. I never could've imagined the success I had. I worked my ass off for it, but to come in and do the things that I did, I never expected it. I mean, I'm a fat kid from fucking Lincoln, Nebraska, on the cover of *ESPN The Magazine*."

A visit to Cleveland derailed Chamberlain's storybook rise. On the evening of October 5, 2007, the Yankees held a 1–0 lead in Game 2 of the American League Division Series, and Torre summoned Chamberlain to relieve a tiring Andy Pettitte. Chamberlain recorded the last two outs of the seventh inning and then returned to the mound in the eighth. He was instantly swarmed by a tribe of Lake Erie midges attracted by the unseasonable 81-degree evening and the bright lights of what was then called Jacobs Field.

As the bugs flapped into his mouth and eyelids, Chamberlain walked Grady Sizemore and threw a wild pitch that advanced the tying run to second base. Head athletic trainer Gene Monahan visited the mound, dousing Chamberlain with insect repellent. Unbeknownst to the Yankees, the spray actually served as a homing beacon for the midges. Torre frequently listed not pulling his rattled team off the field as one of his greatest regrets, adding that the spray had been "like chateaubriand" for the bugs.

Chamberlain threw another wild pitch that allowed Sizemore to score the tying run, hit a batter, and walked another before escaping. The Indians went on to win 2–1 in 11 innings and then took the series in four games. To this day a downtown hotel in Cleveland keeps its guest windows locked during the summer with an affixed explanation that recounts the night that the midges served as the Indians' MVPs. "It wouldn't matter if I went to the Hall of Fame; I'll be most known for the bug game in '07," Chamberlain said. "It's never happened before and, of course, it happens to this kid coming in."

Chamberlain's path from Lincoln to the Bronx was unique and anything but smooth. His father, Harlan, was born on the Winnebago Indian

Reservation in Nebraska and endured a childhood bout with polio that reduced him to having to use a motorized scooter. Chamberlain's mother, Jacqueline Standley, battled drug use for years, including a 2009 arrest for suspicion of selling methamphetamine that resulted in four years of probation.

Chamberlain saw duty as a starter and reliever in 2008, going 3–1 with a 2.76 ERA in 12 starts during a campaign that was interrupted by a right shoulder injury sustained on August 4 in Arlington, Texas. Years later, Cashman acknowledged that Chamberlain was not the same pitcher after that night. "It made me a better person," Chamberlain said. "It made me a better man, it made me a better father, it made me a better teammate. But the only thing I do honestly wish during that whole process was that [they] gave me a chance to start every five days. It's a night and day difference because I got to be on a routine, I got to know my schedule.

"You could never dictate when I get seven days off, when I get 10 days off, trying to pitch in those innings that you're going to pitch in a game. You can beat your legs up, you can work out as hard as you want, you can run until you throw up. It has nothing to do with being on the mound and standing 60 feet, six inches [away]. I wish I got a chance every five days to get on that mound and pitch. I didn't get that opportunity."

As Chamberlain had compiled a 2.31 ERA in 30 appearances out of the bullpen, an argument raged frequently over whether Chamberlain best projected as a starter or reliever, creating a lay-up topic for callers to debate with Mike Francesa or Michael Kay on drive-time radio. "I knew the rules from Day One, so this wasn't a shock to me," Joe Girardi said. "The hardest part was seeing the disappointment in the player in dealing with that, trying to talk to him about the importance of it and how it's going to affect you later on in life. We're worried about your career, not just this year. It was frustrating because Joba loved being on the mound. He loved the adrenaline and the excitement."

Looking back now, Girardi said that his recommendation would be to have Chamberlain—or any pitcher subject to similar limitations—begin the season a month late since frigid April conditions tend to suppress offenses anyway. "There aren't a ton of runs scored when it's 32 degrees with a

25-degree wind chill factor," Girardi said. "You can go out and throw maybe an average starter, but he might put up great numbers for four starts, where it's harder to do in the months of July, August, and September. So I'm a firm believer: start him a month late, have him ready for May 1. That's what I would do if I was king for a day."

Dave Eiland, the Yankees' pitching coach at the time, was in favor of having Chamberlain build strength as a minor league starter. That suggestion was rejected, he said. "Trying to build him back up into a starter and also go out and compete in a major league game was a tough thing to do," Eiland said. "The day Joba pitched, the bullpen was going to have to carry most of the load because of the pitch limits he was on. The other starters put more pressure on themselves that they had to go deep into the game to save the bullpen because they were going to get taxed once every five days when Joba pitched. Joe and I would talk all the time, saying, 'We're going to do what we need to do to win.' Joba didn't like the rules. I don't know how firmly they were going to be enforced because we were trying to win and we were focused on winning a world championship and we were going to do what we had to do to win it. Ban the Joba Rules."

Cashman said that if he was dealing with Chamberlain's situation today, he would not have been as forthcoming publicly. He likened it to the more recent example of Luis Severino, whose innings were monitored closely after promotion to the big leagues late in 2016. "I wouldn't coin the phrase, 'Joba Rules,'" Cashman said. "People have asked, 'Hey, are there going to be restrictions?' about Sevy. I'm like, 'Listen, we'll handle our pitching program the way we've always done.' It took a life on its own, so we're not going to articulate our pitching manual publicly. Back then I did, but I learned from that. Although we and most people are doing the same thing, it created a false narrative that to this day gets asked about."

Chamberlain's preference was to be a full-time starter, and 2009 finally delivered that opportunity. The prospective rotation gathered for a photo that spring. Pettitte was directed to sit in a chair while Chamberlain, CC Sabathia, A.J. Burnett, and Chien-Ming Wang stood behind with their hands resting upon Pettitte's shoulders. Chamberlain keeps a copy framed in his home, a reminder of that winter's free-spending fervor. "To be a part of those guys and learn from them, it's like, we have one great starting pitcher—and holy crap—we have another one," Chamberlain said. "And, oh, you know what? We're going to go ahead and get a great first baseman. Everybody talks about Tex's offense, but to have that dude at first base and save you so many runs with his glove was unbelievable."

Before the season could begin, Chamberlain had off-field drama to handle. He returned to Nebraska on April 1, pleading guilty to having driven under the influence of alcohol the previous October. Sentenced to probation and fined $400, Chamberlain acknowledged that he had made a mistake, but some in the organization wondered if he was having too much fun off the field.

"Look at Matt Harvey. I see Joba all over again," said Charlie Wonsowicz, the Yankees' advance scout and head video coordinator in 2009. "I think when your organization gets you at a young age, they start building you up and putting this build-up on you. If you have the personality like Joba does and that's what fuels your fire, if you don't perform, you're dead in the water."

Eleven days after his court date, Chamberlain was back on a mound, limiting the Royals to one earned run over six innings in his season debut on April 12 at Kansas City, taking a no-decision in a Yanks' loss. Recovering from an April 17 stumble against the Indians, Chamberlain limited the Red Sox to two runs over five-and-a-third innings on April 24 at Fenway Park for another no-decision. Chamberlain picked up his first win on April 29 at Detroit, hurling seven innings of one-run, three-hit ball against the Tigers.

His season story largely followed a similar pattern—some brilliance (eight scoreless innings on July 29 at the Tampa Bay Rays), a few clunkers (seven runs allowed on August 25 vs. the Texas Rangers and September 20 at Seattle Mariners) and a bunch in the middle. As some in the organization mulled a demotion to the minors, some of Chamberlain's magic seemed to be missing. "The expectations of Joba as a starter were that he was going to do what he did as a reliever. That's virtually impossible," Girardi said. "I don't think Mo could've done that. What he did as a reliever, I don't know if he could have a 0.70 ERA as a starter in the playoffs. That's almost impossible. The expectations of Joba were always somewhat unfair and hard to meet."

As a reliever, Chamberlain had electrified the stadium with fist pumps and primal roars when he escaped big spots. Such displays are now commonplace, but they constituted a novelty in Chamberlain's first seasons. "The crazy thing to me is: when I showed emotion 11 years ago, everybody was like, 'Holy shit, what are you doing?'" Chamberlain said. "And now you see CC and Severino doing things, and they're like, 'Oh my God. I love the emotion.' I don't know what the separation is. I showed my emotion and I did what I did. Love me or hate me, I'm going to give you everything I've got. It wasn't like it was fake. I was genuinely excited. When I would get talked to about fist pumping, part of me would get mad because I'm just a kid playing a game that I love. I'm showing emotion, and you're yelling at me for it. Do you want me to be your puppet? If I'm not doing it, then I'm not being myself. I'll be the first person to admit there were times where I wasn't myself because I didn't feel like I could."

Chamberlain said that the pushback did not come from his teammates or management. Rather, Chamberlain specifically recalls a moment when his meal at The Cheesecake Factory in Tampa, Florida's International Plaza shopping center was interrupted by an urgent message. Asked about Chamberlain's expressive antics, Hall of Famer Rich "Goose" Gossage had opined that there was "no place for it in the game" and that it was "not the Yankee Way."

Forget dessert and please bring the check. Chamberlain lost his appetite. "You can call me out and say, 'It's not the Yankee Way,' but what the fuck is the Yankee Way?" Chamberlain said. "Frank Thomas came and gave me a hug and said, 'Kid, keep doing what you're doing. I love what you're doing.' What do you want me to do? You don't want me to be excited about executing a pitch and striking somebody out? I know some guys [don't] do that, but that's just not who I was. When you've got one Hall of Famer telling you one thing, and another Hall of Famer saying it's not the Yankee Way, yet I hear stories about [Gossage] fighting [with teammate Cliff Johnson in 1979]…that's not my place to call him out by any means, but if you think it's that big of a problem, why didn't you be a man and say it to my fucking face instead of going to the newspaper?"

Chamberlain's colorful commentary was a godsend for the beat reporters, who found his candor a refreshing change of pace from the workaday clichés frequently spouted in clubhouses. Chamberlain recalls one moment during the summer of 2009 that tested his patience with the press, a July 10 loss to the Angels in Anaheim, when he'd served up a three-run homer to Kendrys Morales and was knocked out in the fifth inning. "That is the only time I never wanted to talk," Chamberlain said. "I was 4–2 going into the break with almost 100 innings and I just got my shit pushed in by the Angels. I looked at [director of media relations Jason] Zillo and went, 'Zillo, get them away from me right now. I'm going to need about five minutes before I snap.' For all the shit we've been through together—from finding out my mom got arrested for selling meth and those questions from the DUI and all the other stuff—that was literally the only time I was like, 'I'm going to fucking lose it. I'm going to snap.' I wasn't getting any run support, I was frustrated, I wasn't pitching great. I wasn't giving us a chance to win sometimes."

After that start Chamberlain returned to Nebraska for the All-Star break and a much-needed vacation. He spent most of his time with his three-year-old son, Karter, playing with Transformers action figures and backyard water slides, which he called at the time "probably the best four days I've had in my life."

When Chamberlain returned to a mound nine days after the averted clubhouse explosion in Anaheim, he felt like a new man. Chamberlain struck out eight Tigers over six and two-thirds innings of one-run ball in a 2–1 victory that followed the first Old-Timers' Day game played at the new Stadium. That effort completed a three-game sweep of Detroit, moving the Yankees within a game of the division-leading Red Sox. As he said that afternoon, referring to both his Nebraska roots and his adopted residence in the Bronx, "Home is where the heart is."

It would come as no surprise to Chamberlain that there were more bumps in the road to follow, but at that moment, the Yankees had won 16 of 21, and his first victory at the new Stadium was in the books. Finally, Chamberlain felt like he was exactly where he belonged. "I never could've imagined I'd do the things I've done with the New York Yankees," Chamberlain said. "To have that legacy—whatever it is, good or bad—I don't have a regret. I'm so grateful and humble to even have that opportunity. The Yankees took a chance on me, and it turned out all right."

• CHAPTER 17 •

CATCH ME IF YOU CAN

It was late afternoon at Fenway Park on August 22, 2009, and the usual catcalls accompanied each of A.J. Burnett's tosses from the bullpen mound. Jorge Posada's glove popped while pitching coach Dave Eiland offered occasional nods of approval. This battery had not been the most natural fit, but the memories of their disastrous efforts against the Boston Red Sox in late April and early June seemed to have become a footnote in a successful season.

That lasted all of two outs. A pair of singles placed Burnett into early trouble, and the fearsome David Ortiz waggled his bat at home plate. The index and middle fingers on Posada's right hand signaled for a curveball, and Burnett tossed a spinner without conviction, listening for the clank of ball against tin as Big Papi pounded a two-run double off the Green Monster.

Another run scored in the first inning, and four more came home in the second, and Burnett knew he would have to eat innings to save the bullpen from getting overtaxed. It was obvious that pitcher and catcher could not get on the same page. By the fifth inning, Burnett's back was to home plate, watching an Ortiz drive clear the wall toward Lansdowne Street. Burnett spread his arms wide and lambasted himself—clear as day for the TV cameras to capture: "Why? Why would you throw that pitch?"

In that at-bat Posada's suggestion for a curve was rejected by Burnett, who fired heat. He instantly regretted his choice, and someone brought home a souvenir. The Red Sox stomped the Yankees 14–1, as Burnett allowed a career-high nine runs, and Posada was furious about how many times he had been shaken off. Tossing his chest protector into his locker, Posada hardly minced words, saying, "It's frustrating when he wants to throw a certain pitch, and I want him to throw another one."

A decade later Burnett can reconstruct that unsightly start in Boston as if it had taken place last week. "I started against Boston, using a lot of pitches that I don't normally use," Burnett said. "And by no means is that Jorge; I'm not saying that. We have the end decision, but I kept getting beat on these pitches I was throwing. This isn't Jorge Posada. This is one of the best catchers around for decades. I'm trying my hardest to work with him, and everything I throw is just getting whacked. I made some gesture, and he felt like I was showing him up. I didn't mean to do that because I don't want to show up my teammate. He followed my career; I've never done that. But I think there I did a little bit, maybe by accident. We talked in the clubhouse."

It was a pivotal moment between a proud "Core Four" member and one of the Yankees' most celebrated offseason acquisitions, authoring a subplot that neither saw coming. Following a July that saw Burnett go 4–0 with a 2.43 ERA in five starts, he was hit hard on August 1 by the Chicago White Sox at U.S. Cellular Field. That 14–4 massacre marked a third straight loss for the Yankees, as Burnett allowed seven runs on 10 hits, plus a pair of bases-loaded walks to No. 9 hitter Jayson Nix. Since Burnett had been 8–2 with a 2.08 ERA in his previous 11 starts, the unfortunate outing on Chicago's South Side seemed like an outlier.

Six days later, Burnett paired with Posada to hold the Red Sox to one hit over seven-and-two-thirds scoreless innings, working around six walks to outduel former Florida Marlins teammate Josh Beckett. Quality efforts against the Toronto Blue Jays and Oakland A's followed, preceding the miserable rout in Boston. Burnett acknowledged that he had a good curveball and should have agreed with Posada to use it more, saying at the time, "He calls it fine back there. It's a matter of me throwing what I want to throw. You don't throw a pitch unless you're 100 percent behind it. I've had a great run with Jorge. There's no fingers to point but at me."

Burnett and Posada had experienced more success than failure to that point, and even during the right-hander's poor starts, their communication never appeared to be an issue. Posada had caught each of Burnett's starts during his strong summer run, so there was little reason to believe the Fenway flop would result in anything other than an ugly pitching line and a Yankees loss. Some contention between Burnett and Posada may have been evident—neither player had a particularly strong poker face—but teammates hardly gave it a second thought. "The fact of the matter is that we're grown men; you put 25 grown men together for six months, I'm surprised there's not more in sports," Mark Teixeira said. "I'm surprised there's not guys that just all-out pound on each other during games. We're competitive, we all have egos, we all have goals and wishes. Jorge and A.J. weren't best friends, but they both wanted to win. So when we knew that they might've butted heads about pitch-calling or whatever, okay, that happens all the time. I mean, Greg Maddux had a personal catcher his entire career. Did Javy Lopez like it? Probably not, but everyone understood that it was all about winning. It wasn't a big deal for us."

Burnett, Posada, and Joe Girardi were peppered with questions about the relationship and whether a change might be in the works. Girardi had fallen victim to a similar scenario in 1996, when Joe Torre installed Jim Leyritz to serve as a personal catcher for Andy Pettitte. That year Pettitte had a 3.49 ERA in 27 starts with Leyritz compared with a 5.32 ERA in 10 starts with Girardi. "Unfortunately, pitchers are sometimes a little mental, and you feel like you and another guy are in sync a little bit better," Pettitte said. "A lot of times throughout the course of the season when big games are coming up, it's hard to not go with who you feel is a good combination."

Girardi insisted that there were no plans to make such an accommodation for Burnett, promising that he would continue to rotate the catching between Posada and Jose Molina. As the inquiries continued to flow, Girardi expressed irritation, barking, "This story has become bigger than it really is."

Posada was on the back nine of a career that would clear space for his uniform No. 20 in Monument Park, but the catcher had experienced something like this before. Only a few years earlier, Randy Johnson famously snubbed Posada, making it clear that he preferred backup John Flaherty to handle his starts.

Burnett tried to squash the controversy, but Girardi tossed kindling onto the fire when he filled out his lineup against the Texas Rangers on August 27. Molina was behind the plate, though that hardly seemed newsworthy given that it was a day game after a night game. Burnett rebounded from the Fenway fiasco, striking out a dozen over six innings. He allowed two hits, but one was a three-run Ian Kinsler homer that proved to be the game-winner.

Posada returned to catch Burnett on September 1 in Baltimore. The catcher enjoyed one of his best days of the season at the plate, going 2-for-4 with two home runs, three runs scored, and three RBIs against the Orioles, but he and Burnett continued to struggle. Burnett gave up six runs on 11 hits over five-and-one-third innings, taking a no-decision in the Yankees' 9–6 victory. This wasn't working. "It wasn't a bad relationship in the clubhouse; it wasn't bad anywhere else," Burnett said. "We felt like we let each other down, to be honest with you. It just never got better."

The start at Camden Yards marked the final time that Burnett and Posada worked together that year. Girardi never made an official announcement, but each time Burnett made that walk across the outfield grass throughout the remainder of 2009, Molina was wearing shin guards. "Posada had a great career, but A.J. wasn't the first one to have issues throwing to him," general manager Brian Cashman said. "Most of them overcame it through forced effort, but in A.J.'s case, he couldn't. For whatever reason, that matchup didn't get the best out of A.J., so we eventually had to make tough decisions."

"They were two stubborn personalities," said Charlie Wonsowicz, then the Yankees' advance video scout and head video coordinator. "I don't think it fizzled out as bad as everybody made it out to be because even today you have guys now in the game that have certain catchers. As a pitcher all you want to do is get in sync with your catcher. At that time of the year, you're not going to keep fighting over it. As a staff we've got to try to find a remedy."

One of the team's emotional leaders for more than a decade, Posada was devastated. Beginning with studying videos of Burnett's Blue Jays starts prior to spring training, Posada said that he had spent a great deal of time trying to figure out how to help Burnett be more consistent. The mystery was that on any given day nobody knew which version of Burnett might show up. Girardi said that benching Posada in favor of Molina was "one of the tougher decisions I've ever had to make." "Jorgie was a winner and was willing to do anything, but I just felt like it was a better pitcher-catcher relationship [with Burnett and Molina]," Girardi said. "I felt like I was doing what was in the best interest of the team. I think as a leader that's what you have to do. I had grown up with Jorgie and I knew what Jorgie was about. It just seemed to work better."

Pitching coach Dave Eiland dismissed the idea that Posada was the problem, though he admitted that once things clicked between Burnett and Molina, there was no reason to switch back. "You or I could be catching; the catcher can only put a finger down and tell you what to throw," Eiland said. "If you don't like it, you shake your head. Whatever pitch you decide to throw, whether it's your call or the catcher's call, you have to execute that pitch. We made that switch, and the other catcher got him going again, so why change it? If it's not broke, don't fix it."

Clearly upset with the situation, Posada would stalk around the club-house carpet on the days Burnett was scheduled to pitch. Nearly a decade later, that feeling had not subsided. "I felt like he stabbed me in the back," Posada said. "I really was passionate about making him be what I thought he could be. I got the news I wasn't catching one day because he didn't want me to catch; the media kind of ran with it. He hurt me deeply. To this day, I would love for him to answer that question because I have no idea why. I thought we had a good thing going. He gets one bad one in Boston and all of a sudden he can't throw to me anymore."

Burnett denies that he requested to be paired with Molina over Posada. "I didn't go in there and ask for a [different] catcher," Burnett said. "I won my first game with the Yankees—five-and-two-thirds strong against Baltimore—when Jorge caught me, punched out a dozen with Jorge. I hope he knows that. I hope he knows I didn't go in there and ask to not work with him because that's totally not the case. It wasn't a bad relationship; it was just something didn't click on the field for some stupid reason."

CC Sabathia seemed to have no trouble pitching to Posada that season, though he did generate lower ERAs with Molina and Francisco Cervelli. While Sabathia said that he doesn't believe Burnett ever approached anyone to ask for a different catcher, Sabathia revealed that he was among those pushing Burnett to do so. "I don't think A.J. ever said a word," Sabathia said. "We saw that there was a problem, me and Andy or whoever. I was always saying, 'Bro, you got to go tell [Girardi] that you need Josey to catch you.' I saw that, so I would tell A.J. to go say something. He never, to my knowledge, said anything. I don't know who made the change and who didn't, but I don't think it was A.J. at all. He wouldn't say anything. I think that he didn't want that to be a problem. He didn't want people to think that he needed a special catcher."

Molina caught each of Burnett's final six regular-season starts, a season-ending stretch that saw him post a 2.92 ERA while holding opponents to two or fewer runs in five of those games. What was it about Molina that seemed to work better for Burnett? "Communication, maybe," Burnett said, "the way that he talked…I don't know because Jorgie did a good job of that, too."

Posada and Burnett had grown so frustrated with each other and the situation that it was difficult to tell which one was more exasperated. Burnett said that bled into the clubhouse between starts. "We just got to the point where we couldn't figure anything out together," Burnett said. "He couldn't tell if I was mad, he couldn't tell what I was thinking. Maybe I wasn't saying anything or I didn't want to go up to Jorge because I knew he was pissed. I know a few times he said, 'I'm scared to go up and talk to you right now because of how mad you are,' and I'm like, 'Yeah, me too, same thing.'"

That wasn't the case with Molina, a veteran backup who specialized in his defensive work. Burnett said that Molina simplified things for him, taking the stress away from worrying about his deteriorating relationship with Posada. "A.J. was pretty hard-headed and committed to what he did," Phil Hughes said. "He had a plan that he wanted to go out there every night and execute. Sometimes that differed from Posada's plan. [Posada] put a lot into not only his offensive game, but what he was as a catcher. Sometimes when you have two guys that believe in different things, they can clash a little bit."

Burnett said that he would feel a pang of guilt prior to each of his starts, as it was difficult to see Posada sitting at his locker preparing for another day on the bench. That increased tenfold once the Yankees advanced to the postseason. "I had to walk by him every day in the playoffs when I was pitching and he's not catching because of me," Burnett said. "And that's kind of the first thing I would think of, like, *Fuck. Is he thinking that way about me?* He's not probably, but I'm looking at him and thinking it. I think I even told him that at some point, 'I just feel so bad, Jorge, that you're not catching.' He was just like, 'You need to go out there and do your job. You need to go out there and pitch. If this guy handles you better and you're more comfortable, I'm okay with that. I want that. I want you to succeed. I want our team to succeed.' It meant so much because I'll be honest with you: it hurt me to walk by him. He wanted to play."

Once they were paired, Molina said that he took time to sit down with Burnett, trying to get inside the pitcher's head. Why did he prefer to throw a curveball behind in the count against a tough lefty? Did that mind-set change based on how good he felt about his fastball on any given day? Molina wanted to know Burnett's habits better than Burnett did. "I don't know if Jorgie took his time to know him well," Molina said. "I learned in my career that you have to sit down with pitchers and let them know that you're on their side and you're not against them. I think that helped me a lot with A.J."

Molina couldn't feel sorry for Posada. As a backup catcher, his job was to stay ready, play when the opportunity presented itself, and in some ways, act as an assistant to the pitching coach. Burnett's connection with Molina was not an indictment of Posada's skills but a credit to the work the understudy had put in. Posada's griping behind closed doors rubbed Molina the wrong way. "When you hear somebody saying things like, 'Why is Molina catching and not me?' instead of being the other way around: 'Hey, don't worry about it. Go ahead and do your job,' I think I would've taken it better," Molina said. "I wasn't mad; I was just kind of disappointed because a teammate is a teammate in the good times and the bad. If Joe is the one making the lineup, why are you going to be mad at me instead of supporting me? That's not right. That's not the way a teammate supports a teammate. That was the only thing that kind of bothers me. Not anymore. I just threw it in the trash. I didn't care anyway. I did my job, and that's what matters."

For Posada, it is difficult to regret much from a career that spanned 17 seasons and included five All-Star appearances, five Silver Sluggers, and a fistful of rings, but the inability to make things right with Burnett continues to upset him. "You have to take it personally," Posada said, "because you're trying to do everything you can to help a guy out and then all of a sudden you felt stabbed in the back."

Burnett wishes that the relationship could have been repaired, knowing his time in New York will always be defined to some extent by that complicated relationship with the iconic catcher. "We're all tough athletes, but everybody's got a heart," Burnett said. "I could tell his was hurt and I hope he knew mine was. I haven't spoken with him since I left New York about any of it, but I felt like I let him down so many times. It was all mental for sure. Like I said, I love that man. That sucks that he feels that way."

• CHAPTER 18 •

SIGMA CHI

As the Yankees padded their growing tally in the win column, the corporate atmosphere of the pinstripes had melted away. No team with Johnny Damon and Nick Swisher playing starring roles could remain buttoned down, and as Alex Rodriguez had observed, their clubhouse more closely resembled a college campus than Goldman Sachs.

This team of fraternity brothers needed a common area to hang out, a place where the doors would always be open for swapping laughs and war stories. Enter Sigma Chi, the unofficial name that Mark Teixeira bestowed upon the coaches' locker room, where players spent a considerable amount of that season. "We always hung out in there," CC Sabathia said. "It was where we could go and get away. It's a big deal to be able to come to the field and be comfortable. Now we have a room with some TVs in it and some couches where guys can hang out and lay down, but that wasn't finished before '09, so we just hung out in the coaches' room all the time."

Joe Girardi's staff of pitching coach Dave Eiland, hitting coach Kevin Long, bullpen coach Mike Harkey, first-base coach Mick Kelleher, bench coach Tony Pena, third-base coach Rob Thomson, and head video coordinator Charlie Wonsowicz were happy to have the company. "If we won, we'd have big speakers, telling them to turn it up loud," Eiland said. "It was a little party—loud, laughing, and carrying on. Tex walked in one day and goes, 'It's like a frat house in here.' It got to a point where he would stop by all the time: 'All right, Sigma Chi, see you boys tomorrow.'"

With decades of professional baseball experience among them, Girardi's coaches worked hard between the white lines and in their pregame preparation, but they always seemed to be up for a good time after a victory. Sensing that, many of the players pledged their allegiance to the frat. "They were players' coaches," Joba Chamberlain said. "If you look at that staff, every one of them played and every one of them knew the grind and understood what it meant to have a coach that got it. We used that fraternity team loosely, but that's what it was. I felt like that's what our team emulated because that's how much we cared for each other and that's how much we wanted to fight for each other."

Compared to his previous stops in Miami and Toronto, A.J. Burnett sensed an unusually tight bond between the players and coaches in 2009, crediting that to the manager's influence. "That goes back to Joe and his family. Family is first here. Family is welcome here," Burnett said. "The coaches' room was in the perfect spot, too. When you left you had to walk by them. I think everybody loved everybody so much. We couldn't wait to pop in and say 'bye' every day."

Even the wives of players and coaches, who were normally not permitted beyond the clubhouse doors, were welcome to attend Sigma Chi following big wins. "We could kind of let our guard down for three or four hours," Long said. "Those were good memories. It was one story after another. The cool part was the wives were in there almost every time, which I thought was a pretty neat part of it. We'd wait, we'd celebrate, and then we'd open up the doors and stay there for hours."

No wonder the Yankees were in high spirits as they rolled into August, carrying a three-game winning streak and a two-and-half-game American League East lead into their anticipated showdown with the Boston Red Sox at the Stadium. After Boston had manhandled them through their first eight meetings, the Yanks were intent upon returning the favor. Hal Steinbrenner sensed as much when he took the temperature of the clubhouse prior to first pitch, observing that his team seemed "focused, yet loose, which I like." If there was anxiety, they were doing a good job of hiding it. "Everyone's on edge when you play the Red Sox," Girardi said. "You walk into the grocery store, you hear, 'You've got to beat the Red Sox tonight.' You go into the mall, you can't really go anywhere where someone's not saying something to you. I don't know if I'd call it extra pressure, but you were always aware when you were playing them."

First on the menu was John Smoltz, a 42-year-old righty chugging toward the finish line of his illustrious career. Playing before a crowd of 49,005, the stadium's first sellout since Opening Day, the Yankees thumped the future Hall of Famer for eight runs and nine hits in three-and-one-third innings. Damon, Melky Cabrera, Jorge Posada, and Teixeira homered in an eight-run fourth, supporting Chamberlain's winning outing in a 13–6 rout. The Yankees couldn't do anything to get those first eight games back, but as Damon said that night, it was definitely better to be 1–8 than 0–9. "Obviously having A-Rod come back, our lineup was deeper," Damon said. "We underachieved for most of the first half; we just got it rolling. The team got healthy and we did very, very well."

They posted another victory the next evening, though it required more work. Rodriguez cracked his first homer in three weeks to give the Yankees their 10th walk-off win of the year, a two-run blast that snapped a score-less tie and ended a 15-inning heavyweight battle that took five hours and 33 minutes to complete. "We always measure ourselves against the Sox, and I think vice versa," Rodriguez said. "Every game is memorable, but obviously there's some that stick out. That one does for me because it was one of the longest games I've ever been involved in. To end at home with a walk-off to left-center field, I still have it crystal clear in my mind. That was a big moment for us. Those are the games that stamp who you are as a team."

After Victor Martinez scared the crowd in the 14th inning with a drive that Eric Hinske flagged just in front of the right-field wall, Derek Jeter singled to lead off the 15th against Junichi Tazawa, who had replaced Smoltz on the roster and was making his big league debut after being signed out of a Japanese industrial league earlier in the year.

Two outs later at 12:42 AM, Rodriguez lined a shot into the left-center field bullpen. "I was probably just happy it was over," Girardi said. "The funny thing about when you get into those long games, your mind starts turning so much about how is this going to affect your roster, roster moves that we're going to make, what are we going to do? I think I was probably just ecstatic to have it over."

Burnett vaulted the dugout steps and slammed a whipped cream pie into Rodriguez's face. "We never worried about it. We never said, 'Here comes Boston again, man, here we go,'" Burnett said. "It was never like that. It was like, 'All right, our turn.' It didn't matter if it was our first loss or sixth. It was our turn and it just stayed that way and eventually it did turn around."

The victories kept flowing, as Sabathia matched Burnett with another seven-and-two-thirds scoreless innings in a 5–0 win, delivering the one-two punch that the Yankees envisioned they could be. Retiring the first 13 batters before a full-count walk to David Ortiz in the fifth inning, Sabathia held Boston hitless until Jacoby Ellsbury broke up the bid with a two-out single in the sixth. At the time Girardi called it Sabathia's best outing as a Yankee. The back-to-back shutouts over the Red Sox marked the first time that the Yankees had done that since blanking Boston in both ends of an August 27, 1963 doubleheader. Burnett, Sabathia, and friends had limited the Red Sox to eight hits over those 24 frames.

Sabathia said he had been amped by Rodriguez's walk-off blast the previous evening. "I was pitching the next game and I didn't want to leave early and I was like, 'If we win this game tonight, we're going to roll the series. This is it. This is the game,'" Sabathia said. "Then he hit the walk-off, and I came out there the next day, then we swept them after that. I stayed for all 15 innings of that game and then I pitched the next day."

Teixeira helped make it a clean sweep of the four-game series, cracking a tie-breaking homer two pitches after a Damon blast helped the Yankees celebrate a 5–2 win. Teixeira carried his bat down the first-base line after connecting with a hooking shot off Daniel Bard, fearing it might curve foul. The blast remained fair long enough to give New York a commanding six-and-a-half-game division lead. "We got to a point where we felt like we were never going to lose, and that's when we got to the point where it's like, 'We're winning the World Series,'" Teixeira said. "We got over the hump with Boston, we're starting to pile up the wins, we had a really nice rhythm."

Long said that in the Yankees' minds the four-game sweep served as an official confirmation that they—not the Red Sox—were the team to beat in the AL East. "Them beating us eight straight, that was a fluke," Long said. "We were the better team and we proved that."

As they had earlier in the year with Brett Gardner's inside-the-park homer, the Yankees had some good karma on their side. The 2009 season marked the introduction of the Yankees' HOPE (Helping Others Persevere and Excel) Week initiative, which sprang to life from a whiteboard in the office of Jason Zillo, the team's director of media relations.

Zillo received enthusiastic approval for the program after presenting it to the Steinbrenners, president Randy Levine, chief operating officer Lonn Trost, and general manager Brian Cashman. A schedule was constructed for five consecutive weekdays during a homestand that summer, during which players, coaches, and front-office personnel would join forces to bring attention to a different individual, family, or organization worthy of public recognition and support. "It was something near and dear to my heart, and I was so proud of the organization to embrace such an outside-of-the-box community concept," Zillo said. "For all of them to say, 'Run, don't walk, on tackling this,' it was a neat moment in my career because you don't know the type of feedback that you're going to get outside of my office."

Each day was designed so that the honorees could share their inspirational stories with players, fans, and the media while being surprised with a day of their dreams tailored especially for them. The outreach typically took place at a location within the community, culminating with a visit to the stadium and—assuming the Yankees won—a chance to join the postgame handshake line.

That first year the Yankees visited the apartment of a Washington Heights couple devoted to mentoring at-risk youth, held a baseball clinic for children with cerebral palsy, hosted a surprise anniversary party for a military veteran with ALS, turned their diamond into an overnight carnival for children with allergies to sunlight, and helped two young men with developmental disabilities deliver mail at a Manhattan law firm. "That started with the players. I knew their buy-in and willingness could make it what it's become,"

Zillo said. "When I addressed the team and explained it to them, to watch them walk up to the sign-up sheet and sign up for the different events was something that I won't forget."

Following the sweep of Boston, the Yankees kept rolling. They took two of three from the Toronto Blue Jays, including walk-off win No. 11 when Robinson Cano ripped an 11th inning, Shawn Camp offering into the right-center field gap on August 12. Chad Gaudin, acquired from the San Diego Padres less than a week earlier, worked two scoreless innings and earned the victory. "It doesn't matter who's up there. Somebody is going to come up with a big hit," Blue Jays manager Cito Gaston said that night. "That's the way you win championships. That's the way you win the World Series."

A 5–2 victory against the Seattle Mariners on August 15 at Safeco Field improved the Yanks' performance to 23–7 since the All-Star break, bolstering baseball's best record. Only Joe DiMaggio's 1941 Yankees had performed better (22–7) coming out of the Midsummer Classic, and that team had gone on to win the World Series.

New York won seven of 10 games on that trip, taking three of four in Seattle and two of three in Oakland before flying back east to face the Red Sox at Fenway Park. Having rattled off winning streaks of eight, seven, and five in recent weeks, the Yanks showed no signs of complacency. Jeter's red-hot surge helped pace the offense. His shift to the leadoff spot paid dividends. "Nothing different hitting first or second," Jeter said, "except the fact that you hit about two minutes earlier."

Jeter and his teammates would get plenty of reps on August 21, as the Yankees and Red Sox engaged in the highest scoring game in the history of the rivalry—a 20–11 rout that belonged to the visitors. Hideki Matsui hit a pair of three-run homers and drove in a career-high seven runs, becoming the first Yankees player to collect seven RBIs at Fenway Park since Lou Gehrig in 1930, but that was not the most controversial development of the night.

Damaso Marte had become a forgotten man on the roster, having returned from the World Baseball Classic in March complaining of shoulder soreness. Activated from the disabled list after missing 98 games, the left-hander was summoned after Brian Bruney loaded the bases with one out in the seventh inning. Marte retired Ortiz and Mike Lowell to hold the Yankees' lead, preventing the Red Sox from creeping back into the game. "He had been on the DL all year," Teixeira said. "It was like, 'Oh, you're still on the team?' And he was throwing 95, hitting the corner with that dirty slider. No one could touch him. I'm like, 'Whoa. That's huge.'"

With Burnett and Posada unable to get on the same page, Boston spanked the right-hander for nine runs in the 14–1 rout the next night. The Yanks tried to rinse the stench of that one away as quickly as possible, but Jose Molina still recalls it vividly, as it marked his first and only career appearance at third base. Molina had pinch hit for Rodriguez in the seventh inning of the blowout and escaped without having to field a ball. "I remember Casey Kotchman was hitting lefty," Molina said. "I was like, 'Don't hit it here.' You know, a left-handed hitter to third base, it's kind of opposite."

In the finale the Yankees blasted five homers off Josh Beckett, handing Sabathia plenty of support for an 8–4 win that placed them seven-and-a-half games ahead of the Red Sox. Matsui enjoyed his second two-homer game of the weekend, while Jeter, Cano, and A-Rod also went deep off Beckett. Sabathia became the majors' first 15-game winner, striking out eight without a walk.

With August drawing to a close, the Yanks returned home and dropped two of three to the Texas Rangers, though Andy Pettitte remained a model of consistency by winning his third straight decision. They rebounded by sweeping the Chicago White Sox in a three-game series, beginning with walk-off win No. 12 secured with Cano's game-winning 10th inning homer off Randy Williams. It was Cano's second pie of the month, following his August 12 heroics against Toronto. "I totally forgot about [the pie]," Cano said. "I heard the guys say, 'Here we go,' and I thought, *Oh, A.J.* It was great."

Another sweep followed in Baltimore. They destroyed the Orioles by a combined score of 24–9 in a three-game series that included A-Rod's 2,500th career hit. That midweek set was more notable for what happened away from the field as the Yankees commandeered the ESPN Zone restaurant in Baltimore's Inner Harbor for their annual fantasy football draft. "That was one of the best ones," Sabathia said. "I remember it was crazy. Brian

Bruney was re-drafting guys. We put in a bunch of rules from that draft that we still have going on today. If you draft a guy and he gets arrested, that's a $200 fine. It was a dope room, it was a nice setting, and everybody was there. It was a blast. Everybody had jerseys on. It was cool."

The ESPN Zone hookup came courtesy of a relative newcomer. Jerry Hairston Jr. had played the first six seasons of his career in Baltimore and still maintained contacts in the city. "I called my boy that was running the ESPN Zone at the time and said, 'The Yankees want to have their draft there. Will you allow us to have it?'" Hairston Jr. said. "They basically shut the whole place down. I wore my throwback Walter Payton jersey. Alex Rodriguez had a horrific draft. He's a big Miami Dolphins fan. He tried to draft Dan Marino. I think it helped us even be more close to make a really good run for the World Series."

This team knew how to win and had fun doing it. With one month remaining before October, now they had to finish the job.

• CHAPTER 19 •

CHASING HISTORY

As they approached the end of the 162-game gauntlet, the Yankees' stated objective was to make it to the postseason as American League East Champions and then rattle off the necessary 11 victories to hoist the World Series trophy. Their path to October seemed clear as they reached the season's final month, offering a perfect time to give consideration to personal milestones. One unintended consequence of Derek Jeter's consistent career was that the Captain was repeatedly headed toward storied numbers. The previous year, he'd charged toward Lou Gehrig's record of 1,269 hits at the original Yankee Stadium, surpassing the Iron Horse during the building's final week of service with a September 16 single off Gavin Floyd of the Chicago White Sox.

Now the focus shifted to Jeter's march toward the top of the franchise all-time hit list, once again pursuing Gehrig. While curiously flipping through the team's record book early in 2009, Jeter learned that no Yankee had reached 3,000 hits. Gehrig's tally of 2,721 had stood as the most since his final at-bat in 1939. "It was amazing seeing that because he did that in a quiet way," Mariano Rivera said. "He was just playing hard and being Derek: playing to win. At the end he ended up having more hits than any Yankee. You name Babe Ruth, Mickey Mantle, Joe DiMaggio, Gehrig, all those guys, and he got more hits than everybody."

Attention grew as Gehrig's mark neared, and after a three-hit performance on September 6 against the Toronto Blue Jays brought him within four knocks, Jeter displayed signs of pressing. Extending the drama, Jeter went hitless in eight at-bats during a September 7 doubleheader against the Tampa Bay Rays and was retired another four times the next day, when

193

Nick Swisher's ninth-inning homer gave the Yanks their 13th walk-off win of the year. "They had me mic'd for YES [Network], and we couldn't get the hit," first-base coach Mick Kelleher said. "I'm like, 'Come on Jeet, I'm tired of wearing this mic.'"

Jeter stroked three hits in a 4–2 victory against Tampa Bay on September 9, equaling the mark Gehrig had held alone for more than 70 years. Following the third hit, Jeter stood at first base and waved his batting helmet, later saying that he was unsure of how to absorb it because the Yankees were trailing at the time. His closest friend on the team, Jorge Posada, addressed that dilemma with a pinch-hit, three-run homer in the eighth inning. "I went to eat with him every day on the road, and we spent a lot of time together on and off the field," Posada said. "Derek's my brother. When I saw him [pass Gehrig], I mean, I still get chills right now. That's the type of friendship we have."

Jeter surpassed Gehrig on the evening of September 11 at Yankee Stadium, flicking his wrists at a 2–0 fastball from Baltimore Orioles rookie right-hander Chris Tillman. The ball met barrel as Jeter lashed a grounder past diving first baseman Luke Scott, an appropriate opposite-field hit that looked like so many of his 2,722 in pinstripes. The milestone came on a drizzly evening at the stadium, a game that was twice delayed by rain. Spreading his arms wide after rounding first base, Jeter clapped his hands emphatically as he returned to the bag and then saw his teammates rushing from the first-base dugout to congratulate him. A thrilled Alex Rodriguez was the first to arrive. "I can't think of [another accomplishment] that stands out more so—and I say that because of the person that I was able to pass," Jeter said. "Lou Gehrig, being a former captain and what he stood for, you mention his name to any baseball fan around the country, it means a lot."

Jeter's parents and his sister, Sharlee, celebrated in an upstairs suite alongside the shortstop's girlfriend at the time, actress Minka Kelly, and rain-drenched fans wearing bright ponchos delivered an ovation that lasted about three minutes. Jeter waved his helmet to all corners of the ballpark and then pointed to the box where his friends and family were seated. "Anything

Derek did from the time I met him when he was 18, I knew there was going to be history involved. I really did," said Suzyn Waldman, the Yankees' color commentator. "Maybe it was because I knew his parents well and his sister, but there was something about Jeter when he got all these records. The Gehrig thing, it's amazing to think of. I can't say that I knew he was going to be a first-ballot Hall of Famer or get his 3,000th hit on a home run [in 2011]. Who knew that? But there was always something special about Derek Jeter from the second he walked in the door."

Asked then what would stand out about the night in future years, "The fans," Jeter said. "It wasn't ideal conditions and for the fans to stick around it really means a lot. Since Day One they've always been very supportive. They're just as much a part of this as I am."

As Jeter awaits induction into the National Baseball Hall of Fame, seemingly a first-ballot lock for the Class of 2020, Joe Girardi said that he believes accomplishments like surpassing Gehrig probably mean more to Jeter now than they did in the moment. "Derek was concerned about one thing, and that was winning," Girardi said. "I was hopeful that every milestone he accomplished he actually was able to enjoy it and soak it up. Sometimes I think he wasn't able to. The pursuit of 3,000 [hits] really weighed on him, and I felt for him. I just wanted to see him enjoy it."

The outcome of the game, a 10–4 Orioles victory, likely saved Jeter from wearing one of A.J. Burnett's pies. Jeter hadn't collected a walk-off hit since 2007 and he wouldn't notch another until his final stadium hit on September 25, 2014, by which time Burnett would be three years removed from his final game in a Yankees uniform. If there was ever a time for Burnett to dare slamming one on the Captain, moving past Gehrig was the opportunity. "I remember some of us kind of wondering if they would," YES Network reporter Kim Jones said. "Do you think they just didn't have the guts? That would've been the pie to end all pies."

As Jeter headed to the interview room that night, Jerry Hairston Jr. said that he texted the shortstop with a message of admiration. "I told him, 'I really appreciate watching you go to work, being your teammate,'" Hairston Jr. said. "The way he played the game, the way he handles success, the way he handles stardom—you wouldn't know that he was a superstar player if he was your teammate because he just went about his business. He was a team guy. Winning was everything to him."

In a preview of the playoff theatrics to come, the Los Angeles Angels of Anaheim returned to the Bronx on September 14, making up a May rainout. After years of the Yanks appearing sluggish against the Halos, Brett Gardner's pulsating pinch-running flipped the script. Having returned from the DL only a week earlier, Gardner slid into third base on the front end of an eighth-inning double steal, popped up, and scored the go-ahead run as catcher Mike Napoli's throw rolled into left field. The Yanks won 5–3. "It was good to have a nice game for everyone to know we can play well against the Angels," said Mark Teixeira, who hit a two-run triple in the fifth inning during which center fielder Torii Hunter lost a shoe while pursuing. "I told Torii and all those guys when I signed with the Yankees, 'Hopefully we'll see you guys in October.'"

With a happy clubhouse and little to fight for in the division, they found a reason to go to war the next night at the stadium. Still upset about his fractured relationship with Burnett, Posada took that aggression out on the Blue Jays' Jesse Carlson, elbowing the reliever after crossing home plate in an otherwise sleepy contest. The players scrapped near the first-base dugout, leading to a frenzied brawl.

Toronto's Edwin Encarnacion and Aaron Hill had been hit by pitches earlier in the game by Sergio Mitre and Mark Melancon, respectively. With the Jays leading by seven runs, Carlson responded by airing a fastball behind Posada in the eighth inning. Posada glared at the hurler and appeared to say, "You don't want to do that." Carlson motioned toward Posada, and the benches and bullpens emptied, though order was quickly restored by home-plate umpire Jim Joyce.

That peace did not last long. Posada worked a walk and then scored on Gardner's double. As he did, Posada jabbed at Carlson, who was on his way to back up the plate. Joyce would say that it was a "cheap shot" and immediately ejected Posada. Carlson cursed at the catcher, who spun around, sidestepped Joyce, and approached Carlson. The two wrestled as the benches and bullpens emptied. "I don't want my kids to see that," Posada said then. "Somebody could have gotten hurt. I'm glad that nobody did."

Not exactly. Girardi had scrapes on his ear and near his left eye, which he said had come while the manager tried to separate players, and Carlson sported a purple welt on his forehead. Johnny Damon pursued Blue Jays catcher Rod Barajas, who got into a particularly rough tussle with big-bodied reserve Shelley Duncan. At one point spindly reliever Edwar Ramirez was seen dragging the 250-pound Barajas by the straps of his chest protector. "I remember Shelley Duncan in that brawl, getting right in the middle of that whole thing and moving bodies," said Billy Eppler, then the Yanks' assistant general manager.

Approximately 15 minutes were needed to restore order, and Toronto held on for a 10–4 victory. In a postgame meeting Girardi questioned his team's judgment. "I told them, 'There's a lot at stake here, and we can't afford to get anyone hurt or lose anyone or get people suspended,'" Girardi said. "You're just hoping and praying: 'Stop this. Stop. Stop. Break it up.' That is not what we want. And this is not what they want. Unfortunately, it's what we got."

Posada and Carlson were slapped with three-game bans, and several other participants were fined. Yet there were those in the Yankees' dugout who thought the brawl—the first at the new Stadium—had been a worthwhile exercise. Pool parties, karaoke machines, and whipped cream pies were fun, but sometimes players need to display a willingness to defend one another. "A team gets close when a team has a fight," strength coach Dana Cavalea said. "When Jorge got into that altercation in September against the Blue Jays and the benches cleared, that was hostile bonding, but it worked."

It was back to business as usual the next night, as the Yanks celebrated walk-off No. 14, a 5–4 win against Toronto. Hideki Matsui belted a two-run homer in the eighth inning, and Francisco Cervelli laced the deciding single in the ninth, a few innings after the effervescent backup catcher said that he alerted a teammate that he was due for a game-winning hit. "You know what's crazy?" Cervelli said. "We had like 15 walk-offs that year, and every one was exciting. I saw everybody chasing me to right field. The emotion was special. That group, it didn't matter who they were—Mariano, whoever—they made you feel like you belonged there. It was unbelievable."

Rivera experienced one of his rare stumbles a couple of days later. Seattle Mariners outfielder Ichiro Suzuki's two-out, two-run homer handed the Yanks a stunning 3–2 loss in Seattle. It was Rivera's second blown save of the year, snapping a string of 36 straight conversions. Credit to Ichiro: after studying Rivera's movement earlier that year, Joba Chamberlain wondered how anyone ever could square him up. "He was throwing to [bullpen coach Mike] Harkey one day, and [Rivera] goes, 'Joba, stand in. Stand on the plate. I'm not going to hit you,'" Chamberlain said. "We were standing in the outfield, and to watch the way that his ball moved at the last second, it was literally straight, straight, straight, and I bailed. I knew it wasn't going to hit me, but the way that his ball moved was unbelievable. To see it from that perspective gave me a whole different understanding of how good he is. Other than his hairline, nothing else has changed. It was amazing. I actually gave a look like, 'Man, he is that damn good.' Then he started to throw a two-seamer, and everybody was all discombobulated. Impressive is not even the word for him."

The Yankees handled the formality of their postseason berth with a 6–5 win against the Angels in Anaheim on September 22, exchanging a few handshakes on the field, eschewing bubbly and plastic sheeting on their lockers. Alone in first place since July 21, they saved the wet and wild celebration for the stadium, giving their new home its first champagne bath on September 27. Their 4–2 win against the Boston Red Sox was win No. 100, clinching the American League East title and home-field advantage throughout the postseason. Standing on the interlocking "NY" at the center of the clubhouse carpet, Teixeira donned protective goggles and doused teammates, screaming, "It tastes good!"

Andy Pettitte said that the playoff miss in 2008 had made them "a little more hungry to get back," and the clinch afforded six games to rest regulars in advance of the playoffs. That was how seldom-used reserve Juan Miranda joined the walk-off list on September 29 with an infield single that caromed off the leg of Kyle Farnsworth and secured a 4–3 victory against the Kansas

City Royals. The ninth different Yankees player with a game-ending hit in 2009, Miranda raised his arms in jubilation, and his teammates rushed out of the dugout, celebrating as if they'd won a playoff series.

New York concluded the regular season with a three-game visit to Tropicana Field. Instead of logging what would have been his first 20-win season, CC Sabathia couldn't make it through the third inning, matching a personal worst by allowing nine runs—five earned—in two-and-two-thirds innings. Sabathia accepted his first loss in more than two months as B.J. Upton hit for the cycle in the Rays' 13–4 win. "I got my ass kicked pretty good," Sabathia said. "Everybody was panicking going to the playoffs, but I felt good about it, like I was going to have a pretty good playoffs."

The final regular-season game gave A-Rod even more momentum heading into the postseason. Rodriguez had slugged at least 30 homers and exceeded 100 RBIs in each season since 1998 and he had all but given up hope of extending that streak, considering his late start to the campaign. Strutting through the dome's access tunnel, eyes pinned to the ceiling, and whistling along with the Steve Perry vocals blasting through his earbuds, Rodriguez owned 28 homers and 93 RBIs. "I was so far away that Joe said, 'Do you want to play? Do you not want to play?'" Rodriguez said. "I said, 'Let me just get one or two [at-bats].' He may have said on the way out that if you hit a home run, I'll have to leave you out there. I'm thinking, *I'm hungover. I'm not going to.*"

That day began with an intensive batting cage session, as hitting coach Kevin Long analyzed side-by-side video of Rodriguez's recent at-bats. Though Rodriguez seemed to have his usual leg kick and rhythm, Long identified a small hitch with his hands, and Rodriguez brought that knowledge out to the field. "He incorporated it in batting practice," Hairston Jr. said. "Alex could sense something, like, 'This feels good.' He looked at me and goes, 'J-Hair, it's on. Look out.' And when superstars say that, I knew Alex was going to have a great postseason."

Wade Davis kept the Yankees off the scoreboard until the sixth inning, when Johnny Damon doubled and Teixeira walked to bring up Rodriguez, who launched the right-hander's first pitch over the left-field wall. The

Yankees had a 3–1 lead, and after returning to the dugout, Rodriguez told Eric Hinske that he might have one shot to extend his 30-homer streak to a 12th season. "Sure enough, kind of in the Alex way, I hit a home run and then I stay in the game," Rodriguez said.

The opportunity improbably materialized later in the same inning, as New York had six runs home, and Andy Sonnanstine issued an intentional walk to Teixeira that loaded the bases for Rodriguez. The free pass kept Teixeira tied with the Rays' Carlos Pena for the American League home run lead with 39, and, though Teixeira said he didn't care, Sabathia believes that Tampa Bay manager Joe Maddon was protecting his slugger's place on the leaderboard. "That was crazy," Sabathia said. "I hit Carlos Pena [on September 7, breaking two fingers], and they were pissed off about it. Joe Maddon, everybody was mad about it the whole time, thinking I threw at him on purpose. He check-swung. Them being pissed off at us got Alex that last one."

Whatever the reason, Rodriguez made Tampa Bay pay. He fouled off Sonnanstine's first offering and then smoked a drive over the wall in right-center field for a grand slam that provided unexpected symmetry to his turbulent year. Rodriguez's first swing of the season had produced a homer, and his last regular-season drive cleared the wall as well. "We were in awe," said Posada, who had been tabbed by Girardi to manage the season finale, a team tradition. "I said, 'You want to get another at-bat or you want to finish right there?' And he starts laughing and said, 'I'm out.'"

All of Rodriguez's seven RBIs came in the same inning, establishing an AL record. The grand slam marked A-Rod's 583rd career homer, equaling Mark McGwire for eighth on the all-time list, having powered past Reggie Jackson (563), Rafael Palmeiro (569), and Harmon Killebrew (573) earlier that year. "It was just like, 'What?'" Swisher said. "You're not even supposed to be up with that many men on two times in a row—and to land exactly on 30 and 100? Some people were put on this Earth to do certain things. I think his purpose was to be a baseball player. That capped off the most amazing regular season that I've ever been a part of."

Indeed, it had been a remarkable journey. That gave Rodriguez hope that the storyline of his postseason was ripe for rewriting. "I felt like I cleared the deck and the tent," Rodriguez said. "I had a very good year, but I finished with the maximum momentum. That signaled to me that this year may be different."

· CHAPTER 20 ·

OCTOBER LIGHTS

The chatter about Yankee Stadium's expensive, vacant seats and the mysterious wind tunnel that seemed to suck lazy fly balls over the right-field wall had been mostly silenced by early October, as workers were affixing red, white, and blue bunting in anticipation of the first postseason games to be played on the grounds.

As the Minnesota Twins arrived for their supporting role in the American League Division Series, the deafening roars that made the old place quiver were thought to be lost to time. That lasted through the first two-and-a-half innings of playoff baseball on the other side of 161st Street, and Derek Jeter was front and center in making it feel like home. "You know the old Stadium, how it used to shake? That's how we felt," Jorge Posada said. "The Stadium was rocking. We're like, 'We've got the same people that were coming back then in the Stadium.' It was good to have that vibration again."

Coming off 19 wins and a self-sabotaged effort to end the regular season, CC Sabathia was entrusted with Game 1, taking on Ron Gardenhire's 87-win Minnesota club. It was the sixth playoff start of Sabathia's career, having taken the ball four times with the Cleveland Indians and once for the Milwaukee Brewers, but the largest Yankee did not seem certain that he could rise to the occasion.

Wearing long sleeves on a blustery night, Sabathia worked around a leadoff double in the first inning and a single in the second inning, but the Twins broke through with three straight two-out hits to grab a 2–0 lead in the third. Michael Cuddyer lined a single that scored Orlando Cabrera, and a Posada passed ball allowed another run to score. Sabathia ended the

203

inning but seemed unnerved when he returned to the bench. "I was really nervous," Sabathia said. "Jeet asked me about it. He was like, 'Man, you all right?' I was like, 'I'm a little nervous.' He was like, 'All right, I got you.'"

Jeter was due up third that half-inning as the Yankees faced 26-year-old rookie Brian Duensing, who had pitched to a 3.64 ERA in 24 regular-season games (nine starts) after spending the first three months of his season in Triple A Rochester. Melky Cabrera reached base on a one-out infield single and advanced on a wild pitch as Jeter waited on a 1–0 offering. The lefty floated an 80-mph change-up that hugged the center of home plate, and Jeter mashed it down the left-field line for a two-run homer, setting off a mad scramble some 20 rows beyond the foul pole. "He came up and— boom—hit the ball to left," Sabathia said. "I hadn't seen him hit the ball to left field the whole season. He turned on that ball, and I just got hyped. I took off in the playoffs from there. He would always talk to me like that; sometimes it didn't work. That was just kind of our thing."

With a crowd of 49,464 roaring, stomping their feet, and banging on seats, you could close your eyes and imagine you were in the old Stadium. "It felt just like the old place," Jeter said. "We couldn't have drawn it up any better."

The Twins had punched their ALDS ticket by winning a one-game playoff to take the American League Central from the Detroit Tigers, resting their hopes upon the broad shoulders of catcher Joe Mauer, a sweet-swinging 26-year-old from St. Paul, Minnesota, who would be celebrated as the AL's Most Valuable Player after leading the majors with a .365 batting average and a .444 on-base percentage.

Outfielder Denard Span and first baseman Justin Morneau highlighted the rest of the roster fielded by the Twins, who were playing their final season in the cavernous Hubert H. Humphrey Metrodome before moving outdoors to Target Field in Minneapolis' historic North Loop warehouse district.

The Twins were scrappy, but the Yankees' 7–0 record against Minnesota in the regular season inspired confidence that the ALDS was a mismatch. "You had that feeling of: holy shit, here we are," Joba Chamberlain said. "I loved playing the Twins because we knew we were going to beat them. It didn't matter."

The Yankees took their first lead in the fourth inning, as Nick Swisher laced a two-out double to drive home Robinson Cano. In the fifth Alex Rodriguez broke a personal 0-for-29 postseason skid with men on base by chasing Duensing with a two-out RBI single. A-Rod may have been a playoff dud in years past, but he was surrounded by a new cast that hardly knew or cared about that. "I never paid much attention to the non-success he had in the postseason," Swisher said. "I never even knew that until I got to New York. I just remember that was his time to shine. That was his time to shake off all that stuff and that's exactly what he did. He came up crucial for us."

Johnny Damon said that he suspects the Yankees' powerful lineup freed Rodriguez from being the focal point of the Twins' meetings. "Every time A-Rod went to the playoffs, they always said, 'Don't let this guy beat you,'" Damon said. "Maybe they weren't thinking that way as much. Maybe he found something in his swing because he did work very hard. He got locked in at the right time."

Gardenhire called upon left-hander Francisco Liriano to face the left-handed Hideki Matsui, who historically seemed to make managers pay for this supposed strategy. In the dugout Jeter and Posada would crow, "Don't do it!" During the regular season, Matsui had hit 13 of his 28 homers off lefties to tie for the big league lead among left-handed batters.

On a night with 20-mph gusts carrying forward the outfield, Matsui delivered again, mashing a two-run homer over the center-field wall into Monument Park. The Yankees had a four-run lead, and as he managed his first postseason game in pinstripes, Girardi laughed when he looked into the crowd and saw liquids flying. "The crowd was electric, and it was waiting to explode every day," Girardi said. "The next time I really saw that was [2017]. I don't like to see people getting wet and someone's beer falling, but it is kind of fun to watch."

Rodriguez padded the advantage in the seventh with a run-scoring single off Jon Rauch, giving Sabathia plenty to work with. The ace had settled down after Jeter's homer, striking out eight while limiting the Twins to two runs (one earned) and eight hits over six-and-two-thirds innings. Phil Hughes, Phil Coke, Chamberlain, and Mariano Rivera combined to handle the remaining seven outs.

A.J. Burnett had the ball for Game 2 against 27-year-old Nick Blackburn, who had pitched to an 11–11 record and 4.03 ERA in his second full big league season. As expected, Girardi paired Burnett with Jose Molina, relegating Posada to the bench. Posada was peeved but had caught Burnett only once since their August 22 meltdown at Fenway, so he couldn't be surprised. The righties matched scoreless innings through five frames before Minnesota broke through against Burnett in the sixth when Brendan Harris ripped a pinch-hit, two-out RBI triple.

"They battled us all year," Burnett said of the Twins. "I remember going out and being confident. I remember strolling in with Eiland, and he couldn't wait, telling us, 'I can't wait to watch you.' I was pumped. I was ready to go. I was excited. I felt like it got more intense as far as the games and the crowds the further along we kept winning, but we had to start with them. We had to beat them."

The Yanks answered immediately. Jeter raked a one-out ground-rule double, and the new and improved postseason version of A-Rod cashed the game-tying run, hammering Blackburn's 92nd and final pitch into left field for a two-out RBI single. "Every time we were on the field, we were better than you," Rodriguez said. "As long as we didn't beat ourselves, we were deep in everything. We knew we had better pitching, we didn't chase, we hit good pitching. We had dominant starters, a great bullpen, the best closer in the game, an iconic infield, iconic closer. It was a matter of saying, 'If we play long enough, we are going to beat you.'"

Burnett completed six innings of one-run ball, handing of ball to Chamberlain and Coke, but Minnesota pushed back in the eighth as Hughes' dominant run hit a speed bump. After two quick outs, he issued a walk to Carlos Gomez and permitted singles to Harris and Nick Punto that put the Twins back on top. Span greeted Rivera with another run-scoring hit, and the Yanks had six outs remaining to make up a two-run deficit.

A-Rod came to the rescue once more. New York went down in order against Matt Guerrier in the eighth inning, but Mark Teixeira opened the ninth with a single off closer Joe Nathan. When Rodriguez worked the count to 3–1 against the 34-year-old pitcher, Girardi sensed a rush of confidence. The manager's ever-present binder of statistics showed that Rodriguez was 6-for-12 lifetime against Nathan, including a pair of extra-base hits in the 2004 ALDS. "Alex had great numbers off Joe Nathan," Girardi said. "I just felt like we're going to do it again. That's the feeling: *here we go again, we're going to be fine.* That's the importance of all those walk-offs and the ability to come back during the regular season and what it does to the dugout during the postseason. You're shocked when it doesn't happen."

Rodriguez said that he was thinking, *Base hit*, when Nathan challenged with a 94-mph fastball. Instead the pitch was slugged into the right-field bullpen, tying the game. Rodriguez knew it was gone immediately, dropping his bat and looking into the home dugout before clenching his fist to begin his trot around the bases. Matsui said the accompanying auditory explosion was deafening. "When Alex hit the home run to tie the game in the ninth inning, I remember that was when the fans erupted," Matsui said. "It felt very close to what I experienced in the old Stadium. You could say that series might have been a key point when I felt like this was our home."

With the score knotted 3–3, Alfredo Aceves pitched around a walk and a hit in the top of the 10th, and the Yanks wasted a first-and-third, one-out spot in the home half as Jose Mijares induced Damon to line into a double play. The Twins threatened again in the 11th, as Girardi called upon lefty Damaso Marte to face lefties Mauer and Jason Kubel. Mauer led off by slicing an opposite-field drive down the left-field line that eluded Cabrera and bounced into the seats for what appeared to be a ground-rule double.

Except it wasn't. Despite having a clear view of the play from his vantage point in left field, umpire Phil Cuzzi inexplicably ruled the ball foul. The Twins howled, and, though Cuzzi's missed call would help push baseball toward expanding instant replay, there was no mechanism in place to challenge the call. Cuzzi was surely relieved when Mauer and Kubel stroked back-to-back singles.

Girardi tapped his right arm to summon high-socked 24-year-old David Robertson, who was three years removed from the University of Alabama campus and about to make his postseason debut. A year prior Girardi had answered his cell phone and greeted Tino Martinez, then a special advisor to the club. Martinez was gushing about a pitcher he had just seen with the Double A Trenton squad. "Tino called me and said, 'I just watched this kid, David Robertson. He's going to help you. You wait,'" Girardi said. "That probably stuck in my head."

Robertson got ahead of Cuddyer with a 1–2 count, but his fourth pitch was stroked into center field, loading the bases with none out. The pitching coach typically makes the first mound visit to a pitcher, but Girardi trotted out instead, offering words of encouragement. "I remember coming in and it being kind of quiet when I got in there," Robertson said. "I felt I could do it because I'd gotten myself into jams like that in college over and over again. I'd walk the bases loaded, then I'd have to strike my way out of it."

As Robertson nodded, Posada, Jeter, Cano, and A-Rod stood near the mound with their hands resting upon their hips. In the outfield Swisher told Brett Gardner and Cabrera, "We need some Houdini action right now."

They got it. Delmon Young hacked at Robertson's first pitch, a looping curveball, and scorched a line drive that Teixeira flagged. "If Tex doesn't grab that line drive from Delmon Young, I think we lose that game," Robertson said.

Carlos Gomez followed by tapping a soft grounder to first, and Teixeira fired to catcher Francisco Cervelli for a force-out. Two pitches, two outs. The TV cameras focused on a frustrated Gardenhire, who stomped down the dugout steps, ripping his cap off his head. "I got lucky," Robertson said. "They knew everything I was throwing. In my head I didn't even think twice about it. I just went back and threw it. I was so green I didn't understand what tipping was and what I was doing. I remember thinking, *Don't walk anyone. Throw strikes. Make them hit the ball.* After I got the first two outs, I knew I could get the third. I just had to make one more decent pitch."

The final obstacle was Harris, a light-hitting infielder, who looked at a 93-mph cutter for a called strike. Cervelli called for the same pitch twice more, and Harris whipped his bat at the third offering, lifting a lazy fly to Gardner in center field. Say hello to "Houdini," a nickname Robertson would carry for the rest of his big league career. His first great escape was complete. "Every time I see him, I remind him about that," pitching coach Dave Eiland said. "That was a neat thing. It was like, what's the worst that can happen here? We lose the game? So what? We'll come back tomorrow. We'll be fine. Just one pitch at a time. That's when I think he proved to himself, 'I'm a big leaguer, and I'm pretty good.'"

Teixeira intended to ensure that Robertson's hard work would be rewarded. Waggling his bat on his right shoulder as he led off the 11th inning, Teixeira said that he was trying to hit a home run off of Mijares, a 24-year-old Venezuelan left-hander who had surrendered seven long balls in 61 ⅔ innings that year. "I was trying to go deep. I think I missed the first pitch by three feet," Teixeira said. "I had to calm myself down, like, 'Yeah, you're trying to hit the ball hard, you're trying to get the ball up in the air and do damage but make sure you look at the ball.'"

Teixeira's eyes bulged at a 2–1 cutter, and he barreled a laser toward the left-field foul pole. Teixeira initially thought that it was a double, but the drive had just enough height to clear the wall. Jubilation reigned as Teixeira dashed around the bases, flipping his helmet into the air and charging into a swarm of his teammates. "Running around the bases, I'm just thinking, *I can't believe I hit a walk-off home run in the playoffs*," Teixeira said. "There's not a better feeling, I don't think. Maybe Game 7 of the World Series, but how many people ever do that? I still get chills. It doesn't get old."

Teixeira's blast was the Yankees' first postseason walk-off homer since Aaron Boone's pennant-clinching shot toppled the Boston Red Sox in the 2003 American League Championship Series. In Teixeira's view the Yankees' 16th walk-off win of the season was one of their most crucial because it strapped them into the driver's seat of the best-of-five ALDS. "We knew how tough it was going to be going into Minnesota," Teixeira said. "The old Metrodome was a tough place to play for many reasons. If we would've gone into that game tied 1–1, we may not get out of the first round…Personally, it was very gratifying, but when you look at: all right, now we're going 2–0 to Minnesota, the team feels so much better about where we were in that series."

Following an off day, the Yankees trotted onto the artificial turf for what would be the final game played at the Metrodome. They had a familiar foe in Carl Pavano, who had been given the hilarious and unfortunate nickname "American Idle" during his injury-marred Bombers tenure from 2005 to 2008. New York's $39.95 million investment in the surly righty yielded nine wins and a 5.00 ERA in 27 starts, as teammates openly questioned Pavano's work ethic while laughing at his continued maladies, including a 2006 disabled list assignment for what the team announced was a "bruised buttocks."

Pavano attempted to restore his value by signing a one-year deal with the Indians, who swapped him to the Twins for a low-level minor leaguer in August 2009. As fate would have it, that placed Pavano directly in the Yankees' crosshairs as the final obstacle standing between them and the next round of postseason play. A motivated Pavano pitched well, matching zeroes with Andy Pettitte until the sixth inning, when Mauer drove home the first run of Game 3 with a single to left field. Pettitte retired 17 of the first 18 he faced, and coming off a campaign in which he went 14–8 with a 4.16 ERA in 32 starts, the value of the lefty's presence and intensity could not be understated. "His teammates had a great feeling when he took the mound that he was going to give you a good night, and the effort would be incredible," Girardi said. "It might be entertaining at times, the way he talked to himself. He was going to be special every time he took the mound."

In the seventh inning, Rodriguez and Posada slugged solo homers off Pavano, providing what would prove to be the margin of victory. Both were to the opposite field; Rodriguez's drive carried over "The Baggie," the 16-foot plastic wall extension in right field of the Metrodome, while Posada's long ball soared into the seats in left-center. When Pavano's night was done, some in the Yankees' dugout yelled that the Twins should keep him in.

Rodriguez went 5-for-11 with two homers and six RBIs in the three games against Minnesota, which hitting coach Kevin Long credits to a clearer mental approach. "I knew he was going to be our light," Long said. "We talked about it daily. Every day, it was, 'Stay in the strike zone. If they don't come to you, pass the baton.' He was a lot more relaxed. I remember we'd go out and have a drink. I'd say, 'Come on, let's have a drink tonight—just to relax him, get his mind off some things. We did that a couple times. I think that helped as well."

Posada and Cano added run-scoring singles in the ninth off Nathan, and the Bombers' bullpen locked things down after Pettitte's six-and-a-third sharp innings. Chamberlain and Hughes recorded two outs apiece, and Rivera got the final four outs to complete the sweep, sending the Yankees to their first ALCS in five years. "We were happy that we were moving on," Posada said. "[The ALDS] is probably the toughest series. Now the wild-card game is probably the toughest, but back then, three-out-of-five is not easy."

The visiting clubhouse at the Metrodome was a narrow, rectangular room that did not provide much space for a celebration, especially with an influx of reporters clogging the arteries. Because traveling secretary Ben Tuliebitz had decided to have the team fly home the next day, the Yankees did their requisite splashing and drinking at the ballpark and then kept the party rolling well past midnight at Minneapolis' posh Grand Hotel. "I have never had more champagne on me than when they won that series at the Metrodome," said Kim Jones, who handled postgame clubhouse duties for the YES Network. "I remember going back to the team hotel, went back upstairs, and I ended up throwing away that pantsuit. There was just no saving it. I was absolutely soaked."

A private reception with a bar and hot food was set up in one of the four-star hotel's ballrooms where players and their families were invited to mingle. Play-by-play broadcaster Michael Kay recalled that A-Rod, Jeter, Kate Hudson, and Minka Kelly sat at the same table for part of the evening. "Everybody was happy. It was a real kumbaya," Kay said. "It wasn't raucous by any stretch of the imagination. People were really cool. They knew that their job wasn't done. It was just one step. It just shows you how close that team was."

Some members of the coaching staff rested their plates upon a grand piano, and Long remarked to no one in particular, "It would be great if someone could play a song on this thing rather than just us eating on it."

Joe Lee, who'd been hired as a clubhouse attendant in 1995 at age 15, cracked his knuckles and volunteered his services. Lee's duties maintaining uniforms and equipment behind the scenes at the Stadium typically did not present an opportunity to tickle the ivories, and the team was wowed to learn of his hidden talent. "We pushed the piano out a little bit from the wall, opened up a lid, and I started playing, and within seconds the entire team gathered around the piano," Lee said. "I must've played for over an hour. I played everything from Billy Joel to Elton John to The Beatles. The team was in great spirits. Everybody just came together."

After a few songs, Hudson joined Lee on the piano bench, singing along and making requests. "I've never been a starstruck person, but that was really cool for me," Lee said. "I'm around these baseball guys all the time, but I went to bed that night saying, 'Who am I? All of a sudden, I'm playing the piano for the Yankees and Kate Hudson?' It was so different to see CC Sabathia or Mark Teixeira hanging out at the piano, singing. I'm playing 'My Life' from Billy Joel, and it's surreal. I'm putting on a concert for these people. It was a fun time."

Still talking about their travails from the night before, the Yankees checked out of the hotel amid a snowstorm. As they boarded buses for the nine-mile ride to the airport, assistant general manager Jean Afterman tapped Lee on the shoulder, telling him that she hoped they won in the next round just so she could hear him play the piano again. "It was a wonderful, old-time celebration," Afterman said. "There were so many parts of the postseason that were echoes of the past we left behind in the old Stadium. A party at a hotel with a grand piano? That was part of the magic of that season."

• CHAPTER 21 •

No Monkeying Around

It had been five years since the Yankees had participated in the American League Championship Series, and, though that seven-game battle against the Boston Red Sox proved to be unforgettable, everyone connected with the franchise wished that they could wipe it from their collective memory banks. Boston had rallied from a three-games-to-none deficit to stun the Bombers, becoming the first team in history to overcome such a bleak scenario. The Red Sox went on to win the World Series, ending the 86-year-old Curse of The Bambino and turning the tables on what had been largely a one-sided rivalry for three generations.

When the 2009 postseason began, the stage was set for another such showdown. The Yankees were facing the Minnesota Twins in the American League Division Series, while the Red Sox were presented with the Los Angeles Angels of Anaheim. With three wins for each AL East powerhouse, the world would be treated to another classic series with a trip to the World Series on the line. "We thought for sure we were going to get Boston," Johnny Damon said.

The Yankees knew an ALCS matchup with the Red Sox would generate more attention than any other, and there was a part of them hoping for it to happen. They had recovered well after beginning the year 0–8 against Boston and, as dominant as the Yankees had been historically against the Twins, they knew the Angels had a similar track record against New York.

Those plans were dashed as the Yankees prepared for Game 3 at the Metrodome, watching the Angels finish off a three-game sweep at Fenway Park to become the first team to punch its ticket to the ALCS. When the Yankees polished off the Twins, it set up a best-of-seven series against the franchise that had sent them home in both 2002 and '05. Assistant general manager Billy Eppler thought, *Oh crap, here's a team that's going to make us look not as athletic and fast.*

With the first game slated for October 16, the Yankees had five days to prepare for the Angels. The Halos had dealt them an embarrassing three-game sweep before the All-Star break, though the Yankees built confidence by beating them three times in four September games, including twice during a three-game set at Angel Stadium. "I knew how difficult it would be facing their club, how aggressive they were, how we really had to be on our toes at all times," Joe Girardi said. "Mike Scioscia was willing to do anything. The amount of scouting that we put in to prepare for that, we were looking for all kinds of trends."

Girardi had warned his team after the humiliating July series that they would run into the Angels again—words that proved to be prophetic. The Angels were all that stood between the Yankees and the World Series. That damn Rally Monkey wasn't going to send them home again.

"I knew how formidable they were going to be, and we knew it was going to be a tough series," said Mark Teixeira, who knew the opponent as well as anybody, having played 54 games with the Angels in 2008. "We were very confident going against the Twins; we felt like we were the better team. With the Angels we knew we had to bring it or we could get embarrassed."

If Teixeira had fears about the series, imagine how those who had fallen victim to the Angels time and time again must have felt. The Angels may not have been able to match the Yankees' powerful lineup and pitching prowess, but Scioscia's club found edges by getting on base, running aggressively, and playing strong defense. Andy Pettitte summarized the Angels' aura perfectly, saying, "They would give us fits."

"We had no success against the Angels, at least in my time," said assistant general manager Jean Afterman, whose Yankees career began in December 2001. "They beat us in the postseason constantly when we played them. They would scramble around the bases, make us look old and ponderous and heavy."

The Yankees had a couple of things working in their favor, however. Their 103 wins during the regular season meant they held home-field advantage, placing the first two games of the series in the Bronx, where frigid temperatures and blustery winds were expected to wreak havoc.

More importantly, the scheduled day off between Games 4 and 5 meant the Yankees could use their top three starters—CC Sabathia, A.J. Burnett, and Pettitte—for the entire series with only Sabathia forced to pitch on short rest. They'd roll with the three-man rotation, having only briefly entertained giving a postseason start to Joba Chamberlain or Chad Gaudin. "It was the only decision," Cashman said. "It was the way we had to go about it to get where we wanted to be. It was the right strategic decision to deploy, and we hoped it worked."

Sabathia had proven he was game for any challenge the previous season with the Milwaukee Brewers, when he volunteered to make his final three regular-season starts on short rest, helping Milwaukee edge the New York Mets for a wild-card spot. When the Yankees discussed the concept of a three-man rotation, the big lefty said that he was ready. "I just wanted to pitch as many times as possible just because I was feeling good and I was healthy," Sabathia said. "I remember Geno [team trainer Gene Monahan] was like, 'What are you doing pitching on three days' rest?' I remember he was going crazy like, 'What's going on around here?' I don't think they had ever done it before that. I was ready to do it."

When the teams took the field for Game 1, light rain fell on the Stadium while 17-mph winds whipped on a chilly, 45-degree night. Even the traditional pregame introductions were scrapped; neither team wanted to stand on the field any longer than necessary. The Yankees were accustomed to playing through inclement conditions, giving them a home-field advantage beyond crowd support and familiar confines. After all, Girardi had kept the team on the practice field through torrential downpours.

During batting practice several Angels took their swings wearing balaclavas, wool caps, and hooded sweatshirts. Though Damon, Teixeira, and Nick Swisher wore fleece-lined caps that evoked images of Elmer Fudd, Robinson Cano opted for a ski mask, prompting his teammates to mock him mercilessly. "Jeter kept saying, 'Look! They've got masks on. They don't enjoy this weather,'" hitting coach Kevin Long said. "But we knew it wasn't going to be easy and we knew that some things were going to have to go our way."

The first inning showed how far out of their comfort zone the team from Southern California was. Left fielder Juan Rivera made a throwing error on the second play of the game, and slick-fielding shortstop Erick Aybar let a pop-up fall near third baseman Chone Figgins, gifting the Yankees a pair of runs. Frustrated by the gaffes, Angels starter John Lackey crouched near the mound and screamed. "It was windy, it was cold, and it looked they hadn't seen conditions like that very often," Girardi said. "It looked like it bothered Aybar, and [Lackey] was really mad when that ball fell."

The Angels made two more miscues, leading to another unearned run. Even Torii Hunter, the eight-time Gold Glove center fielder, allowed Derek Jeter's sixth-inning single to roll past him. The Yankees didn't hit a home run—only the second game played at the new Stadium without a long ball on either side—but the Angels' sloppy play helped New York to an early lead. Sabathia took care of the rest.

The ace fired eight brilliant innings, holding the Angels to one run on four hits and a walk, striking out seven. He faced a three-ball count only twice all night, giving up his lone run in the fourth and then holding the Angels hitless over his final four innings before handing a 4–1 lead over to Mariano Rivera, who closed out the win. "It was about as cold as it gets," Sabathia said after the game. "It was pretty nasty today."

Hunter refused to use the conditions as an excuse. With Sabathia pitching the way he did, they could have been playing on a Caribbean island, and it wouldn't have mattered much. "CC was the cold weather," Hunter said. "CC's the real deal, man."

Sabathia was now 2–0 with a 1.23 ERA in his first two postseason starts for the Yankees, striking out 15 batters while issuing one walk over 14 ⅔ innings. If it was possible to outperform the biggest contract a pitcher had ever signed, the southpaw was doing it. Alex Rodriguez said that Sabathia was proving to be "the complete package" for the squad. "He's left-handed, he's 6' 6", over 300 pounds; he's a monster out there," A-Rod said. "He's durable as hell, he's dependable, he's tough. He has three pitches that are all above major league average: a 95-mph fastball, a wipe-out slider to lefties, and then a change-up that could've been his best pitch that he threw exclusively to righties. He was just a dream."

"CC's performance during that series was huge," Hideki Matsui said. "Him winning that first game to set the tone made a big difference."

Indeed, starting the series with a victory was better than the alternative, but the Yankees had done the same in 2002 and again three years later. Each time, they were sent home within a week. Game 2 provided no reprieve for the players, who took the field with a game-time temperature of 47 degrees, intermittent rain, and a steady 15-mph wind that caused more chaos.

Cano's second-inning RBI triple gave the Yankees an early lead for the second straight night, and Jeter hit a solo home run in the third to make it 2–0. Burnett cruised through four innings before running into trouble in the fifth, as the Angels scored twice to tie the game. Burnett pitched into the seventh inning but departed with the score still tied thanks to an equally effective outing by left-hander Joe Saunders.

Mariano Rivera entered with two outs in the eighth inning, recording the next seven outs as the game moved to the 11th. Figgins had been a Yankee killer during the regular season, hitting .333 with a 1.025 OPS in 39 at-bats against Bombers hurlers, but he opened the postseason hitless in 18 at-bats. The speedy switch-hitter was due, and Figgins gave the Angels a lead with an RBI single off Alfredo Aceves in the 11th, pushing the Yankees to the brink of losing their home-field advantage.

The clock struck midnight as rain continued to fall. The sellout crowd seemed deflated, and despite 15 regular-season walk-off wins and another in the ALDS, there was a familiar feeling about the way this series was shaping up. "The Angels didn't scare you, but they small-balled you to death," said John Sterling, the Yankees' radio announcer. "Something always went wrong."

Brian Fuentes, an All-Star left-hander who led the AL with 48 saves that season, jogged in from the bullpen with the assignment of finishing off the Yankees and sending the series across the country tied. He got ahead of A-Rod with two quick strikes and then tried an 89-mph fastball on the outside corner. It caught too much of the plate.

Rodriguez poked a drive to right field and dropped his bat, sprinting out of the box. He wasn't sure if it had enough to get out of the park, especially given the blustery conditions. As Bobby Abreu leaped against the padded wall with his glove hand outstretched, the ball traveled just far enough. It struck a fan in the front row and fell back onto the warning track, where Abreu scooped it on a bounce and fired to the infield. Rodriguez raised his right index finger, signaling home run, and received confirmation from second-base umpire Jerry Layne. The game was tied. "I loved facing their pitchers," Rodriguez said. "They always attacked you. They just didn't want to walk you, and that just played into my strengths."

Following a scoreless 12th inning in which the Yankees left the bases loaded, Girardi called on Jerry Hairston Jr. to pinch hit for pinch-runner extraordinaire Freddy Guzman as New York came to bat in the 13th. The veteran had played more than 900 regular-season games, but this would be his first in the postseason. "I'm getting loose in the tunnel, and Girardi says, 'Hey, you're leading off the inning,'" Hairston said. "As he said that, Derek looks at me. Derek had this little place next to Girardi where he sat when he wasn't hitting. He turns to me and goes, 'I told you you're going to do something special. You're going to do it right here.' And I said, 'I got this.'"

Hairston's grandfather, Sam, and uncle, John, each had cups of coffee in the majors, while his father, Jerry Sr., and brother, Scott, enjoyed lengthy careers in the big leagues. Sam's career spanned four games with the 1951 Chicago White Sox, while John's lasted three with the 1969 Chicago Cubs. Jerry Sr. played two postseason games during his 14-year career, going 0-for-3 for the 1983 White Sox during their ALCS loss to the Baltimore Orioles. Scott would play 11 seasons in The Show without sniffing the playoffs. "I felt kind of an energy like, 'This at-bat's for my family,'" Hairston said. "I remember thinking, *I'm going to do something. I'm getting on base to help us win tonight.*"

Facing Ervin Santana, Hairston delivered, stroking a single to center field and moving to second on a Brett Gardner sacrifice bunt. As the game inched past the five-hour mark, Scioscia signaled to intentionally walk Cano in order to face Melky Cabrera, whose three walk-off hits led the Yankees that season. Cabrera stroked a grounder into the hole between first and second, where second baseman Maicer Izturis moved to his left, spun, and threw to second, attempting to start a double play. His throw sailed to Aybar's left, and, though Figgins had backed up the play, he bobbled the ball, allowing Hairston to score the game-winning run. "I looked back and I saw the ball being kicked around a little bit and I made a break for home," Hairston said. "I thought we needed that game because in a seven-game series anything can happen. It was a big game for us, a big moment for me personally. Getting an opportunity to play in the postseason, get an at-bat, and help the team win was special."

A banner had waved from the upper deck earlier that night, reading, "We Want Pie!" That order was filled. After Hairston's teammates pummeled him on the dirt behind home plate, he savored the sweet flavor of whipped cream, becoming Burnett's latest victim. The Angels trudged off the field with no wins to show for the most frigid eight hours and 28 minutes of their lives. "The first two games at Yankee Stadium were two of the coldest nights I've ever been a part of," third-base coach Rob Thomson said. "Those guys were all bundled up and they weren't used to that. They were dropping pop-ups, and no one wanted to catch anything. They were making mistakes that they normally don't make just because of the cold. I think the confidence and the momentum flipped at that point."

The average first pitch temperature for the next two games in Anaheim was a much more palatable 73 degrees, and as the Yankees headed west toward Disneyland's backyard, they knew the ALCS was far from over. Mickey Mouse wasn't the concern; they had fallen victim to the Angels and their hyperactive furry friend too frequently throughout the decade. Still, there was an unusual confidence that spread from the clubhouse into the front office. "I remember getting on the plane late at night out of New York so excited," Eppler said. "At that point I felt like we were going to get this one."

Solo homers by Jeter, A-Rod, and Damon built a 3–0 lead against Jered Weaver in Game 3, but Pettitte served up a Howie Kendrick blast in the fifth, waking up the sleepy crowd at Angel Stadium. That's when the Rally Monkey appeared on the scoreboard. House of Pain's "Jump Around" blared through the public-address system as the Angels staged one of their trademark rallies. Vladimir Guerrero mashed a two-run homer off Pettitte in the sixth, tying the game 3–3. "You have to be ready all the time because they can come back, and they can hurt you," Cano said. "We always said, 'Don't look to the board. It's the Rally Monkey. Don't look at it.'"

Chamberlain replaced Pettitte with one out in the seventh, quickly giving up a triple to Kendrick, who scored on Izturis' sacrifice fly. Jorge Posada answered with a solo home run off Kevin Jepsen in the eighth, tying the game once more. Home or away, the Yankees refused to give up.

Like Game 2, it took more than 27 outs to decide Game 3. Phil Coke, Phil Hughes, Mariano Rivera, and David Robertson combined for three-and-two-thirds scoreless innings, but Aceves could not record the final out to the 11th inning. Kendrick singled, and light-hitting catcher Jeff Mathis doubled to deep left-center, driving home the game-winning run. "Anyone who thought we were going to breeze through a series with the Angels is crazy," Teixeira said.

The setback lasted mere hours. The Yankees hammered Scott Kazmir for three fourth-inning runs in Game 4, and A-Rod hit a two-run homer in the fifth. It was his third straight game with a home run and it also marked Rodriguez's eighth straight postseason game with at least one RBI, tying a major league record. The five-run cushion was plenty for Sabathia, who seemed unfazed by working on short rest, firing eight dominant innings of one-run ball. The lefty allowed five hits and two walks, striking out five in a 10–1 win that seized control of the ALCS. "He pulled teams together," Girardi said. "But he also gave everyone on the field confidence when he was there and basically a don't-worry attitude [of] 'I got your back.'"

As he analyzed the Angels, Posada said he didn't see the same fire that had been their trademark during the previous postseason meetings with Scioscia's club. "The Angels would always have a little run during the middle of the game and make sure that they'd come back or they'd do something," Posada said. "This team—I don't know what was going on. It felt like they were not together. They were not the same team. They were not the same Angels anymore."

Sabathia and A-Rod had delivered the Yankees to the precipice of the World Series, but they needed one more win. If those 2004 holdovers had learned anything, it was that the fourth win can sometimes be the toughest one. The teams had an off day between Games 4 and 5, and with a commanding lead in the series, the Yankees enjoyed some rest and relaxation. "We were there for five days because we had the two off days," Sabathia said. "It was great. We were at Disney and shit. I remember having to kick myself and remind myself that this was a business trip."

Burnett took the mound in Game 5 with a chance to power his team to the pennant, but the Angels pounced on him for four first-inning runs, opening the game with a walk and four consecutive hits. Six days after being visibly frustrated by his club's sloppy defensive play in Game 1, Lackey cruised through six scoreless innings before Cabrera cracked a one-out double in the seventh. Posada and Jeter worked walks to load the bases.

Lackey had starred for the Angels as a rookie during their 2002 World Series run, but he was out of gas. Teixeira greeted left-hander Darren Oliver by belting a bases-clearing double on his first pitch. After an intentional walk to A-Rod, Matsui singled in Teixeira, tying the game. Jepsen relieved Oliver, though he was equally ineffective as Cano tripled in both A-Rod and Matsui, capping the six-run inning.

The Yankees were nine outs from the pennant, but they should have known that it would not come that easily in The House of the Rally Monkey. Burnett opened the seventh but exited after allowing a single and a walk, and three runs came home against Damaso Marte and Hughes. The 7–6 lead held thanks to Weaver and Fuentes; Swisher popped out with the bases loaded to end it, sending the ALCS back to the Bronx.

Despite losing two of three in Anaheim, the Yankees jetted home loving their chances. Having won 35 of their last 43 games at the Stadium, they had Pettitte ready to take the ball on regular rest. After tough losses

Pettitte was always the correct choice to restore order and hope, peering over his glove while balancing fire and peace. "It was huge because there would never be a moment too big for Andy Pettitte," pitching coach Dave Eiland said. "He's never going to back down from any moment or situation. He's going to stay in control and he's going to continue to make pitches in big moments. That's how we felt about it. You hand Andy Pettitte the ball in a big game. You know he's going to do his part."

Pettitte and the Yankees would have to wait an extra day for Game 6, as rain washed away the originally scheduled contest. When the teams took the field on October 25, they did so on a mild 58-degree night—much to the Angels' relief—that bore no resemblance to the inhospitable conditions they faced in the same building eight days earlier.

Abreu opened scoring against his former team with a third-inning single off Pettitte, but the Yankees answered in the fourth, tagging Saunders for three runs as Damon stroked a two-run single, and A-Rod worked a bases-loaded free pass. Pettitte used his vast postseason experience to hold that lead into the seventh, when a Juan Rivera single prompted Girardi to summon Chamberlain, who recorded the final two outs of the inning. With six outs separating the Yankees from the pennant, Girardi called on Mariano Rivera, but the closer surrendered a Guerrero RBI single in the eighth that drew the Angels within one run.

Assisted by two Angels errors, the Yankees tacked on two insurance runs in the bottom of the inning, giving Mariano Rivera breathing room in the ninth. When Posada squeezed the closer's final pitch, a swinging strikeout of Gary Matthews Jr., the Yankees had secured the 40th pennant in franchise history. "It brought back so many wonderful moments as a player," Girardi said. "I wanted to see Alex enjoy it, Tex enjoy it, Swish, and these guys that have never done it. And I wanted to pay it back to Mr. Steinbrenner for trusting me. It was like, 'Okay, we're two-thirds of the way, we've beat two pretty good teams, we've got one more to go.'"

Mariano Rivera calmly raised his right fist as Posada ran to embrace him. He laughed and repeatedly thumped his longtime catcher on the back. The rest of the team gravitated toward the dirt near third base, where A-Rod was swarmed by his teammates on the way to his first—and, as it would turn out, only—trip to the Fall Classic. "I couldn't be more excited; I felt like a 10-year-old kid," Rodriguez said. "That's what you play for: in order to win a World Series. You have to get there first."

The Yankees went through the traditional clubhouse celebration, dousing one another with champagne and beer. A proud Hal Steinbrenner glowed that his team had "been a family. They play like that every single day, and that's why they're here." But as they popped corks, it was clear that they were choosing to follow Jeter's "this is what you play for" lead. If this was to be the final celebration of 2009, it would be a grave disappointment. "I was excited, but I didn't want to get too excited because I knew this meant nothing," Sabathia said. "If I was in Cleveland or Milwaukee, winning the ALCS or NLCS would be huge, but it's not here. This was not the time to celebrate, so I wouldn't let myself get there yet." "It wasn't finished business," Teixeira said. "But for one night—or a half a night—you could enjoy it."

A-Rod had posted huge numbers for a second straight series, finishing the ALCS 9-for-21 (.429) with three home runs, six RBIs, and a whopping 1.519 OPS. But when the ALCS Most Valuable Player award was announced, Sabathia brought home an honor that he hadn't even been aware of. "I thought that we could've been co-MVPs for sure," said Sabathia, who was 2–0 with a 1.13 ERA against the Angels. "Before that, I guess I didn't pay attention to the playoffs enough. I didn't know they did MVPs for the ALCS and NLCS. That award was cool."

There was a sentiment that if the Yankees could finally get past the Angels, there was no stopping them. As the celebration raged on, Teixeira excused himself to the clubhouse washroom, where he found A-Rod sitting on the countertop. His legs dangled, as he was lost in thought. "He was just soaking it in," Teixeira said. "I forgot that it was his first World Series. The best player in baseball over the last 10 years, this was his first World Series. I was happy that I got to experience that with him."

• CHAPTER 22 •

BOASTFUL BRAVADO

Seventy-seven years before Jimmy Rollins agreed to be booked as a guest on *The Jay Leno Show*, Babe Ruth had appeared in the Wrigley Field batter's box during Game 3 of the 1932 World Series. As the legend goes, the Bambino responded to catcalls from the Chicago Cubs' dugout by pointing his bat toward the center-field grandstand, slugging Charlie Root's next pitch into that general area. Historians debate whether the Babe actually called his shot, but the tale of Ruth's bravado stood the test of time.

Following through on a bold boast could cement a reputation, as Joe Namath discovered 37 years after Ruth's homer. Three days before Super Bowl III, the New York Jets quarterback appeared at the Miami Touchdown Club and brashly guaranteed victory over the Baltimore Colts, who were favored by 18 points. The Jets' 16–7 victory gave birth to a legend that Namath parlayed into a half-century in the public eye, remaining relevant long after his final snap.

For every Sultan of Swat or Broadway Joe, there was the danger of becoming another Patrick Ewing, who promised his New York Knicks would defeat the Indiana Pacers in Game 6 of the 2000 Eastern Conference Finals and then missed his final six shots. As he appeared on NBC's air two days before the Yankees and Phillies were to open the Fall Classic, the loquacious Philadelphia Phillies shortstop placed a public wager on his team. "Of course, we're going to win," Rollins said. "If we're nice, we'll let it go six [games], but I'm thinking five. Close it out at home."

Rollins was known for this brand of bombast. Prior to the 2007 season, the eventual National League MVP said his Phillies, not the New York Mets, were the team to beat in the National League East. Rollins guaranteed that Philadelphia would win 100 games in 2008; the Phillies notched 92 in the regular season and 11 more in the playoffs, celebrating the club's first championship since 1980. The switch-hitter kept the braggadocio going into the spring of '09, when Rollins told *Playboy,* "The Fall Classic? I see our boys vs. the Yankees. They spent all that money. They've got to be there. We've got a title to defend, so we're going to be there."

As the Yankees returned to their lockers following a rain-soaked workout on the stadium turf, they largely yawned when quizzed about Rollins' boast. Jorge Posada referred to Rollins as "Nostradamus," and Derek Jeter quipped, "He predicted we'd play them in the World Series about seven years ago, too. You make enough predictions, I guess you'd be right most of the time, right?"

In private some members of the team were incensed. "I remember we heard that Jimmy Rollins said, 'Phillies in five,' and that was a turning point for us," Robinson Cano said. "We didn't like that. It pissed a lot of guys off, and we said, 'You know what? We're not going to let that happen.' I remember the year before he said something, and they won, so he came back and said the same thing again."

"That was fuel to our fire," Posada said. "He woke us all up because we were already determined to do it, but this one helped us do it a little more."

Rollins' prediction became bulletin board material in the clubhouse. Joba Chamberlain recalled seeing the quote posted somewhere, and CC Sabathia said that it raised his confidence in advance of the Fall Classic. "When Jimmy Rollins guaranteed that they would win the World Series, I knew that we were going to win," Sabathia said. "That was a guarantee for me. I was like, 'All right, cool, we got this.' Nobody ever talked about it or said anything about it, but for me when I heard him say that, I was like, 'All right, cool. Too cocky.' They obviously hadn't played us yet and didn't know how good we were."

A rematch of a 1950 Fall Classic (won by the Yankees in a four-game sweep) that predated the completion of the New Jersey Turnpike by 13 months, the New York-Philadelphia World Series opened at the Stadium on the evening of October 28 with Sabathia and Cliff Lee reprising the pitching matchup from the Yanks' historic home opener.

A 30-year-old left-hander from Benton, Arkansas, Lee had made 22 starts for the Cleveland Indians before being swapped to Philadelphia in late July. Cleveland netted a four-player package headlined by pitching prospect Carlos Carrasco, and Lee went 7–4 with a 3.19 ERA in 12 regular-season starts for the Phils, using his spiked curveball, deceptive change-up, and pinpoint fastball to help his new club breeze past the Colorado Rockies and Los Angeles Dodgers to claim the pennant.

Phillies manager Charlie Manuel viewed the lefty as the obvious choice to take the ball in Game 1. Girardi had the same easy call to make with his starter, coming off an American League Championship Series in which Sabathia secured MVP honors by going 3–0 with a 1.19 ERA. Sabathia was incredulous that the former Tribe Cy Young Award winners were seeing each other again and on the game's biggest stage. "Pitching against Cliff was surreal," Sabathia said. "A year or two ago, we were on the same team, hanging out literally every day together on and off the field. Having us pitch Game 1 was nuts."

With George Steinbrenner looking on from an upstairs suite, the pre-game ceremonies featured First Lady Michelle Obama and Second Lady Dr. Jill Biden escorting Yogi Berra to the mound. Jeter caught a first pitch from Anthony Odierno, an Army lieutenant who lost his left arm in Baghdad when a rocket-propelled grenade smashed through his Humvee.

As the teams were introduced on the baselines, snipers stalked along the top of the massive scoreboard in center field, keeping close watch on a crowd that showed only a few pockets of Phillies red. The World Series was underway, and the fans booed loudly as Rollins prepared to take his hacks against Sabathia. At third base Alex Rodriguez pounded a fist into his glove, reflecting on his good fortune at that moment. "Game 1 of the World Series was honestly a dream come true," Rodriguez said. "I played 25 years professionally and only got a chance to play in one World Series and I cherished every moment. I'm so thankful that I was able to capture the moment and not waste it. I grew up watching Dan Marino, and it still breaks my heart that he went to one Super Bowl, and he couldn't finish it. I came up watching Charles Barkley—same thing. I just wanted to enjoy it, cherish the moment, and play well. I enjoyed the hell out of it."

Chase Utley opened the scoring, winning a nine-pitch duel in the third inning by pulling a 95-mph fastball over the wall—the first homer that Sabathia had allowed to a left-handed batter at the Stadium that season. Utley struck again in the sixth inning, mashing a 96-mph heater into the right-field bleachers to give Philadelphia a 2–0 lead, stunning what had been a raucous crowd.

Though Utley was a four-time All-Star who hit 31 homers during the regular season, he was an unlikely candidate to rock Sabathia. Utley had been 0-for-7 with five strikeouts against Sabathia to that point, and there were whispers about Utley's injured right foot and balky right hip going into the series. It proved to be the only damage that the Phils were able to inflict upon Sabathia, who took the loss as the Yankees flailed against Lee. "I felt like I pitched pretty good," Sabathia said. "We lost, and I was like, 'Damn, man. He just dominated us.' That was the first time we got dominated in the playoffs and looked like we couldn't hit. He made us look bad. It was a little bit of like, 'Oh, we can lose?' I had so much confidence in that team and felt so good about that team that I always felt we were going to win every game. It was humbling for sure."

Pitching in short sleeves on a drizzly 52-degree evening, Lee seemed to be toying with a lineup that led the majors with 915 runs scored during the regular season. Chomping on a wad of gum, the hurler extended his glove and easily—almost dismissively—snagged Johnny Damon's sixth-inning pop-up to the mound. The Phils' bench laughed, and, though Lee said that he was trying not to be cocky, some of the Yankees took it that way. In the eighth Lee made a nifty stop behind his back on a Cano one-hopper and then flipped the ball to first baseman Ryan Howard, who later remarked, "Wow, am I missing something? It was so nonchalant, so casual."

"It was exciting," said the Phils' J.A. Happ, the current Yankees pitcher who had transitioned into a relief role for Philadelphia that autumn. "It was loud. It was intense. I remember Cliff being Cliff. He doesn't get rattled.

It's another game to him. He had that outlook in general. He dominated. It was unbelievable. He pounded the strike zone. That's something I'll never forget."

Three of the Yankees' six hits belonged to Jeter, and the Bombers were kept off the scoreboard until the ninth inning, when a Rollins throwing error allowed Jeter to trot home. How good was Lee? He became the first pitcher ever to strike out 10 without a walk in a World Series start, in which he permitted no earned runs. "We were completely shut down by Cliff Lee," Hideki Matsui said. "I remember going back to the clubhouse, and everybody was a little stunned."

Raul Ibanez added a two-run single in the eighth inning off David Robertson, Shane Victorino tacked on an RBI single against Brian Bruney in the ninth, and Howard doubled home the Phils' sixth and final run facing Phil Coke. Girardi had wanted to get some of the younger relievers into Game 1 if possible just to get their feet wet. "It's tough to slow yourself down a little bit sometimes," said Bruney, who had been left off the postseason roster in the first two rounds. "You know however many million people are watching the game. You just know it's the biggest stage in the world that night. It's just exciting."

By that point Girardi had turned some of his attention toward A.J. Burnett and the next night's lineup card and was relieved that Lee couldn't face them for a few more days. "Just thinking about the importance of Game 2, for whatever reason I felt really good about A.J. against their lineup," Girardi said. "They knew what they needed to do. I didn't say anything. And maybe it's because I had a calmness about it."

The damp disappointment of Lee's Game 1 smackdown did not last. After recovering from a 15–17 start to their season, including going winless in their first eight meetings against the Boston Red Sox, they hadn't come this far to go down without a fight. "I remember after Game 1, we were down one, and everybody knew I was starting Game 2 [in right field]," Jerry Hairston Jr. said. "After BP there were 150 reporters at my locker and microphones in my face, going, 'Are you nervous? How do you guys feel? You're down 1–0. Are you still confident? Are you nervous for Game 2?'

I remember telling the reporters, 'Look at our clubhouse right now. You have Johnny Damon and Eric Hinske wrestling in the middle of the clubhouse. We've got an hour and a half until game time and we're arguing about fantasy football.' That's how loose we were, and that's how confident we were in winning the World Series."

CHAPTER 23

EMPIRE STATE OF MIND

Cliff Lee made the Yankees' vaunted offense look meek and overmatched in the World Series opener, and his efforts ensured that they wasted CC Sabathia's solid effort. Now the weight of the World Series was upon A.J. Burnett's shoulders, and no one ever knew which version of the enigmatic hurler would show up on a given night.

Lee's performance did not represent the only disappointment for the fortunate home team faithful who held tickets for the first World Series contest at the new Stadium. Inclement weather had postponed an on-field performance by Jay-Z and Alicia Keys, who had been slated to perform their hit single, "Empire State of Mind," as part of the pregame ceremonies.

The orchestral rap ballad had become an anthem for both the team and the city that year, name-checking the Yankees as well as various neighborhoods and famous residents. Derek Jeter chose it as his walk-up music before the song was released to the public, and the Captain's at-bats were hardly the only times it had been played over the stadium's public-address system.

From his frequent appearances in the expensive seats behind home plate to attending parties thrown by star players, Jay-Z was viewed as an unofficial part of the team. In fact, Alex Rodriguez planned to ensure that the Brooklyn-born musician received his own World Series ring—should they claim one. His presence on the field was a perfect way to begin Game 2. "I was by the bullpen warming up and I see Jay-Z right there," Jose Molina said. "That was unbelievable. It was special. I think that's how the adrenaline starts."

Following batting practice, a stage was erected on the grass behind second base, providing Jay-Z and Keys the same view of the Stadium that Jeter and

Robinson Cano enjoyed each night. Jay-Z sported a field model hat with the interlocking "NY" on the front—the one that the song claims he "made more famous than a Yankee can"—and a leather-sleeved varsity jacket. Keys opted for a purple jacket with matching thigh-high boots. Two guitarists, a drummer, and a keyboard player wore pinstriped jerseys. Four Yankees flags fluttered at the back of the stage, while Keys' glossy black piano was graced by an image of the Statue of Liberty. There was not a stitch of Phillies gear to be found during the performance. Talk about your home-field advantage. "Jay-Z was looking at us like, 'Hey, come on boys, got to get this Game 2,'" Jerry Hairston Jr. said. "We knew we were winning that night and we knew we were going to take it home. Even though we were down 1–0, we were so confident that we were going to find a way to win that World Series. That song was our battle cry."

The two Grammy-winning artists pumped up the crowd, and the performance captured the players' attention as well. Members of both clubs hung on the railings of their respective dugouts as though they were attending a concert, enjoying the show before they had to put on one of their own. Seated on the bench next to an excited Cano, Jeter bobbed his head to the beat. With a bemused grin on his face, Mariano Rivera watched from beneath the comfort of a hooded sweatshirt. Ramiro Pena, who wasn't even on the World Series roster, held a small video camera to record the performance as a keepsake. "It was a reminder that, 'This is New York,'" Joe Girardi said. "This isn't going to happen everywhere. This is New York, and things are different here."

"I was excited that I wasn't pitching that day," Sabathia said. "That was cool to be able to go out and rock out and be a part of that and not have to pitch that game. It would've sucked to have to pitch that game."

Burnett didn't have that luxury. While the musicians were electrifying the Stadium, Burnett was attempting to hit the checkpoints of his pregame routine. Prior to the performance, Joba Chamberlain had crossed paths with Jay-Z, who was enjoying a pregame meal. They exchanged pleasantries, and Jay-Z noticed that Chamberlain was carrying a baseball. "He was like, 'Let me touch this ball,'" Chamberlain said. "Then I went and gave it to A.J., and that's the ball A.J. actually warmed up with before that game."

While the artists performed, Burnett said that he was long-tossing with Molina across the outfield grass about 30 feet behind the stage. "That whole thing—who's going to get to experience that?" Burnett said. "I'm warming up behind Jay-Z in a World Series. What's going on here, man? They were in the outfield, and we were jamming and warming up like it's any other day. It was really weird how that night went down."

In each of the first two rounds, Burnett had taken the mound in Game 2 following a Sabathia victory in Game 1. There was pressure, but because Sabathia pitched the team to victory in the openers against both the Minnesota Twins and Los Angeles Angels of Anaheim, the Yankees hadn't been in danger of falling into an 0–2 hole in either series. That wasn't the case now. Burnett had received an $82.5 million payday to be Robin to Sabathia's Batman, and if Burnett couldn't save the day, the Yankees would have their backs against the wall when the series shifted to Philadelphia's Citizens Bank Park. "I'm sure the weight of the world was on his shoulders," Brian Cashman said. "Obviously, he was a big acquisition for us, and we had high expectations, but unlike CC he was struggling with pitching here for whatever reason."

Burnett had pitched well at home throughout the season; his 3.51 ERA in 16 starts at the Stadium was a full run better than his 4.59 mark in 17 road outings. Although he had pitched well in his first two starts of the postseason, Burnett was knocked around by the Angels in Game 5 of the American League Championship Series, raising questions about how he would handle the Phillies' powerful lineup. Would "Good A.J." or "Bad A.J." show up? If it was the latter, the Phillies would be halfway toward a successful defense of their crown, something no team had done since the 1998–2000 Yankees won three straight titles. Burnett said that he remembers hoisting his eight-year-old son, A.J. Jr., in the tunnel outside the clubhouse after Game 1. "He was all sad," Burnett said. "I'm like, 'Hey, Daddy's got it. Don't worry.' I remember telling him that. That's just kind of how I felt; I don't know why. I felt it that night, I felt it that day. I was just, 'Daddy's got it.' I went in the next day, and it wasn't like, *Shit, I'm pitching Game 2. What am I gonna do?* It was like, *Okay, I've got Game 2.* I felt like, *This is why they brought me here, so we've got to stop the bleeding and turn it around right here.* It was a no-brainer. It was just going to bed that night with that mind-set. I couldn't tell you why, man. Everything was so relaxed with that."

Girardi said he felt confident handing the ball to Burnett, recognizing his ability to "dial up a start and completely dominate a team." But Burnett was an emotional competitor who wore his heart upon his tattooed sleeves. Pitching coach Dave Eiland admits to being concerned that the start might not go well. "I expected him to be scattering balls all over the place in the bullpen because of what a big game it was, one that might've broken us had we not won," Eiland said. "A.J. was on point. He had a calm look on his face and a different look in his eye. I knew he was ready. It was coming out so nice and easy, jumping out of his hand in warm-ups. I'm thinking, 'Okay, if he takes this out there, he's going to have some fun tonight.'"

Another factor in the Yankees' favor, Girardi said, was that the Phillies' scheduled starter, Pedro Martinez, "wasn't the same Pedro we had seen five or six years ago." The stuff of the longtime Yankees nemesis had diminished, but four days removed from celebrating his 38th birthday, the future Hall of Famer remained a formidable presence on the mound. After joining the Phillies in mid-August, Martinez went 5–1 with a 3.63 ERA in nine starts. He had been passed over in favor of rookie J.A. Happ during the National League Division Series against the Colorado Rockies, but Martinez returned to throw seven scoreless innings against the Los Angeles Dodgers in Game 2 of the National League Championship Series before Philadelphia's bullpen blew a late lead.

Now here Martinez was, back in the Bronx, where he had experienced so many highs and lows while pitching for the Boston Red Sox. Late in the 2004 season, Martinez was hit hard by the Yankees, prompting him to remark, "What can I say? Just tip my hat and call the Yankees my daddy."

Even after the Red Sox stunned the Yankees less than a month later with their historic ALCS comeback, fans never forgot Pedro's memorable words. Each time he would appear at the Stadium, chants of "Who's Your

Daddy?" were sure to arise, a reminder that the Yankees were among the few teams to give Martinez fits during his legendary career. Before Game 2 he'd been asked about it as part of an entertaining press conference. "When you have 60,000 people chanting your name, waiting for you to throw the ball, you have to consider yourself someone special," Martinez said. "Maybe when I said that quote out of frustration, I had the purpose of hearing it now. Every time I hear it, it reminds me not to make the same mistakes."

With the crowd charged by the concert and Burnett's breezy 12-pitch first inning, the phrase was heard loudly from the first pitch Martinez threw. Proving that he could still pitch effectively without the high-octane arsenal he once had, Martinez responded by striking out Jeter and Johnny Damon and then got Mark Teixeira to pop up to shortstop.

The Phillies struck first, using Raul Ibanez's two-out ground-rule double and a single by Matt Stairs to score the game's first run. It was only 1–0, but the anxiety in the crowd was apparent. Burnett had a history of imploding at times, especially in high-pressure situations. He didn't let the early run faze him, working around a pair of third-inning walks to post another zero. Burnett got some help in the fourth from Molina, who picked off Jayson Werth in the fourth inning following a leadoff single. "It was his chance to step out from behind CC," said Suzyn Waldman, the Yankees' color commentator. "CC was always the guy, and A.J. never was. That was his chance. He always had great stuff, he was always capable of doing it. Sometimes people have extraordinary moments out of nowhere."

Martinez was humming along, striking out four Yankees through three innings. A harmless single by Hideki Matsui and a Molina walk were all the Yankees had been able to scratch together against Martinez, and Teixeira believed there may have been some carryover effect after Lee silenced them in Game 1. "Cliff Lee just made us look bad; he came into our house and dominated us," Teixeira said. "We were a little shell-shocked. I remember the first couple innings when Pedro was out there, we were like, 'Oh my goodness, are we never going to score a run?'"

Teixeira took care of that, drilling Martinez's second pitch of the fourth inning into the right-center field bullpen. The blast injected life into the sellout crowd, but there were no fist pumps or exaggerated high-fives as he returned to the dugout. Teixeira celebrated his first (and only) World Series homer as though he had gone deep during a spring training game. "The home run was a little bit of a reminder that we're a great team," Teixeira said. "We all know that Yankee fans get impatient. Whether it's one game or a couple innings, you start seeing some bad at-bats, you start seeing guys chasing pitches, popping up pitches down the middle. They get antsy. Remembering the reaction, the crowd noise, feeling the stadium shaking, I think it reminded Yankee fans that, 'Hey, we're a good team. We'll be all right here.'"

No. 9 hitter Carlos Ruiz stroked a one-out double in the fifth, presenting Burnett with the challenge of handling the top of Philadelphia's lineup. Jimmy Rollins struck out swinging, and Burnett retired Shane Victorino on a pop fly, stranding Ruiz in scoring position and keeping the game tied. Dazzling with his heater and hook, "Good A.J." was in the house. "He was special," Molina said. "He was throwing strike after strike. I think he was perfect that night. He was just hitting his spots."

The score remained tied into the sixth, where Martinez struck out Teixeira and A-Rod to open the inning. Ahead of Matsui with a 1–2 count, Martinez tried to get the slugger to chase a curveball. Matsui obliged, golfing a pitch below his knees a few rows into the right-field seats. The Yankees had their first lead of the World Series. With his pitch count at 97 through six innings, Burnett returned to the mound for the seventh. Girardi had used five relievers to navigate the final two innings of Game 1, though none had thrown more than 15 pitches, so he had a full bullpen at his disposal.

Burnett froze Ibanez and Matt Stairs looking at third strikes, and Pedro Feliz grounded out to Jeter. The Yankees were six outs from tying the series. With Burnett having thrown 108 pitches, his work was done, and the crowd gave him a massive standing ovation as he walked off the field. In what would be remembered as the most important game of Burnett's career, he held the Phillies to one run on four hits and two walks, striking out nine. "I thought he was going to pitch well, but to have him come out and do it, that was so exciting," Sabathia said. "Just watching him be able to do his thing, he was locked in, mean, and dominating. That was fun to watch."

Later, Burnett credited Lee for helping his focus. When Lee met with the media after his Game 1 gem, Burnett said that he paid close attention to his fellow Arkansas native's words, hoping to emulate what made him successful. "He talked about confidence and he talked about belief in his stuff, and all I told myself was the same thing," Burnett said. "I went out with confidence, and the game rolled by."

The Yankees tacked on an insurance run in the seventh, and then Rivera fired a pair of scoreless innings to polish off a 3–1 victory. The World Series was now a best-of-five, and after no-decisions in his first three postseason starts, Burnett earned a win at the best possible time. "That was the biggest game of the year for us," first-base coach Mick Kelleher said. "He pitched the game of the season for him, maybe the game of his life. There's no way we could lose two games in New York and go to Philadelphia, you know? That was a must-win game, and he rose to the occasion. He saved us right there."

The World Series wasn't over, but Game 2 established an indelible response to Burnett's critics on the sports radio circuit and in the burgeoning social media world. The start was something that his supporters could point to. As Eiland said, "It justified the signing."

"New York's tough; I don't care who you are," Andy Pettitte said. "It doesn't matter how big of a superstar you are in some other city. When you come to New York, it is different. It takes time, it's an adjustment. We spent a lot of time with A.J., talking to him and trying to build him up. I had a great relationship with A.J., so it was awesome to see him be able to do that."

Burnett would pitch again in that World Series, but his calling card remains the way he handled a pressure-packed assignment in Game 2. Burnett said a decade later, the night of October 29, 2009, has been mentioned in nearly every text message exchange that he and A-Rod have shared.

"I still get texts from Al with '#09Game2,'" Burnett said. "It doesn't matter what he sends: 'Hey, how you doing? Tell the boys hi. #09Game2.' It gives me goose bumps to talk about. Maybe I don't get how much it meant to everybody else, but I know it meant a lot to me as a Yankee. I'm happy to be known for that one game. I want to be known for more, but hey, I'll take it."

• CHAPTER 24 •

NOT-SO-BROTHERLY LOVE

Short of perhaps Benjamin Franklin, there is no person—real or imaginary—more closely linked with Philadelphia than Rocky Balboa. The fictional story of a down-and-out boxer and part-time debt collector who trained to go the distance against the world's heavyweight champion, *Rocky* made Sylvester Stallone into a household name, winning three Academy Awards after its December 1976 release. Backed by Bill Conti's triumphant score, the images of Stallone's Balboa running through the streets of working-class Kensington and ascending the steps of the Philadelphia Museum of Art have become cinematic treasures. Though the opponents in the 2009 World Series had more in common with the well-heeled, battle-tested Apollo Creed, the Yankees had an opportunity to walk a few yards in Balboa's leather shoes.

As the Fall Classic shifted from the Bronx to Citizens Bank Park—separated by 91 miles in the air and 108 via asphalt—the Yankees opted to travel by rail. Mark Teixeira said that Alex Rodriguez likened their hostile reception to scenes in 1985's *Rocky IV*, when Balboa is greeted with hatred and suspicion upon arrival in the Cold War-era Soviet Union for a match against national hero Ivan Drago. "I remember getting off the platform and there being hundreds, maybe thousands, of Phillies fans yelling at us," Teixeira said. "Alex said it was like when Rocky went into Russia. That's exactly what it was. Drago was like the entire Philadelphia Phillies team. Howard and Utley and Rollins and Cole Hamels and Pedro and Cliff Lee—they had some players. So we knew we had our work cut out for us playing Philly."

The team had reported to Yankee Stadium that morning, boarding buses to Penn Station, where awed commuters halted their morning rush to gawk at Derek Jeter's star-studded team walking the corridors in their suits and ties. With private cars and catered meals, the chartered Amtrak experience was largely enjoyable until the train squealed into Philadelphia's 30th Street Station. Their warm Gotham send-off morphed into an icy reception in the so-called City of Brotherly Love, as word of the Yankees' arrival had spread among swarms of rabid Phillies fans. As Joe Girardi and traveling secretary Ben Tuliebitz disembarked, they were greeted by a pair of Philadelphia transit police officers. "I'm within earshot; I can hear the conversation," said then-assistant general manager Billy Eppler. "There's a couple of police officers there, and they said, 'There's some people up there on the platform waiting for you.' Then he goes, 'I have a feeling it's going to be loud up there, guys.' So we get on this moving escalator, and it comes up, comes up, comes up. I think as soon as the people in the terminal area of the train station saw the police officers and Benny, it just rained down. Boos rained down, and they were the loudest I had ever heard. I thought it was pretty cool, so I grabbed my Blackberry—I was still using a Blackberry then—and I'm hitting record. I wanted that on video."

Each of the seven dirty words that George Carlin once identified as being unsuitable for public broadcast rained upon the traveling party, many of whom had brought their significant others along. "When we got off that train, man, that was the worst," CC Sabathia said. "I was not ready for that. I was half groggy because I had been sleeping, and that was unreal—those people unleashing on us. It felt like the cops were holding people back and shit. That was an ill fucking morning. Those people were ruthless."

"There were 10 or 11-year-old kids flipping us off," Joba Chamberlain said. "I'm like, 'Shouldn't you guys be in school?'"

As they lugged bags toward another fleet of buses, one prominent member of the roster wondered aloud why the team had chosen this method of travel. "I was not happy about how we decided to travel," Johnny Damon said. "So we go to Penn Station, and everyone is cheering for us, and train rides are always fun, but as soon as we get to Philadelphia, we're bombarded with boos and people screaming at us. We could've avoided it if we would've just taken that bus from Yankee Stadium all the way to Philly."

Opened in 2004, Citizens Bank Park was constructed on the site of a vacant food warehouse. Offering a baseball-only design, natural grass, and intimate seating for more than 43,000, the Phillies' new home was viewed as a welcome replacement for decrepit Veterans Stadium. A product of the 1970s trend of circular artificial turf stadiums that could host both baseball and football, the Vet performed neither task particularly well.

The Phillies had raised the Commissioner's Trophy in their new home the year prior, prevailing over the Tampa Bay Rays in a rain-prolonged five-game Fall Classic. As the World Series resumed on Halloween night, one member of the Yankees hierarchy was doling out more tricks than treats. In the visiting clubhouse, Brian Cashman startled players by wearing a mask from the 1996 slasher film *Scream*, which he insists disappeared into Nick Swisher's possession. Hours before the first pitch of Game 3, Cashman produced another fun item from his luggage—a battery-powered fart machine, which the general manager stashed in the players' lounge. "I was keeping myself loose, more than anything else," Cashman said. "That's how I'm wired. If I have too much time on my hands, I tend to stray. I remember being in the visiting clubhouse in Philadelphia, and the dining room had some windows. I could be in another room with a remote control, so I had the fart machine underneath the table where players were sitting around. I kept hitting it, and they're all looking around like, 'Dude!' They're confused who had the problem, and I'm in the other room giggling. I know Swisher was in the middle of it. It was funny."

The gag device also made an appearance in Joe Girardi's office, according to Eppler. It was a gift from assistant general manager Jean Afterman, who said that she still keeps an extra in her desk drawer at the Stadium because Cashman wears them out so quickly. "I would like to point out that I was the person that gave him his very first fart machine," Afterman said. "He may have had some worthless cheap version of a burp or a fart machine, but this is what Amazon was created for. I went online and searched for the most reliable fart machine. As a matter of fact, in the first few years of the fart machine, it used to be a gift Brian would give to visiting GMs. It's like *omiyage* in Japan. The fart machine was a key element in our clubhouse during the postseason in 2009. I think, because the job is so high-pressured, because he spent so many years having to deal with George, the outlet is to be a prankster. It keeps it loose around here because the job is brutal, and the hours are brutal. I think it's refreshing when people expect one thing and get another. They expect somebody who's going to be hyper-intense and they get somebody with a fart machine."

Sabathia had been in that Philadelphia visiting clubhouse with the Milwaukee Brewers a year earlier, when he was charged with the loss in Game 2 of the National League Division Series. As he prepared for his return to the hill, Sabathia's thoughts drifted from how to handle Chase Utley and Ryan Howard to…cheesesteaks. Alarmed by a memory of Prince Fielder gorging on sliced ribeye, Sabathia sought out Lou Cucuzza Jr., the Yankees' longtime visiting clubhouse manager. "Lou Cucuzza gets credit for this because in Philly they had those cheesesteaks when I played in Milwaukee," Sabathia said. "I told them, 'Man, we had so many cheesesteaks before the game it fucked us up.' Like, Prince ate like five one day before the game. Lou was like, 'No cheesesteaks before the game!' during the World Series. He made it a rule so we couldn't have it before the games—only after."

The Phillies came out swinging after a rain delay in Game 3, scoring three second-inning runs off Andy Pettitte. The towel-waving crowd had been rowdy even before Hamels' first pitch, and the early advantage whipped them into a frenzy to the chagrin of the visiting executives seated behind home plate. Afterman, Cashman, and Eppler had agreed not to wear their Yankees gear for Game 3, having been advised that it would be wiser to go incognito. If that recommendation had reached Gene Michael, the former sure-handed shortstop whose front-office acumen is credited with building the late 1990s dynasty, "Stick" disregarded it. "We're all in our seats, and Stick comes walking in, head-to-toe Yankee," Afterman said. "He's got his 1996 leather World Series jacket. He's got a Yankee cap on. He's wearing a World Series ring. He has that shock of white hair. As the game starts, there's a guy in back of us who is nonstop talking the most egregious, vile shit. I couldn't tell when he was taking his breaths. At one point, Stick turns around and looks him straight in the eye and says, 'You've got a bad mouth.' That was good ol' Stick. We just kind of raised our eyes and sort of murmured, 'Great, Stick, thanks.' We didn't hear a word after that. That shut him up completely."

No stranger to that brand of fan reception, Rodriguez made history in the fourth inning, blasting a Hamels offering toward the right-field corner. Initially ruled a double, the umpires determined that Rodriguez's drive had clanked off of a TV camera positioned above the 330-foot marker on the wall, making it the first instant replay call in World Series history. "I couldn't believe that ball went out," Rodriguez said. "I had no idea because it's so rare to hit a ball on a line that low that literally goes out right over the first baseman's head. I didn't have time to look up and I don't think anybody's eyes can determine if that ball hit the camera. You have to see it on camera three or four or five times to actually see it hit the camera. So I thought it was a double and then, when I looked in the dugout, I saw the guys rumbling around a little bit. I was like, 'Oh, shit. Maybe it's a home run?'"

Swisher was 4-for-36 in the postseason and had been benched in Game 2, but he broke through with a fifth-inning double off Hamels, mashing a 73-mph curveball down the left-field line for a double. One out later National League rules permitted Pettitte to relieve the stress from what he called "an absolute grind" of a start, looping a single to center field on a first-pitch breaking ball to tie the game. "I just saw a ball up in the zone, so I'm not trying to hit a home run. I'm trying to slap the ball around," Pettitte said. "I was joking with a few of the guys. I've got a few World Series knocks now and now I've got an RBI, so I'm pretty happy about that."

The FOX broadcast picked up Jeter telling home-plate umpire Brian Gorman, "We're going to have to listen to Pettitte now. He's been bragging about his hitting all year." Jeter followed with another hit, Damon roped a two-run double to center, and after a walk to Teixeira, Hamels exited with the Yankees leading 5–3.

Swisher said that he was "heartbroken" when Girardi told him to enjoy Game 2 from the bench, believing he needed a break. Being in the lineup was better. He padded the lead, taking a long look at a solo homer off J.A. Happ in the sixth. Though Jayson Werth clubbed his second homer of the night with a mammoth shot off Pettitte in the sixth, the cushion was restored by Jorge Posada's run-scoring single off Chad Durbin in the seventh. The hometown fans were not pleased. "I remember standing out in that outfield and getting pelted with batteries and quarters," Swisher said. "Anything people could throw at me, man, they were throwing. I love that stuff. That's rivalry stuff, you know what I mean? That's passion."

Relegated to pinch-hit duties by National League rules, Hideki Matsui came off the bench and belted a solo homer in the eighth. Damaso Marte pitched a clean home half of the eighth, striking out Howard and Werth before getting Raul Ibanez to line out. "He came back from rehab and he was throwing 98 when he came back," Posada said of Marte. "I don't know if it was because he just felt rested, but obviously his arm speed was so much better, and his slider was so much better. He was key for us."

Though Carlos Ruiz hit a ninth-inning blast off Phil Hughes, Mariano Rivera recorded the final two outs to seal the 8–5 victory. Rollins' prediction of "Phillies in five" was officially dead. "I can remember the guys saying stuff in the cages: 'Now what, Jimmy? Now what?'" hitting coach Kevin Long said.

Part of a wild weekend in Philly, Game 4 was scheduled for November 1. An afternoon kickoff at Lincoln Financial Field saw another Philly-New York contest; Donovan McNabb threw for three touchdowns as the Philadelphia Eagles trounced the New York Giants 40–17. Many fans who attended that game walked across the street to Citizens Bank Park, trying to add nine innings to their marathon sports day. "Football fans and baseball fans are the same," Jerry Hairston Jr. said. "The environment was there before batting practice. You were hearing 'Let's go Yankees' chants all over the stadium. You're hearing 'Let's go Phillies' chants all over the stadium. The fans were so hyped up for an 8:00 start time around 4:00. It was electric."

Game 4 would be remembered for Damon's base-running display, which many of his teammates point to as *the* moment when the 27th championship was assured. Before Damon's daring dash, Sabathia received immediate support when the bats pounced on Joe Blanton for a pair of first-inning runs, scoring on a ground-out and sacrifice fly. The Phils punched back against Sabathia. Utley stroked a first-inning RBI double, and Pedro Feliz connected for a run-scoring hit in the fourth. Jeter and Damon reclaimed the lead with RBI singles off Blanton in the fifth. After Utley continued to torment Sabathia in the seventh, launching yet another homer, Feliz hit a game-tying blast off Chamberlain in the eighth.

"Utley just killed CC," Posada said. "We couldn't throw the slider where we wanted to. [Sabathia] felt like if we threw it off the corner, he would take it. We couldn't run anything inside; everything would leak in the middle of the plate. He hurt us."

That set the stage for Damon. Brad Lidge took over in the ninth, and the closer recorded two quick outs, retiring Matsui on a pop-up and striking out Jeter. Damon worked the count full in a nine-pitch at-bat, raking a single to left field. "The biggest thing is to battle," Damon said. "I saw the two outs he got before me, and he was just nasty. I was able to work the count to get a fastball on the outside corner. He would rather me get a hit instead of walking me, and I got that hit to left field. After that I knew I had to create something because he was absolutely on."

First-base coach Mick Kelleher greeted Damon with an update of the situation. Both Damon and Kelleher knew that the Phillies infield would shade for Teixeira to pull the ball to the right side, and Kelleher remembers telling Damon, "Hey John, if you're safe [on a steal], take a look because there's nobody covering third." Damon nodded, read Lidge's move, and broke for second base. Teixeira took the pitch, and Ruiz made a one-hop throw. "Fortunately, [Lidge] picked up his leg," Damon said. "I was shocked because it's like, I'm still fast, I can still run bases. He might have been a 1.5 or a 1.6 [seconds] to home, and I'll take that any day of the year. Even today, I'll still be able to steal that bag. I was seeing the shift, and we discussed it all year if there was an opportunity. Obviously, if there was a chance to be out, I never would've gone."

Damon popped up, and his eyes darted toward third base. As Kelleher had predicted, it was unmanned because Feliz was standing close to where a shortstop would traditionally be positioned. That essentially made it a foot race between Damon and the plodding Feliz, one that Damon knew he could win easily. He bolted to complete the rare double steal, arriving safely without a slide. "Our dugout was right there in front of third base,"

Posada said. "We saw it with our own eyes. Derek started screaming, 'Go! Go! Go!' And all of a sudden, he starts running."

There were gasps in the dugout and throughout the ballpark, as those observing needed a few extra seconds to absorb the opportunity that Damon had identified. "I remember kind of being panicked," Girardi said. "You're like, *No, no, no...go, go, go!* Like, oh, I saw that coming all the time, right? It was just such a heads-up play. Johnny was a special player. Johnny had an amazing year. You didn't always look for those brilliant plays, but that's as smart of a play as I'd seen all year. You can't prepare for that. It was instinctual."

"I thought, *What is he doing?*" said Yankees broadcaster John Sterling. "And he had a two-step lead and he turned it into such a lead...He made third easily."

Damon said that by reaching third, the pressure increased for Lidge, forcing him to throw his slider higher in the strike zone for fear of bouncing a wild pitch. A postseason star in '08, Lidge had struggled for most of '09, though he regained his mojo in October. November wasn't so kind, and the unnerved righty plunked Teixeira to place runners at the corners. "I had not had a lot of success off Brad Lidge. The guy had some of the best stuff in baseball," Teixeira said. "[Lidge] ends up hitting me because he's trying to be really careful."

That brought up A-Rod, who was 1-for-13 to that point in the series. He had, however, homered off Lidge on May 23 in New York, a blast that set up Melky Cabrera for walk-off win No. 6. Rodriguez looked at a first-pitch fastball, and Lidge threw him the same pitch again. Rodriguez lashed it into left field for a solid tie-breaking double. "As I'm rounding first base with this euphoric feeling—I remember this so vividly—my four or five steps before I touched second base, I went *Holy shit, we are world champs*," Rodriguez said. "And the only reason I thought that, as Mariano Rivera gets up, I knew we had [Pettitte] pitching Game 6. So regardless of what happened [in Game 5], we had Game 6 covered at home."

Posada followed with a two-run single to left field, and the game was as good as won. Rivera saw to that, retiring Matt Stairs, Rollins, and Shane

Victorino to seal a 7–4 victory. Now the Yankees were nine good innings away from the best celebration of the year. They placed their trust in A.J. Burnett, who would pitch on short rest but was riding high off his Game 2 performance.

As Burnett prepared to depart the ballpark after Game 4, reliever Brian Bruney made an offhand comment that he would regret. "We're going home for the night, and Bruney walks up to me and goes, 'Hey, good luck out there tomorrow, man. Go out there and get yourself that MVP,'" Burnett said. "And I was like, 'What the hell is he talking about?' Then I'm thinking and I'm like, 'Oh shit, he's right.'"

Burnett's chances at hardware fizzled when he gave back a one-run lead almost immediately. Rollins singled, Victorino was hit by a pitch, and Utley homered to stake Philadelphia to a 3–1 lead. In the third inning, Burnett walked Utley and Howard and then permitted run-scoring hits to Werth and Ibanez. Out came Girardi, calling to the bullpen. Burnett had recorded just six outs. "I left everything up," Burnett said. "I didn't have anything. Bro, that's a bad feeling. Guys still came into that locker room in the fourth and fifth inning, saying, 'Hey man, we ain't here without you. Don't worry about it; we've got you. We couldn't have got here without you; we got you.' I mean, everybody—even Jeter. It didn't matter. I believe Jorge came in. Everybody came in, saying, 'Hey, don't beat yourself up, man.'"

Utley and Ibanez homered in the seventh off Phil Coke, giving Utley five dingers in the series, equaling Reggie Jackson's 1977 record. Philadelphia used its same winning formula from Game 1: Utley homered twice, and Cliff Lee pitched a six-hitter, though the Yankees pushed five runs across against the southpaw this time.

New York chipped away at an 8–2 deficit by scoring three times in the eighth, including A-Rod's two-run double off Lee, but a ninth-inning rally died when Ryan Madson got Jeter to bounce into a double play, and Teixeira struck out for the final out of the 8–6 loss. Bruney had forgotten about his remark to Burnett until recently, when he was reminded about it for this book. "Clearly, that's something I shouldn't have said," Bruney said. "I always try to motivate guys and get them going. A.J. was an emotional player. That obviously didn't go well, but it's the same reason why he pitched well when he came to New York with the Blue Jays. It's more emotion, it's more excitement, and he pitched well on bigger stages. A.J. and I were pretty good friends, and, trust me, I wasn't trying to jinx the guy."

The Yankees played 15 postseason games in 2009, and with that Game 5 start, Burnett was the only starter who did not record at least 17 outs. Burnett swears that the next time he and Bruney cross paths, Game 5 will be discussed. "I'll say, 'Hey, you put a lot of pressure on me, Bruney. It's all your fault,'" Burnett said, trying to hold back a laugh. "Obviously, it wasn't him. I didn't even think about that; it never crossed my mind. I could care less. I'm trying to get ready and then I'm like, 'Damn, if I show up tonight, he's right.' It didn't work out that way, but I'll laugh and throw it on Bruney."

The rest of the Yankees took the loss in stride, too. Each full-time employee received two free tickets to the road games, and entire sections waved the 'How May I Help You?' signs that were seen at the Stadium that season. Some eschewed the bus back to the Bronx, opting to gamble in Atlantic City—confident that No. 27 would be wrapped up at home. After all, they had lost three straight just twice after the All-Star break, dropping consecutive home games only once after mid-June.

Girardi also skipped the bus ride, opting to drive his own vehicle. His wife, Kim, rode shotgun, and the back seat was occupied by his two older children, Serena and Dante. As the Empire State Building came into view from the darkened New Jersey Turnpike, Girardi was confident that the building would be lit in Yankee blue and white to celebrate a championship, especially because Pettitte had Game 6. "I felt great about the position we were in," Girardi said. "Andy had clinched first round, second round. It's only fitting."

CHAPTER 25

GODZILLA'S FINAL ROAR

The bulging, dripping ice packs were strapped to Hideki Matsui's swollen knees as he walked across the clubhouse throughout the summer of 2009, prompting more than one observer to wonder aloud how the international icon was still able to walk, let alone run. He was not setting any speed records on the base paths, and his time patrolling the outfield had been mercifully reduced, but "Godzilla" could still hit as well as anyone on the planet.

As you would expect of a proud athlete who once apologized to his teammates because a fractured wrist cost him three months of the 2006 season, Matsui did his job daily without complaining about the sacrifices necessary to remain on the field. Amidst immense stardom, that focused nature prompted Derek Jeter to frequently refer to Matsui as "one of my favorite teammates," a stance he maintains to this day.

So the Yankees didn't fret when Matsui missed their pregame stretch prior to the second game of the World Series. Though Matsui was 45 minutes tardy for batting practice, having been ensnared in traffic near his Manhattan apartment, he'd always shown up for a big game. Having keenly noted that Pedro Martinez seemed to be surviving on breaking balls, Matsui atoned by sitting on one for the game-deciding homer. "Before I came in 2003, the team was in the World Series almost every year," Matsui said. "When I joined the Yankees, that was my only goal: to win the championship. It's what I worked toward every year to help the team get there. Looking back, I didn't realize that it would take that long to win a championship—seven years. To be honest with you, I thought it would happen much faster."

No one could have predicted the evening that Matsui was about to enjoy, but as the Yankees took the field for Game 6, they expected victory. That confidence was largely derived from the left arm of Andrew Eugene Pettitte, as Mark Teixeira would learn. On most nights, Teixeira exhibited the assured strut of a state trooper, but the magnitude of being 27 outs away from a crown had shaken him. Charlie Wonsowicz, the Yankees' advance scout and head video coordinator, called him on it. "I was a nervous wreck, just trying to channel all of my emotions," Teixeira said. "Wonz asked me, 'You doing all right?' I was honest. I was like, 'Dude, I'm a nervous wreck. It's hard for me to focus right now.' He said, 'Don't worry; we've got Pettitte on the mound.' That completely calmed me down. You can talk about how important youth is, but when you're in the playoffs and you have veterans that go about their business and don't change, it relaxes you."

Drafted by the organization in 1990, Pettitte made his big league debut in 1995 and was a key member of the "Core Four," winning at least 12 games in each of his nine seasons with New York. Acquired by way of a third-grade move from Louisiana to Texas, Pettitte's easygoing drawl camouflaged his intensity. "Andy is a big-game pitcher, man," Jorge Posada said. "When you have a guy like that who can be so professional, so into his craft, doing his scouting report, the little things—he's got his little notes—having him is just important. The key piece of each championship was him."

That had not always been so clear to the Yankees' decision-makers, which was nearly Philadelphia's gain. At George Steinbrenner's urging, the Yankees had explored trading Pettitte during the 1999 season with parameters of a Philadelphia Phillies deal agreed upon. For Pettitte the Yankees would have acquired a pair of former first-round picks in pitcher Adam Eaton and outfielder Reggie Taylor, among others.

Impassioned pleas by general manager Brian Cashman, manager Joe Torre, and pitching coach Mel Stottlemyre saved Pettitte's place on the roster, though Steinbrenner issued his standard warning to those who supported keeping Pettitte: "You'd better be right." They were; Pettitte and his No. 46 landed in Monument Park, while Eaton went 71–68 with a 4.94 ERA in

209 games for five big league teams from 2000 to 2009. Taylor batted .231 with 14 homers for three organizations from 2000 to 2005.

Following a three-year stint during which he helped pitch the Houston Astros to the 2005 World Series, Pettitte returned to the Yankees for '07, though his heart continued to be spread across a span of 1,600 miles. During '09 Pettitte jetted home whenever possible, opting for quality time with his wife, Laura, and their four children over nights in American League hotel rooms. "I really appreciated the whole postseason in 2009 because I didn't know how things were going to turn out," Pettitte said. "It was difficult to get on that team in '09 as far as the contract negotiation, so I wasn't real sure. I know that whole deal for me was icing on the cake. To be able to do what I did and pitch well, I really feel like I took all that in, where I never did before that. I was able to really enjoy it and savor it and realize that I was getting on my last leg. At that time every year, I was thinking, *Do I really want to go through this again? I don't want to do this again.* I mean, my family is in Texas, and I'm flying home every off day. I'm older and I'm feeling it. When I land in Houston at 2:00 in the morning and I've got to come back the next evening and meet the team in Oakland or whatever, it was pretty tough."

Moments like this—pitching with a title on the line—fueled Pettitte's desire to come back for more, as they would in 2012 after a failed first attempt at retirement. Pitching on three days' rest, Pettitte took the mound following Bronx native Mary J. Blige's rendition of the national anthem and retired the side in order in the first inning. He then kept Philadelphia off the board in the second inning despite a walk and a wild pitch.

With the chants of "Who's Your Daddy?" again ringing throughout the grandstands, Matsui led the charge as the Yankees pounced on Martinez, their familiar nemesis. Thanks to his reputation for throwing at batters and—on one occasion in '03—spilling lovable septugenarian coach Don Zimmer to the turf, Martinez would never win any popularity contests in the Bronx

In the second inning, Matsui worked the count full and then thumped Martinez's eighth pitch into the second deck in right field for a two-run homer. "All year he was always getting huge hits every time we needed them, but in that World Series, he was hurting," CC Sabathia said of Matsui. "I remember him walking around the clubhouse [with] double ice and getting his knees drained every other day. I remember thinking it was a perfect matchup. Pedro was pitching, and I knew once he got that first hit it was going to be a big night for him."

An inning later, the 35-year-old Matsui connected for a two-run single to center field that chased home Jeter and Johnny Damon, giving the Yankees a 4–1 lead. Bedlam sparked throughout the Stadium's five decks, as an announced crowd of 50,315 could sense they were on the precipice of a celebration.

Pettitte pitched out of trouble to strand two runners in the fourth inning, barking at home-plate umpire Joe West as he left the field, and then worked a perfect fifth. Phillies manager Charlie Manuel turned the pitching over to Chad Durbin, and when Teixeira snapped a slump with a one-out single that drove home Jeter, the beers and Brut bubbly could safely be chilled in the home clubhouse.

Matsui wasn't done yet. He strode to the plate, following Durbin's walk to Alex Rodriguez, and Manuel called upon left-hander J.A. Happ, again prompting the jovial cries of "Don't do it" from Jeter and Posada. Matsui took four pitches—three of them balls. Happ floated one that Matsui pummeled off the auxiliary scoreboard in right-center field, driving home Teixeira and A-Rod. "He was a monster that series," Happ said. "I remember hanging a slider, and he hit a double with a couple guys on base. When I saw it go in the gap, I knew it was not the place I'd like that ball to end up."

Standing atop second base, Matsui reached for his belt, exhaled, and fiddled with his gloves while ignoring the pandemonium he had unleashed. The Yankees had seven runs on the scoreboard; Matsui drove in six, tying a World Series record. The only previous player to have six RBIs in a World Series game was the Yankees' Bobby Richardson, who did it against the Pittsburgh Pirates in 1960. The feat has since been equaled by Albert Pujols (2011) and Addison Russell (2016). "Coming back from Philadelphia and being penciled back into the lineup again, it felt good to be back," Matsui said. "And to be able to have that kind of performance in the game that decides the world championship, that was just surreal."

If this was destined to be Matsui's final game as a Yankee, what better note could there have been to go out on? "I've said it about a thousand times: he's not American, but he's the all-American boy," Yankees broadcaster John Sterling said. "You didn't have to do anything with Matsui, just write his name down. He really is one of my favorites—such a nice guy, such a gentleman. That phenomenal last game made me feel so good."

Ryan Howard trimmed the deficit in the sixth with a two-run homer off Pettitte, but Philadelphia's hopes of a repeat were fading fast. Joe Girardi clapped his hands and claimed the ball from Pettitte after five-and-two-thirds innings. The lefty had earned a standing ovation by having limited the Phils to three runs over a gritty 94-pitch effort. Pettitte slowed near the dugout steps, lifted his cap, and shook it.

His pitching move having been executed, Girardi needed to make another call—to a car service. His eldest children, Serena and Dante, had been instructed to watch the first five innings from their home in suburban Purchase, New York, but now that it looked like there would be a celebration, they needed a ride to the Stadium. "My kids had the flu and wanted to come to the game, and I said, 'No, you're not going to sit in the kids' room' because if we have to play a Game 7, I didn't want them getting the fathers sick," Girardi said. "They said, 'Will you send a car if you're winning in the sixth inning?' I said, 'Absolutely.' They made it."

Joba Chamberlain finished the sixth but ran into trouble in the seventh, allowing a hit and a walk. He was bailed out when Damaso Marte fanned Chase Utley on three pitches. Marte also dispatched Howard to open the eighth. He fired two-and-two-thirds perfect innings across four World Series appearances, striking out five. Marte also hurled one-and-one-third perfect frames in three American League Championship Series outings. "The World Series MVP, to me, came down to Hideki Matsui or Damaso Marte," Cashman said. "The field staff didn't want him on the postseason roster. We forced him to be on. They didn't know what they were getting because he missed most of the year. I was like, 'This is a guy who can get lefties out,' and obviously he saved his only bullets for the postseason."

Third-base coach Rob Thomson admitted to being among those who doubted Marte's place. "That kid was unbelievable during the playoffs," Thomson said. "This is how dumb I am: I didn't think he should be on the playoff roster. He got some of the biggest outs throughout the playoffs."

With five outs separating the Yankees from a championship, the phone rang in the right-field bullpen for Mariano Rivera, who had recorded the final outs of the 1998, 1999, and 2000 titles. No other pitcher could claim more than two clinchers, and he'd now get to add 2009 to that list. "Mo's a champion. That's what those type of guys do," pitching coach Dave Eiland said. "It's like Michael Jordan hitting a jump shot at the buzzer with the game on the line. That was Mo. I remember he always called me 'Boss.' 'You got four tonight? Five tonight?' He'd go, 'Whatever you need, Boss. Whatever you need, I got it.'"

Rivera struck out Jayson Werth, surrendered a double to Raul Ibanez, and then induced Pedro Feliz to foul out. Three outs away. The Yanks went down around a Jeter single in the eighth, and Rivera returned to the mound. His left oblique still ached from Game 2, but if Rivera finished the job, he'd have an entire winter to recuperate. "Nobody knew [about the injury], but I talked to him a lot about it," Jose Molina said. "He didn't want anybody to know about it. He kept it really quiet. Even half of Mariano was more dominant than anybody in the league."

Pinch-hitter Matt Stairs lined to Jeter for the first out, and after a six-pitch walk to Carlos Ruiz, Jimmy Rollins lifted a fly ball to Nick Swisher in right field for the second out. The Yankees disregarded Ruiz, who advanced to second base on defensive indifference. The only assignment was to get Shane Victorino, and he refused to give up. The 10th pitch of the at-bat was chopped on the ground to Robinson Cano, who danced a few steps to his left and flagged it. The Yankees bolted from the dugout while Cano's toss to Teixeira was in the air. Eight years to the night that Rivera surrendered a broken-bat single to Luis Gonzalez, marking the final breath of their 1996–2000 dynasty, the Yankees were back on top.

The Yankees were World Series champions, winning it all in the first year of their fabulous new home—just as Babe Ruth and the 1923 squad had. Chamberlain and Swisher emerged from a crush of humanity near the mound to pace a victory lap around the warning track, carrying flags that read: "2009 World Series Champions," and players high-fived fans while spraying bubbly. "I was glad I didn't get kicked in the face on the dog pile," Chamberlain said. "The coolest thing for me was to be able to have my son there, to have my father there, and to be able to say thank you to those guys who grinded with me. It was awesome."

For the "Core Four" of Jeter, Pettitte, Posada, and Rivera, it was ring No. 5, having been cornerstones of the roster that celebrated four titles in five seasons leading into the turn of the century. Rivera said they may have taken winning for granted back then, but what turned out to be their final moment on top tasted just as sweet as they had remembered. "When you're winning so many like that, you think you're going to be there every time," Rivera said. "When you don't go for a few years, you figure out how hard it is. When you get there again, you appreciate it even more. I believe that's what I experienced. When we won before, it was, 'Oh, this is easy. We will be there again.'"

It was the outcome that George Steinbrenner had spent more than $1 billion chasing. Fittingly, the title was dedicated to The Boss, who watched the festivities on television from his Tampa, Florida, home. The video screen in center field flashed the words, "Boss, This Is For You," as Hal Steinbrenner accepted the 20-pound, Tiffany & Co.-produced sterling silver championship trophy from commissioner Bud Selig. "At that time George was a little sick, and to win it one more time, especially at the stadium that he built, it was priceless," Rivera said. "When Hal raised the trophy and said, 'That was for you, Dad,' it was amazing. I still remember that like yesterday."

Cradling the trophy Jeter proclaimed, "We play the game the right way and we deserve to be standing here." Matsui was honored as the World Series MVP, having gone 8-for-13 (.615) with three homers and eight RBIs in the Fall Classic. "That experience [of being named MVP] was also surreal, just like my performance," said Matsui, who had been crowned MVP of the 2000 Japan Series while with the Yomiuri Giants. "I felt like that was a continuation of that. It felt very surreal, and that was really what was going through my mind."

"There's so many stars on that team. You tend to overlook somebody like Matsui," hitting coach Kevin Long said. "But he was Steady Eddie. He had a knack for getting big hits. He loved the spotlight—like a lot of our guys did—and he shined. He was really one of many stars in that World Series."

On the field Yankees color commentator Suzyn Waldman scrambled to find guests for live radio appearances. The first player she encountered was Marte, who had only granted interviews in Spanish that season. Marte waved to Waldman, inviting her to speak with him. "I couldn't believe it, like, *Wait, you speak English?*" Waldman said. "And he said, 'Of course I do.' I remember him being fantastic, very well-spoken, and so happy."

In Cashman's suite there were hugs shared between the baseball operations team who had assembled and maintained the roster. An attendant wheeled in bottles of bubbly, and a toast was made before Jean Afterman, Billy Eppler, Gene Michael, and others descended to field level. "The emotions of *Holy cow, we did it*, it's ingrained in your mind like any other monumental life event," Eppler said. "In my office there's a photo of me and my wife and one of me and my sons. There's no other photos except for my photo of me and 'Stick' [Michael] on the field in that 2009 World Series. We both have our credentials on. Our arms are around each other, and it's just me and him. I see it every day."

As the Yankees left the field and made the turn into the oval of their clubhouse, plastic sheeting draped the lockers, laptops, and televisions once more. A.J. Burnett followed through on his promise to hit Girardi with a pie, screaming, "Come on, Skip!" Girardi loved it.

The manager then signaled that he was calling one final meeting of the 2009 Yankees, asking security to halt the press and family members from entering. They had achieved the objective set eight months prior in Tampa, and Girardi wanted the players and coaches to appreciate that. Mission 27 was complete. "Joe did a great job," Chamberlain said.

"Before we let anybody else in, we had a team moment. Just everybody in there without all the craziness that we knew was about to happen."

Protective goggles were strapped on as the clubhouse became a mob scene for their wildest, wettest celebration yet. The Yankees wielded golden bottles of champagne and doused the 37-year-old Pettitte, the first pitcher ever to start and win the clinching game of three postseason rounds. "It's all fun," Damon said. "The champagne, the eyes hurting, just trying to get to family. That's so huge that you can finally share something with your family after the long year. You're playing baseball, you're trying to win, and you end the year on the most positive note ever."

The largest Yankee was carrying the largest bottle. Jay-Z had gifted a comically oversized Magnum of his exorbitantly expensive Ace of Spades bubbly to the team, and Sabathia hoisted the 15-liter container between rooms, pouring glasses for teammates and coaches. "That big giant bottle of champagne that only CC could carry," first-base coach Mick Kelleher said, "he was the only one strong enough. It was so funny."

Considering where his season had begun with the shame of a performance-enhancing drugs confession and the grueling return from hip surgery, no one seemed happier than A-Rod. Wearing his cap backward, he puffed on a cigar and laughed. No matter what came next in his unpredictable life, Rodriguez would always be a World Series champion. "I felt like I was playing with the house's money," Rodriguez said. "I felt grateful and appreciative. I think that was the most fun I've had."

An ecstatic Hal Steinbrenner opened the Legends restaurant behind home plate, where Jennifer Steinbrenner Swindal donned a chef's toque and gleefully doled out sushi to reveling employees. When the managing general partner made a brief appearance in the clubhouse, his sister dared reliever Brian Bruney to douse the Baby Boss. "I remember Jenny told me to go pour champagne on Hal and I stopped and said, 'Well, can you promise I won't get fired for this?'" Bruney said. "She said, 'Yes, I promise.' So I went and poured it, and the next thing you know, I get traded. Who knows? I remember we had all the goggles and everything. We just had a lot of fun. We shut it down."

The off-limits areas of the ballpark took on a dreamlike haze filled with the warring aromas of booze and cigars. Within the coaches' room, Sigma Chi gathered. A-Rod appeared with Kate Hudson and Kurt Russell, and Teixeira recalls speaking to bench coach Tony Pena about his faith. Some players offered a toast to their vanquished rival, Jimmy Rollins. *Phillies in five?* Try Yankees in six. "That's why you close your mouth and let things happen," Molina said. "He had confidence in his team, but you keep it to yourself. I know guys, especially the veteran players, weren't happy about that. We did what we had to do, playing the game on the field, not with our mouths. We shoved it up his ass."

Chad Bohling, the Yankees' director of mental conditioning, shared a private moment with Jeter moments after what would be the Captain's final championship title. "The party kind of died down a little bit, and I remember going back to the food room and grabbing something to eat," Bohling said. "Derek was sitting down there as well. It was his fifth ring, and I remember Derek saying something like, 'Everyone is special.' He just won a World Series but understands how tough those things are to do. He had a good perspective on how tough it is to win but then also appreciating it and not taking it for granted."

While fans hugged, kissed, and shouted on the sticky floors of the taverns across River Avenue, Girardi and his family piled into their SUV for a 20-minute trek to suburbia. The clock read approximately 2:30 AM when Girardi's wife, Kim, spotted a wrecked vehicle on the left side of the Cross Country Parkway. "The kids are in the back of the car and they've got like a 102 [degree] fever, and she's like, 'Stop, stop!'" Girardi said. "So I stopped. I said, 'Call 911.'"

Dressed in a light jacket, T-shirt, and jeans, Girardi sprinted across the eastbound lanes of the parkway. Approaching the vehicle, Girardi found Marie Henry, a 27-year-old Connecticut woman, behind the wheel. Henry had sustained cuts on her face and arms after her Chevrolet Trailblazer blew a tire, slamming into a concrete wall. "There was glass all over her from the window," Girardi said. "I wanted her to get out of the car, but she wouldn't. I said, 'I'm afraid that someone's going to come around the corner, not see you, and smoke you.' She was just out of it. I would say within a minute thirty the police were there."

After Girardi climbed back into his car and sped off, the responding officer, Kathleen Cristiano, filled Henry in on the identity of her Good Samaritan. Days later a thank you note from the motorist appeared in Girardi's Stadium office. "When she told me it was Joe Girardi, I was stunned," Henry told the *Connecticut Post*. "There were plenty of cars that went by and didn't stop, but he did. And he took a big chance to get to my car. That tells me what a good person he is. Most people know him as manager of the Yankees, but I will always think of him as the guy who went out of his way to help a stranger in trouble."

At the moment Girardi was trying to pry open the mangled door of a mid-size SUV, most of his players were shedding their alcohol-soaked gear in favor of something drier. It was too early to head home, and who could guarantee that they'd experience another night like this? As they felt the rush of the cold November air, the Yankees were ready to enjoy the bright lights of New York City as champions.

• CHAPTER 26 •

MISSION ACCOMPLISHED

The clubhouse celebration had died down, though the stench of spilled champagne would linger for weeks to come. Players and coaches hugged as they prepared to head for the streets, subway, or the Stadium parking garage, but this was not good-bye. A parade was already being planned, giving the entire team a chance to soak in the love of more than a million New Yorkers.

A number of players, coaches, and front-office types had decided to keep the party going at 1 OAK, a nightclub on West 17th Street in the Chelsea neighborhood of Manhattan. When Nick Swisher's car ascended to street level, he was stunned to see how many fans were still reveling underneath the tracks for the 4 Train. River Avenue looked like Bourbon Street during Mardi Gras. "I thought everybody in New York would've been at the bars partying," Swisher said. "It was a mob of people. I'll never forget it. I decided I was going to get out of my car, get on the hood, and pump the crowd up. I couldn't quite make it; I got bum-rushed, bro. Getting the hugs and the high-fives that people were giving me, it was so amazing. The love that New York City and Yankees fans have for their team, you can't beat that."

Most of the gang eventually did make it to the trendy nightlife venue, where they exchanged hugs and high-fives with anybody who looked vaguely familiar. Champagne bottles continued to pop all night, and players and coaches passed them around like they were attending a fraternity kegger. "It was rowdy and crazy loud, but we were all just in a little group," A.J. Burnett said. "We were all together in this spot, celebrating this achievement together. I can't even remember how long we stayed. I don't remember a lot from that night after we left the clubhouse. I didn't drive; I know that."

261

Johnny Damon had won a World Series five years earlier with the Boston Red Sox, though they clinched at Busch Stadium, so that celebration took place in a St. Louis hotel. "Winning at home, that's a whole different ball-game," said Damon, who recalled ending up at a karaoke bar in Koreatown at some point after Game 6. "When I won with Boston, we were in St. Louis, so everyone had to pack so we could go home. That took away from us hanging out for a long time. This was just a great, fun night."

The season culminated with the championship the Yankees had envisioned when they first assembled in early February, though their path to the World Series had been anything but smooth. That was part of what made the journey so memorable. "Everything that happened that year, we had so many ups and downs," CC Sabathia said, "A-Rod being hurt, him coming back, us struggling, just all that stuff. We expected to win the World Series, too; that's a tough thing to deal with. I think it was a big exhale. We had a lot of fun. You don't want that night to end."

Swisher said that he remembers being "so excited but yet so exhausted" as he realized the Yankees had accomplished their mission for 2009. Including spring training, the regular season, and the postseason, the team played 212 games, winning 138. "That's unbelievable," Swisher said. "To go through that entire season and be able to celebrate at the end of it, it's a fucking blowout. At that point you know you don't have anything to do for a little bit and you're champs."

Even players that didn't typically partake in such events made it to the club. Derek Jeter, for example, was six years removed from a public tussle with George Steinbrenner over late hours and a bachelor lifestyle. Even though it resulted in a memorable credit-card commercial, Jeter preferred to save his partying for special occasions. This qualified. "I remember being excited that Jeet was out," Sabathia said. "He never goes out to the club, so to have him there was fun. That was the big celebration, the big night. We had a blast. We were out all night."

One unlikely snapshot of the evening included Mark Teixeira against a back wall of the club, swigging from bottles of champagne in both hands as Jay-Z's "Empire State of Mind" thumped at incredible decibel levels. "He was standing on the booth; he was going to work," Joba Chamberlain said. "When Tex lets loose, Tex lets loose. It's fun to be around."

Had it been Teixeira's choice, the team might have spent the entire night together partying at the Stadium—Sigma Chi perhaps—though he went with the flow. "I'm not a big club guy and I didn't really want to party with people I didn't know," Teixeira said. "I would rather stay in the clubhouse for two straight days, but eventually you've got to go to sleep."

Last call in New York City is 4:00 AM, but considering the final out of Game 6 was recorded 10 minutes before midnight, it's likely the establishment bent the ordinance to let the champions celebrate a few hours longer. Billy Eppler, the assistant general manager, said that he remembers that the sun had come up by the time he was ready to call a car service.

"I don't think I recovered from that," Alex Rodriguez said. "We had a great time that night."

Suffice it to say, most of the players' congratulatory phone calls and text messages went unreturned in the early morning hours of November 5. Phil Hughes said that he stayed in bed for an entire day after the post-World Series parties, while some of the support staff—unable to make it all the way home—crashed in hotels.

Less than 36 hours after Robinson Cano zipped the final out of Game 6 into Teixeira's glove, a parade honoring the World Series champions was scheduled to proceed through the Canyon of Heroes. Few of the players were operating at 100 percent that morning. "Everybody needed that time, especially Johnny," Hughes said. "My favorite thing is they gave us copies of that DVD, the MLB Productions one, and seeing these interviews where he's got these bloodshot eyes and bed head. You can tell it's from two days after we had won. It's pretty funny."

Their adrenaline was flowing as the Yankees reunited at the Stadium at 6:30 AM on the morning of the parade. A police escort shuttled them into Lower Manhattan, and the floats moved slowly from Broadway and Battery Place, proceeding north to Chambers Street. "There's a lot of hurry up and wait, so I knew we were hurrying and we were waiting," Damon said. "You can't really go throughout the city of New York because there's so much traffic."

A wide range of estimates pegged the crowd as being between 500,000 and three million people, though most seemed to settle on a number in the million-plus range. Everywhere you looked, fans in Yankees hats lined the streets with many holding signs thanking their favorite players for the team's 27th championship. "It was as good as the first one," Andy Pettitte said. "The parade is absolutely one of the greatest things. You want to win a championship to be able to experience that again and be able to let the guys do it that had never experienced a parade. It's one of America's great events."

For those first-timers, the sight of that many people in one place was awe-inspiring. "New York is a big, impressive place," Teixeira said. "When you pack millions of people into a few blocks, it becomes even more impressive."

"You're used to playing in front of a packed house every night, so 45 or 50,000 people doesn't sound that crazy anymore," Hughes said. "It was a staggering amount of people there. You really got a sense of how many Yankee fans there are in the city."

Fans clamored to see their favorite players, chanting "MVP!" at Hideki Matsui while lauding superstars like Jeter and A-Rod. One of Michael Kay's favorite memories of that morning was seeing the genuine wonder on Rodriguez's face. "He was overwhelmed because a lot of people had been telling him, 'Wait until you see this' and he finally got a chance to experience it," said Kay, the play-by-play broadcaster. "This is a guy that, for whatever reason, never received the love that would be commensurate to his level of talent. He felt the love that day."

When a float would roll by with someone they didn't recognize, fans would shout, "Who are you?" "I was just a rookie; they're like, 'Where's Derek? Where's CC? Where's Andy?'" David Robertson said. "It was a good time. I just couldn't believe how many people showed up."

The ticker tape that rained upon the Yankees for their first two parades through the Canyon of Heroes in 1961 and 1962 was no longer in use, so high above Broadway, observers leaned out of windows and flung tons of shredded office paper, confetti, and toilet paper into the air. "To look down the street and see nothing but people and people sitting outside of balconies throwing paper like 30 floors up," Swisher said, "it looked like it was snowing in November."

Francisco Cervelli was joined by a couple of A-list companions. As his float rolled through the streets, A-Rod was on the catcher's left, sporting dark sunglasses, a fedora, and a Yankees dugout jacket. To Cervelli's right was Jay-Z, who wore a World Series cap and acknowledged cheering fans as though he had led the club in home runs and RBIs. "A-Rod was in the front with Jay-Z and he told him, 'Hey, Cervy is the player; let him live this moment,'" Cervelli said. "I was in the front watching everything; I cannot forget it. People were hanging everywhere off the lights."

As a high school student, Dana Cavalea had skipped class to attend the Yankees' parades in the late 1990s, clamoring for a view of Jeter or Bernie Williams. Now he was part of the team on the other side of the fun. As the strength and conditioning coach marveled at the throngs of fans, all he could think was, *Are you kidding me?* "We just won together, but you felt that it was already over," Cavalea said. "That was the undertone of it all. But you were a part of the greatest team in the world that day, going through New York City. People were just going wild. It was a little bit scary, too, because here you are as a moving target, and people can throw things out the window."

Once the caravan reached city hall, players, coaches, and executives took seats on the stage, walking in to Queen's "We Are the Champions." Jeter carried the World Series trophy, hoisting it high above his head, and the attendees were bathed in brilliant sunshine. "It's been too long, hasn't it?" Jeter said to the crowd. "It feels good to be back."

"You forget how magical this is," Hal Steinbrenner added.

Jay-Z took the stage for another performance of "Empire State of Mind," adding an appropriate closing touch to an unforgettable season. "It was our song," Sabathia said. "Still to this day, that's my song. When it comes on, it's our '09 World Series song. It was cool to have that be our thing."

"It does remind me of what was a very special October and getting to be part of the parade, which was unreal," Hughes said. "But I'd be perfectly happy never hearing that song again. I'd like to keep it in a time capsule with my ring and everything else from that year. It does bring back good memories, but you're not going to find it on any playlists I have."

Mayor Michael Bloomberg delivered a few prepared lines, including a zinger about Jimmy Rollins needing a new crystal ball, and then presented a ceremonial key to the city to each player, coach, and executive. The final one was issued to George Steinbrenner, which Hal accepted on his father's behalf. "I was so happy for Hal; it was his first year as managing general partner, and we were so ecstatic," team president Randy Levine said. "It's a great, great sense of accomplishment, and you're very happy. You're like that for two days and then you've got to start all over again. That's the way the Yankees are."

Joe Girardi said that he had spoken with The Boss before arriving at city hall, delivering a message from the famous owner to his players. "The only thing greater than this celebration is doing it two years in a row," Girardi said. "So he asked me to remind you that pitchers and catchers report in 96 days. Be ready to defend it."

The conclusion of the parade closed the book on 2009. Players dispersed to their respective offseason homes, while the front office began plotting the quest to defend their title. By the beginning of the next week, the pro scouting meetings were underway. Call it Mission 28, an objective that still remains to this day. "We don't get the chance in the front office to enjoy it as much as others because the work starts immediately thereafter," general manager Brian Cashman said. "During the World Series run, I was already talking about Curtis Granderson with [Detroit Tigers general manager] Dave Dombrowski."

When the Yankees opened 2010, they did so without Damon, Matsui, Brian Bruney, Melky Cabrera, Phil Coke, Jerry Hairston Jr., Eric Hinske, Ian Kennedy, Jose Molina, Xavier Nady, and Chien-Ming Wang, all of whom had been traded, released, or signed elsewhere as free agents.

The home opener was scheduled for April 13 against the Los Angeles Angels of Anaheim. The team that the Yankees had defeated in the American League Championship Series the previous fall had signed Matsui as a free agent only five weeks after he was named the MVP of the World Series. It was a happy coincidence that Matsui would be present to receive his ring along with his former teammates.

With Girardi, Yogi Berra, and Whitey Ford handing out the treasures, each player was summoned to receive a ring, which was handcrafted in white gold by Balfour and featured a Yankees blue stone accented by a diamond-clustered "NY" logo. A beautiful rendition of the Stadium adorned the sides, along with the words "Tradition" and "Unity."

When Matsui's name was called, the title team enveloped the slugger in a circle of love and admiration. His red cap and gray uniform stood out in a swarm of navy blue hats and white pinstripes. "It was just so heartwarming for everybody to surround me in that way and appreciate me," Matsui said. "That was probably the one moment that I almost had tears in my eyes. I was so happy."

Jeter played a prank on his friend, replacing Matsui's ring with a fan giveaway that had been distributed that spring. Matsui didn't inspect the ring immediately, but when his Angels teammates cracked open the wooden box, some remarked that it looked cheaper than they expected. Girardi gave Matsui the real ring during pregame introductions. "Knowing Matsui," Jeter said, "he probably appreciated the fake one, too."

A more private ceremony took place in George Steinbrenner's suite, as Girardi and Jeter presented The Boss with his seventh ring. A Michigan fan, Jeter playfully told Steinbrenner that he would need to take off his Ohio State ring in order to claim the new Yankee version. Instead, Steinbrenner removed his 2000 ring, replacing it with 2009. "I consider that one of my most special moments as a Yankee, handing him a ring," Girardi said. "That is probably the best way you can say thank you to George—to give him a World Series ring."

CHAPTER 27

THE AFTERMATH

As the Yankees toured the White House grounds in April 2010, having received their customary post-victory invitation from president Barack Obama, some within the party assumed that 1600 Pennsylvania Avenue would be an annual stop on the travelogue. That was how it had seemed for the franchise in the late 1990s, when four World Series titles in five years placed Joe Torre's squad on the guest lists of both Bill Clinton and George W. Bush.

Some repeat visitors, like Andy Pettitte, could rattle off a typical schedule: there would be a lengthy wait in a holding area and then a tour that included a stop in the Oval Office, where players would have the opportunity to sit in the president's chair. The commander-in-chief would shake hands and make small talk, as Obama did in the East Room, lamenting that his favored Chicago White Sox had not won a title since 2005. "For the millions of Yankees fans in New York and around the world who bleed blue, nothing beats that Yankee tradition: 27 World Series titles, 48 Hall of Famers—a couple, I expect, standing behind me right now," Obama said that day. "From Ruth to Gehrig, Mantle to DiMaggio, it's hard to imagine baseball without the long line of legends who've worn the pinstripes. Last season this team continued that legacy, winning 103 games and leaving no doubt who was the best team in baseball. But what people tend to forget, especially after watching their teams lose, is that being a Yankee is as much about character as it is about performance, as much about who you are as what you do. Being successful in New York doesn't come easy, and it's not for everybody. It takes a certain kind of player to thrive in the pressure cooker of Yankee Stadium, somebody who's poised and professional and knows what it takes to wear the pinstripes."

Obama praised the Yankees for their work on and off the field, citing Mark Teixeira's establishment of a scholarship in the name of a high school friend who was killed in an automobile accident and Jorge Posada's efforts to raise awareness of craniosynostosis, a rare birth defect that affected his son, Jorge Jr. The president also lauded Derek Jeter's work ethic and the organization's commitment to HOPE Week, which continues to this day. "That's something I'll never forget," said Jason Zillo, the Yankees' director of media relations. "The president of the United States mentioned a concept of mine that started on a dry-erase board."

When Joe Girardi presented the president with a pinstriped No. 27 jersey that had been autographed by the title-winning roster, the manager asked Obama to hoist the trophy for a photo opportunity. Standing a few feet away, assistant general manager Jean Afterman made a quip that she would instantly regret: "Let him hold it. He may not get a chance again."

"And you wonder why the other teams don't root for you," Obama replied with a smile.

"I meant to be teasing him about his references to the White Sox," Afterman said. "And then [White Sox executive vice president] Kenny Williams, who's a great friend of President Obama, texted me and said, 'Look at you, talking smack with the president.' So that was my White House experience. I'm sure any dream I had of working for Obama vanished after that."

The players had been wise to savor their time together that final night of the World Series. The group that traveled to Washington, D.C., six months later after Robinson Cano fielded that ground ball seemed representative, but there were several key differences.

Johnny Damon and Hideki Matsui were gone. Damon landed instead with the Detroit Tigers, signing an $8 million contract, while Matsui inked a $6 million deal with the Los Angeles Angels of Anaheim. Swapped to the Atlanta Braves for pitchers Javier Vazquez and Boone Logan, Melky Cabrera also exited. The Yankees had interest in retaining Damon and Matsui, but those key cogs were replaced by a trade for outfielder Curtis Granderson and the signing of injury-prone designated hitter Nick Johnson. "I definitely wanted to come back," Damon said. "My agent [Scott Boras] called me and said, 'The Yankees are offering you two years, $14 million,' and I was like, 'Can we negotiate? Can they go two years, $20 [million]?' And he goes, 'Well, you have to hurry up and make this decision before they sign Nick Johnson.' And I was like, 'Why is this only a couple minutes decision? What's been going on since the season ended?' I was very upset. I wanted to be a Yankee."

Damon said that he spoke to Brian Cashman before the parade, telling the general manager that while Boras would probably ask for four to seven years, Damon was prepared to settle for two. "Matsui, Damon, we were going to try to sign all of those guys," Cashman said. "Matsui pressed us early, and I couldn't guarantee we were going to be with him. I tried to get Johnny back, but the price tag was too extreme. They wound up in Detroit, and we signed Nick Johnson. Nothing worked out for any of us, but I feel like if the options were more realistic, he would've been a happier person staying where he belonged."

While Matsui was front and center for the home opener against the Los Angeles Angels of Anaheim, Damon received a lengthy standing ovation when the Tigers made their first visit to New York in 2010, blowing a kiss to the crowd. That reception was still buzzing in Damon's mind when the Boston Red Sox claimed him on waivers a week later. Damon had a clause in his contract that permitted him to reject trades to all but eight teams, one of which was Boston. "My attachment to New York was so strong," said Damon, who completed the year in Detroit. "I was like, 'I can't do it again. I can't do it to my family. I can't do it to the Yankee fans that just cheered me a couple days before.' The love I felt for New York was a big reason why I said I couldn't go back to Boston."

The Yanks' universe was rocked on the morning of July 13, 2010, when George Steinbrenner died of a heart attack at St. Joseph's Hospital in Tampa, Florida, nine days after his 80th birthday. Steinbrenner's passing came two days after the death of longtime Stadium public-address announcer Bob Sheppard, who was 99. "Simply put, Mr. Steinbrenner and Mr. Sheppard both left this organization in a much better place than when they first arrived," Jeter said. "They've set the example for all employees of the New York Yankees to strive to follow."

That September, the Yankees unveiled a massive monument at the Stadium to honor the colorful and combative Steinbrenner, who led the team to seven World Series titles, 11 pennants, and 16 division titles over 37-plus seasons as principal owner. Giving Steinbrenner the final championship he craved ranks as a proud accomplishment for the '09 team. "He was the one that gave the okay to do all this, he was the one opening up the wallet to get great players to surround us, and it was gratifying to be able to win for him," Pettitte said. "The older we got, the more that I was around, and the more time I got to spend with him, the more you learned to love him and realized his passion for the game. That was extremely special."

Girardi steered the 2010 team to 95 wins, finishing a game behind the Tampa Bay Rays in the American League East and settling for the wild-card. Veterans like Lance Berkman, Austin Kearns, Marcus Thames, Randy Winn, and Kerry Wood passed through the clubhouse, and as they did in '09, the Yanks breezed past the Minnesota Twins in the American League Division Series. Their hopes of a repeat were dashed by the Texas Rangers, who ended New York's season in a six-game American League Championship Series. "With all the increased rounds, it has become more difficult because there's so many little things that can go wrong in one or two games," Girardi said. "If you don't win one game you're supposed to, chances are you're not winning the series. And you've got to do it so many more times. If you're a wild-card team, you've got to win four series. I mean, that's pretty hard to do. If you play four series in a row against teams that aren't necessarily great, there's no guarantee you're going to win all four. It's baseball."

During that season the Yankees had come close to landing Cliff Lee, who had been a thorn in their side during '09 with the Cleveland Indians and Philadelphia Phillies. With their playoff hopes sunk, the Seattle Mariners agreed to swap Lee to the Yankees for three prospects: catcher Jesus Montero, pitcher Zach McAllister, and infielder David Adams. Seattle called off the deal, balking at medical reports concerning Adams' injured ankle. The

Yankees offered pitcher Adam Warren as a replacement, but the Mariners insisted upon pitcher Ivan Nova or infielder Eduardo Nunez.

Lee landed instead with the Rangers, where he fired another dominant gem at the Stadium in Game 3 of the ALCS. Cashman tried again to secure Lee in the offseason, offering a reported six years and $138 million to the hurler, but Lee opted to accept a five-year, $120 million pact to return to Philadelphia. That ALCS may have been a factor; Lee's wife, Kristen, claimed to have been spit upon and doused in beer by rowdy Yankees fans. "You can't control 50,000 people and what they're going to do," Lee said in 2010. "There were some people that were spitting off the balcony on the family section and things like that, and that's kind of weak, but what can you do?"

Even without Pettitte, who announced his retirement prior to the 2011 season, the Yankees reclaimed the top spot in the AL East by winning 97 games. It was a season that saw Jeter reach a storied milestone, homering off the Rays' David Price for his 3,000th career hit on July 9, but the Captain's closest friend on the roster struggled with an increasingly reduced role.

Replaced behind the plate by Russell Martin, Posada was a full-time designated hitter, and the ball no longer exploded off his bat the way it once had. Dropped to ninth in the lineup for a May 2011 game against the Red Sox, Posada told Girardi that he felt "disrespected" and refused to play. Posada ended his career in the ALDS, as the Yankees were eliminated in five games by the Tigers. "The strangest thing for me was when I'd go to spring training, and one of them wasn't there," Girardi said. "Jorgie wasn't standing there as the catchers got done [catching] their bullpens, and then they were hitting. It was like, 'Where's Jorgie?' Jorgie was always in the first group. Jorgie was the leader. That was when it really became strange to me."

CC Sabathia continued to anchor the rotation in 2012, parlaying the opt-out clause Cashman had given him to tack on an additional year to his original seven-year deal. A.J. Burnett's tumultuous tenure in pinstripes ended just three years into his five-year contract. The Yankees would always be thankful for Game 2 of the 2009 World Series, but Burnett was dealt to the Pittsburgh Pirates in February 2012, leaving the Yankees with a 34–35 record and 4.79 ERA in 99 games (98 starts). "I was traded to Pittsburgh for a reason," Burnett said. "I did decent on the mound, but I really didn't do as well as I should have the entire time I was there. CC and I came in together, and we were close, so I wished I could finish it out with him. He stuck, he made it. I don't regret going there. I don't hate pictures of me in Yankee uniforms. Heck no, I enjoyed every minute of it."

Had the Yankees not won a title in the first year or two of the Stadium, Sabathia wonders if he might have had a similar fate. "It's hard to pitch here," Sabathia said. "Everybody's different. It's tough. If we wouldn't have won in '09 or '10, man, I don't know if I would've been able to pitch here the rest of that time. They probably would've ran me out of town, coming in here making all that money."

Cashman has wondered how fans might view the new ballpark today had the club not inaugurated it with a title. "Thank God we won that year because I know that the clock would have started on, 'Oh, they should've never left the old ballpark. It's been one year, 10 years, 15 years, 30 years since they've won a championship. They never should've gone to the new ballpark,'" Cashman said. "Thankfully, we got that out of the way in '09 because the media would've played on that heavily just like when a new player here goes 0-for-21, and the watch is going on."

More than a decade after its groundbreaking was held in Macombs Dam Park, Cashman said that he believes the venue has been transformative for the South Bronx. "I've been in the Bronx for a long time and I feel like this building has uplifted this entire community," Cashman said. "I never used to see kids walking to a pool with towels, for instance. I see more neighborhood people utilizing the track, soccer, football, playing softball or baseball. It was more business/industrial before, and now this whole neighborhood has a new feel. The Stadium is a big reason why."

Feeling the itch to face hitters, Pettitte ended his retirement during spring training of 2012. Mariano Rivera intended for that season to be his final tour, but the plan changed when his right knee buckled in pursuit of a batting practice fly ball during a May series in Kansas City. Defiantly proclaiming, "Write it down in big letters: I'm not going down like this,"

Rivera successfully rehabbed his torn anterior cruciate ligament and would be back on the mound the following year.

Though the 2012 Yankees won 95 games and again claimed the division title, the "Core Four" was breaking down, and the energy that propelled the '09 club was fading. New York edged the Baltimore Orioles in a five-game ALDS, but their season was as good as over when Jeter crumpled to the infield dirt in pursuit of a grounder late in ALCS Game 1 against the Tigers.

Jeter had received several cortisone injections toward the end of that season, weakening his left ankle until it finally shattered under his weight. With their Captain on crutches, the rest of the Yankees limped to the finish as the Tigers swept their way to a pennant. The Yanks cleaned out their lockers and wondered if their glory days were past. For many on that roster, they were.

Though they continued to post winning records, injuries and underperformance kept Girardi's clubs out of the playoffs in 2013 and 2014, the first time the Yankees had endured back-to-back dark Octobers since Buck Showalter's managerial tenure in the early 1990s. "The expectation was this team should have been able to do this for two or three more years in a row [after 2009]. For whatever reason we didn't," Girardi said. "We lost to Texas, and they ended up going to the World Series. We lost to Detroit, and they went to the World Series. We just didn't get it done. I think people understood that we had players that are going to be playing until they're 37 or 38. You knew players would age, and players would leave."

Pettitte retired for good after '13, joining Rivera for their final exits as active players. Rivera enjoyed a season-long send-off that included ceremonies and gifts in each city the Yankees visited, as did Jeter the next year. When Jeter lined a walk-off single in his final home game on September 25, 2014, Burnett and his whipped cream pies were nowhere to be found. Jeter's exit marked the end of the "Core Four," and only whispers remained of '09. "I always feel like I got them one more [ring]," Sabathia said. "That was their dynasty. It's like watching big brothers go out. All of their retirements, I had a chance to be a part of it and play with them and to win, too. It was cool to be here and be a baseball fan and know what it meant historically to play with those guys."

Mark Teixeira remained a formidable switch-hitting presence and leader, though his performance was never the same after a right wrist injury sustained during the spring of 2013. Their depth was incredibly thin. To replace Teixeira, Cashman plucked 36-year-old Lyle Overbay from the scrap heap after he had been released by the Red Sox a day earlier. "We didn't have a lot of young players," Teixeira said. "We didn't have a lot of young talent coming in to fill in for us when we got older, and so between that and some injuries and a couple bad breaks, the window closed pretty quickly."

Cano blossomed into a perennial All-Star, but the Yankees balked at his request for a 10-year contract after 2013, offering seven years and $175 million. Cano agreed to a 10-year, $240 million pact with the Mariners, and the Yankees responded by spending $438 million on Masahiro Tanaka, Carlos Beltran, Jacoby Ellsbury, and Brian McCann.

Years later, cradling a bat in the first-base dugout at Seattle's Safeco Field, Cano said that he misses that time in pinstripes. "That team that we had there, I don't think that's going to happen in baseball again," said Cano, who returned to New York in December 2018 when the Mariners traded him to the Mets. "Man, I came up with a special group and special players. Anyone would miss that time. For me now that's something that I tell young players. I appreciate when you can be around a couple of superstars. I look back and [played with] Jeter, A-Rod, Mariano, Teixeira, Posada, Johnny Damon, CC, Burnett, seeing them, being around them."

His relationship with the right-field Bleacher Creatures fractured by postseason shortcomings, Nick Swisher landed a four-year, $56 million deal with the Indians prior to 2013. His departure had an unexpected benefit for the Yankees. As compensation for losing Swisher, the Yankees were awarded the 32nd overall pick in the 2013 draft. Cashman's director of amateur scouting, Damon Oppenheimer, used it to select Aaron Judge, a hulking, power-hitting outfielder from Fresno State University who would develop into the 2017 AL Rookie of the Year. "In the end Swish was the gift that kept on giving," Cashman said.

Phil Hughes signed a three-year, $24 million deal with the Twins prior to 2014, enjoying two solid years that earned him an extension worth an additional $42 million before injuries took their toll. Joba Chamberlain appeared with the Tigers, Kansas City Royals, and Indians before retiring at age 30. David Robertson scored a four-year, $46 million commitment to close for the White Sox, though he wondered why the Yankees never made it back to the top. "I literally just thought we were going to keep winning every year," Robertson said. "I'd been winning all the way through the minor league system. I had won in the Cape Cod League before I came. I just expected to win every year."

As time passed and baseball instituted tougher bans on performance-enhancing drugs, some corners of the '09 team were stained. Alex Rodriguez was ensnared in Major League Baseball's investigation into Anthony Bosch and his South Florida Biogenesis clinic, taking on MLB in a scorched-earth, litigious battle before agreeing to be suspended for the 2014 season—the most substantial penalty for performance-enhancing drug use in the game's history at the time.

Francisco Cervelli was among 13 players who served 50-game suspensions for their connections to Biogenesis, and while playing for the San Francisco Giants in 2012, Melky Cabrera was hit with a 50-game suspension for a positive testosterone test. After Cano tested positive for a banned substance and received an 80-game suspension in May 2018, Teixeira—now on the media side as an analyst for ESPN—said that the multitude of PED bans changed how he views the '09 team. "I'd be lying if I said it doesn't, but I think every single team that's won a World Series over the past 25 years can probably say the same thing," Teixeira said. "I'm not going out on a limb there. I hate it. I don't like that baseball has this hanging around us, but that's unfortunately the game, and you've got to live with it. I know what I did for the team that year. Being a clean player, I'm proud of what I've done."

When their postseason lasted just nine innings against Dallas Keuchel and the Houston Astros in the 2015 AL wild-card game, change was necessary. Cashman convinced Hal Steinbrenner to allow him to unload pieces in July 2016. Established stars like Beltran, Aroldis Chapman, Andrew Miller, and Ivan Nova were moved for prospects, netting outfielder Clint Frazier and infielder Gleyber Torres, among others.

Rodriguez was released from his contract a week later, and the organization ate $27 million while offering A-Rod a soft landing as a special advisor. Rodriguez played his final game on August 12, 2016, ending his career with 696 homers, fourth all time behind Barry Bonds (762), Henry Aaron (755), and Babe Ruth (714). Girardi even permitted him to play one final inning at third base. Rodriguez admitted to being terrified, as he had forgotten to wear a protective cup.

"At his retirement press conference, they asked me about Alex and what was the legacy here," Cashman said. "I said, 'I don't have this '09 ring on my finger without Alex Rodriguez's contributions.' I put it right there on the table. Enough said."

The moves cleared room for an influx of young talent. Catcher Gary Sanchez almost single-handedly powered the Yankees to a postseason berth in 2016, mashing 20 homers in 53 games, and the trio of Sanchez, Judge (who hit an AL-best 52 homers), and dominant right-hander Luis Severino propelled the Yankees within one win of the 2017 World Series.

New York's ALCS loss to the Astros was Girardi's final game as the club's manager, and his decade at the helm was complete. Despite Girardi's average of 91 wins per year during his tenure (and having overachieved with some clubs that probably deserved less), Cashman and Hal Steinbrenner said that they were concerned by Girardi's issues communicating and connecting with the younger players on the roster. "This is not something that came from two or three weeks. It came from two, three, four years, and everything we observed in that time period," Steinbrenner said. "You've got to consider that you have a young team, and that maybe a different type of leadership, perhaps, is needed for a younger team than it is for a veteran team."

That prompted the hiring of Aaron Boone, who enjoyed a successful move from the broadcast booth to the dugout in 2018 despite having no professional coaching or managing experience. Elsewhere, Jeter followed through on his desire to move from the diamond to the owner's suite, joining New York-based financier Bruce Sherman to finalize a $1.2 billion purchase of the

Miami Marlins. One of Jeter's significant early moves as the Marlins' CEO was to unload outfielder Giancarlo Stanton, trading the reigning National League MVP to the Yankees in December 2017. Stanton slugged 38 homers with 100 RBIs to help Boone's inaugural roster win 100 games, marking the Yanks' most victories since the '09 squad won 103, but they were upended by the eventual World Series champion Red Sox in the ALDS.

Only Brett Gardner and Sabathia remained from '09. Still hoping to celebrate a second championship in New York, Gardner and Sabathia re-signed with the Yankees prior to the 2019 season, though Roberston inked a two-year $24 million deal with the Phillies. Sabathia said that he has yet to open the box that contains his '09 ring. "I still have never tried it on," Sabathia said. "It's in my closet. People know you won a World Series. What the fuck do you need a ring for? For me, I feel like if you wear the ring, you're living in the past. I don't know, maybe when I'm done playing and I'm not trying to chase another one, maybe I'll have a different perspective."

One of the highlights of that '18 season came on a sunny Saturday afternoon as the 1998 championship squad—widely regarded as one of the most dominant in baseball history—reunited at the stadium. As Paul O'Neill, Bernie Williams, Tino Martinez, and Orlando Hernandez slipped the pinstripes back on and were joined by Pettitte, Posada, and Rivera, it was impossible not to envision how an anniversary celebration in the summer of 2029 might look, feel, and sound. "I'll be almost 60, God willing," Rivera said. "It'll be fun, knowing the first year of that stadium, we brought such joy to the city. It was a moment to tell the world that Mr. George did something special for us. Closing one era—but opening another one."

ACKNOWLEDGMENTS

A decade after the last bottle was popped in the clubhouse, the authors of this book believed that the World Series championship had been indelibly imprinted into our minds. We were staggered by the incredible amount of details that were either forgotten or had not surfaced at the time. Many people connected to the 2009 Yankees generously offered their time and experiences during the research phase of this project, and we would like to thank the following: Jean Afterman, Doug Behar, Chad Bohling, Brian Bruney, A.J. Burnett, Melky Cabrera, Brian Cashman, Robinson Cano, Dana Cavalea, Francisco Cervelli, Joba Chamberlain, Johnny Damon, Dave Eiland, Billy Eppler, Michael Fishman, Brett Gardner, Joe Girardi, Jerry Hairston Jr., J.A. Happ, Mike Harkey, Phil Hughes, Kim Jones, Michael Kay, Mick Kelleher, Joe Lee, Randy Levine, Kevin Long, Hideki Matsui, Jose Molina, Xavier Nady, Paul Olden, Andy Pettitte, Jorge Posada, Brian Richards, Mariano Rivera, David Robertson, Alex Rodriguez, CC Sabathia, John Sterling, Nick Swisher, Mark Teixeira, Rob Thomson, Suzyn Waldman, Chien-Ming Wang, Charlie Wonsowicz, and Jason Zillo.

A special shout-out goes to our boy Swish, who authored a foreword that captured his energetic spirit and lived up to our expectations.

We would also like to thank Jordan Bastian, Adam Berry, and Alan Chang for their assistance in tracking down some of the interviews. Ron Berkowitz was also enormously supportive of this project and a great friend throughout the process.

Some of our beat brethren from 2009 helped us brainstorm, so thanks to Peter Abraham, Erik Boland, Pete Caldera, Marc Carig, Chad Jennings,

Tyler Kepner, George King and Sweeny Murti for their friendship, support, and many late-night laughs during that memorable season.

Mandy Bell, our amazing research assistant, was a rock star throughout this project. Thank you for your many hours of work. We could not have reached the finish line without you.

We wouldn't have had a book to write if not for Stacey Glick, our fantastic agent. Jeff Fedotin, our editor at Triumph Books, was a pleasure to work with. Thanks for your suggestions along the way.

Mark would also like to thank Mom, George, Danielle, Dad, and Ellen for their never-ending love and support. Dad, being able to get you into the Stadium for the Game 6 clincher was one of my greatest joys. Thirty years earlier, you brought me to the old Stadium for the first time, kicking off my love for this game that has now become a career. Funny how things work out.

To Laurie and Eric, thanks for being so supportive and such an important part of our lives. And to Richie L., one of the biggest Yankees fans I ever knew, we miss you and love you.

Of course, my biggest thank you goes to Dena, Ryan, and Zack. Everything I do, I do for you guys. I love you all.

Bryan would like to thank Connie, with whom the 2009 Yankees go hand in hand. That season serves as the backdrop for our lives from a first date in spring training to tracking your float through the Canyon of Heroes. The Yankees gave you a first ring; mine will be the last. You are an amazing teammate, and Penny and Maddie have been our '16 and '18 Rookies of the Year, respectively. Thank you for taking on late-night diaper duty throughout this project and keeping my desk stocked with Red Bull. The three of you are my World Champions, filling each day with joy and laughter. I love you all the more than words can express.

In addition, Bryan would like to thank Mom, Dad, and Shawn for supporting the path that took me from watching games in our living room to writing about them from the press box. It all started with a pack of 1987 Topps (I still have the dog-eared, paint-splattered Danny Tartabull) and a Nintendo Baseball cartridge. Thanks also to Jackie, Seth, and Julia for taking on the full Hoch experience; it's never dull.

Shortly after 2009, Bryan began to spend more time with Connie's extended family and was certain that they were too good to be true. It was like having dinner with the Brady Bunch; no group could legitimately enjoy each others' company this much. But much like the '09 team learned that Swisher's over-the-top energy was completely authentic, Ray and Eileen are the real deal. Your generosity and support has been a blessing as we share laughs and create memories together. Thanks for embracing the chaos of a beat writer's life; one minute we're splitting a pizza pie, the next A-Rod is on the phone. (That actually happened during this project.)

Thank you also to Joan, Harold, Steve, Raymond, Linda, Brian, Joanna, Griffin, the Clymers, Joe, and the Long Island Schwabs for welcoming Bryan into their circle. The '09 season had the "Core Four," and this roster is even deeper. Your Grapefruit League visits are a highlight of the year. There's always an air mattress or couch for anyone who needs to escape the snow and get a sneak peek of their beloved Yankees. Our girls are growing up with so much love around them. We could not ask for more.

A special thanks to Connie's late grandfathers: Raymond, one of the original Bleacher Creatures, and Clairmont, who enthusiastically cheered along countless softball sidelines. They both instilled a love of the game that transcends generations and is sure to be rooted deep within our daughters' hearts.

Finally, the authors would like to thank the millions of Yankees fans who avidly watched the completion of "Mission 27" in 2009 and continue to relive the excitement of being the last team standing. It was a privilege to chronicle those games and the move between stadiums—in the moment and again for this project.

Bibliography

Books

Posada, Jorge. *The Journey Home: My Life in Pinstripes*. Dey Street Books (2016).

Rivera, Mariano. *The Closer*. Little, Brown and Company (2014).

Roberts, Selena. *A-Rod: The Many Lives of Alex Rodriguez*. Harper (2009).

Torre, Joe. *The Yankee Years*. Doubleday (2009).

Periodicals

The Bergen Record

Connecticut Post

New York Daily News

The Star-Ledger

Newsday

The Press of Atlantic City

Sports Illustrated

New York Post

The New York Times

Websites

baseball-reference.com

fangraphs.com

mlb.com

espn.com

whitehouse.gov

yahoo.com

yesnetwork.com

About the Authors

Mark Feinsand has been covering Major League Baseball since 2001, spending the first 16 of those seasons on the New York Yankees beat for MLB.com (2001–06) and the *New York Daily News* (2007–16). He returned to MLB.com as an executive reporter before the 2017 season and appears regularly on MLB Network. Mark lives in New Jersey with his wife, Dena, and their sons, Ryan and Zack, and is also the author of *The New York Yankees Fans' Bucket List*.

Bryan Hoch has covered Major League Baseball for the past two decades, working the New York Yankees clubhouse as MLB.com's beat reporter since 2007. Hoch contributes to MLB Network, and his work has appeared in *Yankees Magazine*, *Inside Pitch Magazine*, and various other outlets. Hoch lives with his wife, Connie, and their daughters, Penny and Maddie. Bryan is the author of *The Baby Bombers: The Inside Story of the Next Yankees Dynasty*.